Saving, Investment, and Growth in India

For our families:

Soma, Chintana and Chaturica

and

Shilpi, Kushan and Ayushi

Saving, Investment, and Growth in India

Prema-chandra Athukorala
and
Kunal Sen

OXFORD
UNIVERSITY PRESS

OXFORD
UNIVERSITY PRESS

YMCA Library Building, Jai Singh Road, New Delhi 110001

Oxford University Press is a department of the University of Oxford. It furthers the University's objective of excellence in research, scholarship, and education by publishing worldwide in

Oxford New York

Athens Auckland Bangkok Bogota Buenos Aires Cape Town Chennai Dar es Salaam Delhi Florence Hong Kong Istanbul Karachi Kolkata Kuala Lumpur Madrid Melbourne Mexico City Mumbai Nairobi Paris São Paulo Shanghai Singapore Taipei Tokyo Toronto Warsaw

with an associated company in Berlin

Oxford is a registered trade mark of Oxford University Press in the UK and in certain other countries

Published in India
By Oxford University Press, New Delhi

First published in India 2002

ISBN 019 565857 4

Typeset in Adobe Garamond 10.5 on 12
by Jojy Philip, New Delhi 110 027
Printed at Rajkamal Electric Press, New Delhi 110 003
Published by Manzar Khan, Oxford University Press
YMCA Library Building, Jai Singh Road, New Delhi 110 001

Preface

Issues relating to patterns and determinants of saving and investment, and the role of investment in economic growth have been at the centre of the post-independence development policy debate in India. As part of the emphasis on development planning which dates back to the early 1950s, India has developed a systematic mechanism for generating and reporting saving and investment estimates on a continuous (annual) basis. Unlike many other (if not all) developing countries, in India saving and investment estimates are a part of the key macroeconomic indicators used in the analyses of economic performance and the national policy debate. Consequently, there is a vast literature in the country, both academic and semi-popular, in this area. However, so far, there has not been a comprehensive systematic study of the determinants of savings and investment, and the mechanisms by which capital formation impacts the growth process. This book aims to fill this gap.

The book has its origin in our participation in a debate in the *Economic and Political Weekly*, the influential Indian economic periodical. The debate centered on an observed decline in saving and investment rates in the aftermath of the structural adjustment-cum-liberalization policy reforms initiated in 1991 (Athukorala and Sen 1995). In an attempt to scrutinize the structuralist critique that this decline was an invariable outcome of embracing market-oriented reforms, we closely studied trends and patterns of investment and saving in the Indian economy, with emphasis on the underlying data generation process. Our analysis led to the inference that the reported decline in saving and investment rates was merely an aberration that originated in the nature of the estimation procedure rather than the beginning of an adverse trend that would continue well into the post-reforms era. Based on the experience gained through this exercise, and encouraged by the attention this paper received, we decided to embark on the task of writing a comprehensive book on saving and investment in India. Our collaborative work was unexpectedly interrupted by Kunal Sen's move from the Australian National University (ANU), where we met and forged effective research collaboration, to Massey University, and then to University of East Anglia. But this interruption eventually proved to be a blessing in disguise. It gave us the opportunity to expand the coverage of the book by adding a chapter on the investment–growth nexus in the light of more recent developments in the 'new' growth literature, and to appropriately embody the empirical analysis of the Indian experience in the broader literature on saving, investment and growth in developing countries. Thus the end product takes the form of a comprehensive Indian case study of the role of saving and investment in the process of economic development, rather than a study of India *per se*, which will be of interest not only to the students of the Indian economy but also to others concerned with the process of economic development in developing countries.

In the process of undertaking this study, we have benefited from ideas and criticisms of many friends and colleagues. Among them Max Corden, George Fane, Kirit Parikh, Ross McLeod, Sarath Rajapatirana, James Riedel, Tirthankar Roy, Tony Thirlwall, and Rajendra Vaidya deserve special mention. We are particularly grateful for their willingness to share their insights. We also thank the two anonymous OUP reviewers of the manuscript whose detailed and incisive comments led to major elaborations of some slighted issues.

We wish to express our gratitude to our academic homes—Department of Economics, Research School of Pacific and Asian Studies (RSPAS) at ANU and the School of Development Studies, University of East Anglia, for excellent research facilities and a congenial work environment. We are particularly grateful to the Department of Economics, RSPAS for financing a visit by Kunal Sen to ANU at the final stages of preparing the manuscript.

We also wish to thank Kanhaiya Singh for able research assistance at various stages of the project. A special vote of thanks is due to the editors at OUP Delhi for their unfailing enthusiasm in the speedy publication of the book.

CHANDRA ATHUKORALA
KUNAL SEN

Contents

Tables

Figures

Abbreviations and Acronyms

ADF	Augmented Dickey–Fuller
ADL	Autoregressive Distributed Lag
CSO	Central Statistical Organisation
DF	Dickey–Fuller
ECM	error correction mechanism
HPAEs	High Performing Asian Economies
IMF	International Monetary Fund
FERA	Foreign Exchange Regulation Act
GDCF	Gross Domestic Capital Formation
GDP	Gross Domestic Product
GDS	Gross Domestic Saving
GNDI	Gross National Disposable Income
GNP	Gross National Product
GNS	Gross National Saving
GSM	'general to specific' methodology
LCM	life-cycle model
MRTP	Monopolies and Restrictive Trade Practices
NAS	National Accounts Statistics
NFPS	Non-Financial Public Sector Enterprises
NIC	newly industrialized countries

OECD	Organization for Economic Cooperation and Development
OGL	Open General Licence
OLS	Ordinary Least Squares
OMM	organized money market
RBI	Reserve Bank of India
SAP	structural adjustment programme
TSLS	two stage least squares
UMM	unorganized money market

1

Introduction

This book examines the role of financial factors in economic development. In particular, it looks at the determinants of saving and investment and the inter-relationships between investment and growth. The analysis is conducted in the context of the Indian economy, while drawing upon recent advances in the theoretical and empirical literature. The findings are carefully analysed in the wider developing country context to inform the policy debate on the role of financial factors in economic development. Thus the book intends to be a comprehensive Indian case study of the subject, rather than a study of India *per se*.

In recent years, there has emerged a considerable amount of theoretical and empirical work on the determinants of saving and investment and on the investment–growth nexus, both in developed and developing countries. This has been driven by the widespread concern over falling saving rates in the major OECD countries and the growing divergence in saving and investment rates between countries of the developing world, and the renewed emphasis on the investment–growth nexus triggered by the new growth theories and the related empirical literature.

There is a growing concern that the burgeoning empirical literature in this subject area is lopsided. Given the nature of data availability, these studies have primarily been conducted using multi-country cross-sectional data.[1] Quite apart from general methodological flaws relating to model specification and econometric procedure (Deaton 1989), there are two fundamental limitations that make results from any cross-country study on this subject rather dubious.

First, cross-country regression analysis is based on the implicit assumption

[1] For recent surveys of this literature, see Fry (1995), Gibson and Tsakalotos (1994), Deaton (1989), and Gersovitz (1988).

of 'homogeneity' in the observed relationship across countries. This is a very restrictive assumption. It is common knowledge that there are considerable variations among developing countries in relation to various structural features and institutional aspects that have a direct bearing upon the impact of financial factors on the growth process. Second, given the vast differences among countries with respect to the nature and quality of data, cross-country comparison is fraught with danger (Deaton 1989; Srinivasan 1994). The statistical procedures for measuring saving and investment as well as the magnitude of errors in data in the implementation of these procedures vary significantly among countries. Thus, any attempt to characterize the 'average' developing country in terms of a cross-country regression is unlikely to yield sensible results.

Even if these limitations are ignored, cross-sectional studies are only a means of testing the validity of generalizations. Such tests are of obvious importance for broadening our understanding of economic phenomena. But in order to inform the policy debate, it is necessary to go beyond the general picture and obtain a comprehensive account of the underlying growth process and related social, political, and institutional aspects.

These considerations point to the need for undertaking in-depth analyses within individual countries over time, by appropriately combining quantitative analysis with qualitative analysis in its own historical context, in order to build a sound empirical foundation for informing the policy debate. Unfortunately, systematic country studies of this nature are few and far between. Interestingly, some of the available country studies have, in fact, produced large and quite significant interest elasticities with respect to saving and investment, compared to various cross-country estimates. At the same time, there are significant variations in the magnitude of measured elasticities among countries, suggesting that data should not be pooled without considerable caution. Thus there is a clear need for more systematic historical case studies covering countries at different stages of development and operating under different policy regimes.

India is a very appropriate case study of the subject at hand for the following reasons. First, the Indian saving and investment database is considered relatively good by developing country standards, and data are available on a comparable basis for a period of time, which is adequate for systematic econometric investigation (Srinivasan 1994). Secondly, India has also undergone significant policy transitions relating to the key variables relevant for the analysis, providing an appropriate setting for a historical analysis of the subject at hand. Finally, saving/investment performance and the role of capital formation in growth acceleration have figured prominently in the policy debate in India in the post-independence period and, in particular, following the structural adjustment reforms initiated in 1991 (EPWRF 1995; Athukorala and Sen 1995). However, there is no hard empirical evidence to inform this policy debate.

The few available studies on saving behaviour in India (for example, Krishnamurty et al. 1987; Ketkar and Ketkar 1992; Laumas 1990; Pandit 1991) are dated and partial in subject coverage. Krishnamurty et al. examine the determinants of the saving rate using data from 1954 to 1981. Laumas's test of McKinnon's complementarity hypothesis relates to the period 1954 to 1974. Ketkar and Ketkar examine the impact of bank branch expansion on financial saving, private investment, and growth of gross domestic product (GDP) for the period 1952 to 1984. The most comprehensive study to date of the structure and growth of saving in India is Pandit (1991), but the time period of the study ends in the early 1980s. Surprisingly, to our knowledge there has not been any empirical analysis of investment behaviour or the investment–growth nexus, other than some useful survey of patterns and trends in policy-oriented periodicals (in particular, the *Economic and Political Weekly*) and government policy reports.[2]

This book covers 42 years of the post-independence era of the Indian economy from 1955 to 1996. The reference period for all data series is the Indian fiscal year, from 1 April in the *given* (stated) year to 31 March in the following year. All data series come from the standard official sources.

Throughout the book, we have attempted to maintain an appropriate blend of theory and policy. The key economic relationships examined are carefully specified in the light of relevant theories. The econometric analysis draws upon recent advances in time series econometrics, with a view to minimizing the risk of uncovering spurious relations. The results are carefully analysed with an emphasis on their relevance for the policy debate in India, bearing in mind that the econometric evidence can only be suggestive, rather than definite, relating to any issue at hand.

The econometric methodology used in regression analysis throughout the book is the 'general to specific' methodology (GSM) (alternatively known as the 'Hendry method', or the 'London School of Economics method'). It comprises four 'steps': (i) formulate a general model that is consistent with the economic theory and one that restricts the dynamics of the process as little as possible; (ii) re-parametrize the model to obtain explanatory variables that are near orthogonal and which are 'interpretable' in terms of the final equilibrium; (iii) simplify the model to the

[2] The only exception that we know of is the recent study of investment behaviour in manufacturing by Goldar (1997).

simplest version that is compatible with the data ('congruent'); and (iv) evaluate the resulting model by extensive analysis of residuals and predictive performance, aiming to find weaknesses of the model designed in the previous step.

This four-step procedure aims to redress the 'spurious regression' problem through continuous interplay of theory and data in the process of specification search. Unless there are good reasons for believing otherwise, it is normally assumed that theory suggests which variables should enter a relationship, and the data are left to determine whether this relationship is static or dynamic. A non-technical exposition of GSM, together with a discussion on the reasons for choosing it among the alternative techniques, is provided in Appendix 3.

The rest of the book is structured in seven chapters. Chapters 2 and 3 set the stage for the ensuing analysis. Chapter 2 surveys the debate on the role of saving and investment in the process of economic growth and the investment–growth relationship, and highlights the changing perceptions and emerging new issues. Chapter 3 provides a snapshot picture of the Indian policy context as it relates to saving and investment behaviour, and their growth implications. Chapter 4 surveys the trends and patterns of saving and investment in the post-independence Indian economy. It also provides a comparative picture of India's saving and investment performance in the wider developing country context. Chapter 5 examines the determinants of saving in India, using an analytical framework developed in the context of the life-cycle model of consumption behaviour, with appropriate modifications to the Indian context. Sources of variation of both private and total national saving are analysed. Chapter 6 focuses on the behaviour and determinants of investment, using the neoclassical model of investment. Both corporate and non-residential business investment are examined, with emphasis on their response to the policy reforms initiated in 1991. In Chapter 7, a detailed empirical analysis of the investment–growth nexus is undertaken. After surveying the relevant theoretical literature, we choose the new growth model due to Scott (1989) as the framework of our analysis. The model specification allows for the role of policy in determining the nature of the link between investment and growth. An attempt is also made to shed light on the differential impact of investment in machinery, compared to investment in construction, apart from examining the aggregate investment–growth relation. The final chapter summarizes the key findings and draws policy lessons.

Four separate appendices supplement these chapters. The procedures adopted in measuring saving and investment and the key limitations of these procedures are discussed in Appendix 1. Appendix 2 presents the dataset used in the empirical analysis, with methodological notes where relevant. A note on econometric methodology is given in Appendix 3. Finally, Appendix 4 provides a simple exposition of the neoclassical and endogenous growth models and is specifically related to Chapter 7.

2

Saving, Investment, and Growth: Changing Perceptions

The role of saving and investment in the process of economic growth has long been at the centre of the debate on economic policy reforms in developing countries. This chapter sets out the main themes of the debate, in order to place the Indian case study in perspective. Three broad periods are identified in terms of the changes in perception of the key issues during the post-World War II period.

During the 1950s and 1960s, when import-substitution development strategies were in vogue, Keynesian monetary theory held sway with regard to the financial aspects of development policy. Capital accumulation was considered the prime mover of economic growth and financial repression—keeping interest rates low and reallocating investable funds in terms of non-market means—was the norm of financial sector policies. There was a 'neo-classical resurgence' in development thinking from about the early 1970s. As part of this paradigm shift, there was a swing of the pendulum from capital accumulation (capital fundamentalism) to policy reforms aimed at achieving efficiency in resource allocation through market oriented reforms. There was also greater emphasis on ending financial repression with a view to promoting saving and the efficiency of financial intermediation. From about the mid-1980s, the intellectual climate relating to the role of physical investment in growth has undergone significant change, as part of the emergence of the new growth theory and the mushrooming empirical growth literature.

The Era of Keynesian Supremacy

In the 1950s and 1960s there was a broad consensus in the economics profession that the basic strategy for development should be based on import substituting industrialization, that is the promotion of industries oriented toward the domestic market by using import restrictions, or even import prohibition, to encourage the replacement of imported manufactures by domestic products.[1] It was widely believed that that primary commodity dependent status enforced by the ex-colonial powers was the main cause of economic backwardness of developing countries, and the gap in living standards between developed and developing countries would continue to widen because of an inexorable deterioration in the terms of trade against primary commodities. Industrialization was therefore considered the key to economic development.

Industrialization through greater integration with the world economy was, however, not considered as a viable option. The consensus view was that given the weakness of domestic economic activities and their inability to compete with established industries abroad, industrialization could not be undertaken without insulating the domestic economy from competition from established foreign industries. It was almost taken for granted that there was little room for developing countries to prosper through exporting labour intensive manufactured goods. The theoretical underpinning for this view was provided by the infant industry argument for temporary protection of the manufacturing sector against import competition. Moreover, since most manufactured goods were imported, it seemed to follow logically that the taking over of the ready-made markets of imports by the domestic production of manufactured goods was the main avenue for industrialization. Consequently, controls over foreign trade became the main policy instrument of planning for industrialization. Trade protection was often reinforced by domestic market policy interventions in the form of selective credit policy, industrial licensing, price controls, and the establishment of state owned enterprises to undertake manufacturing activities in key sectors.

Reflecting the Keynesian influence that dominated economic thinking at the time, capital accumulation, with central planning playing a pivotal role, was considered the key to economic growth. National planning models of the day were commonly built around the Harrod–Domar equation, which was an extension of the Keynesian short-run employment theory into long-run growth theory (Domar 1947; Harrod 1948).[2] This equation implied that growth rate could be maximized by increasing the national

[1] The nature and underlying forces of this policy orientation has been well documented in the literature. For useful surveys, see Diaz–Alejandro (1975), Bhagwati and Srinivasan (1979), and Krueger (1997).

[2] Let Y be income (GDP), S saving, K capital stock, I investment, g growth rate, s saving rate, and k the incremental capital–output ratio, where:

investment ratio and by minimizing the capital-output ratio (that is, improving efficiency of capital use). Given the general conviction at the time that the latter was not a feasible policy target in the short to medium term, the former (capital accumulation) received pride of place in national policy making (Meier 1984; Little 1982; Lal and Myint 1996). Most economists in the 1950s subscribed to the view that 'the problem of development is much more that of insufficient resources, especially capital deficiency, than it is that of inefficient use of resources' (Meier and Baldwin 1957). Part of the funds required for capital formation was to come from taxation, deficit financing, and foreign aid. But, it was generally acknowledged that the bulk of finance had to come from an increase in domestic saving (Little 1982; Lewis 1984).

The debate on how an increase in domestic saving would come about and how to promote saving was primarily guided by Keynesian monetary theory. In this theory income is the prime mover of saving. On the premise that the substitution effect and the income effect of a given change in interest rate may work in opposite directions, the interest rate effect on consumption (and hence on saving) was considered 'secondary and relatively unimportant, except where unusually large changes are in question' (Keynes 1936: p. 94). Taken together, these propositions lead to the conviction that interest rates can be repressed to an artificially low level to generate profit and promote investment as a means of breaking the vicious circle of low saving, low investment, and economic backwardness (Ranis and Mahmood 1992).

The postulated relationship between income growth and saving received further justification from the surplus labour (dual economy) model of Arthur Lewis (1954). The model predicted that, as the supply of labour is infinitely elastic in the typical developing economy, the expansion in the modern ('capitalist') sector would lead to a rising share of profits. Under the assumption that marginal propensity to save is greater from an increase in profits than from wages, the increase in the share of profits in turn implied a long-term rise in overall saving propensities as part of the growth process.

The Keynesian approach to the finance of development also stressed that a mild inflation can stimulate saving/investment through two major channels. First, by raising the nominal rate of return on investment and by

---

$g = \Delta Y/Y$ (1)

$s = S/Y$ (2)

$k = \Delta K/\Delta Y = I/\Delta Y = S/\Delta Y$ (3)

Substitution of (2) and (3) in (1) yields the Harrod–Domar growth equation:

$g = s/k$.

reducing the cost of capital (real rate of interest), inflation raises the profitability of investment. Secondly, it helps investment to generate its own saving, by keeping aggregate demand buoyant and by redistributing income from wage earners with a low propensity to save to profit earners with a high propensity to save. This reasoning provided justification for inflationary deficit financing of investment as part of development planning at the time. And many leading development economists argued that governments in developing countries should not be overly concerned with tackling inflation and instead should place more emphasis on remedying unemployment and achieving faster growth of output through deficit financing (Thirlwall 1974: pp. 22–3).[3]

Given the perceived 'endogeneity' of saving in the growth process and the emphasis on deficit financing as a desirable means of financing capital formation, 'development was overwhelmingly thought of in real terms' (Little 1982: p. 109). There was little study of domestic capital markets and their role in the process of development. National development plans in India and elsewhere in the developing world assumed that funds would flow in the direction indicated by the planned patterns of investment. Wider aspects of the role of financial development in the overall growth process, and the role that might be played by improved capital markets were scarcely mentioned in the policy debate.[4]

The critical role of investment in the growth process was challenged by the neo-classical (Solow–Swan) growth model, which began to make inroads in the growth debate in the developed countries in the late 1950s (Solow 1956, 2000; Swan 1956). This model postulated that capital accumulation affects growth only during the transition to the steady state and the long-term growth is determined only by the rate of technological change, which is assumed to be exogenous. This view came under attack by prominent economists in the Cambridge school of thought (for example, Kaldor 1957; Robinson 1962) on the ground that separation between investment and technological change was rather arbitrary as the latter is mostly embodied in new machinery and equipment. Perhaps because of these powerful criticisms the neoclassical model was never considered as a serious challenge to the 'capital supremacy' that dominated the development thinking at the time.

[3] For instance, Little (1962) was critical of the Third Five Year Plan in India for its unwarranted concern about the danger of monetary expansion resulting from deficit financing.

[4] As early as 1955, Gurley and Shaw pointed to the importance of paying attention to the financial aspects of the growth process. But this view remained hidden beneath the dominance of the Keynesian approach to the finance of development until the early 1970s.

RESURGENCE OF NEOCLASSICAL ECONOMICS

Many developing countries experienced rapid growth at the early stage of substituting domestic production for imports of consumer goods and other light manufactures. But, as these easy import-substitution opportunities dried up, further growth was naturally limited to the rate of growth of domestic demand, and that was generally not high in most developing countries. In almost every country, and particularly in small countries, import-substitution policies encouraged high-cost, inefficient activities that showed little productivity gains over time, partly due to their sheltered position in the domestic market. Consequently, the original expectation of catching up with the advanced countries never materialized. Further, in terms of equity considerations, such policies were often associated with regressive shifts. Most of the newly established industries relied heavily on imported intermediate goods. To make matters worse, the protectionist policies pulled resources into high-cost import competing industries and discouraged export production. As a result, periodic foreign exchange shortages and 'stop–go macroeconomic cycles' usually emerged, with deleterious effects on output and employment.

In contrast to the dismal overall performance of the import-substitution addicted developing countries, Hong Kong—a prototype free economy—and three other East Asian countries—Singapore, South Korea, and Taiwan—that shifted early to more market-oriented trade, industry, and financial sector policies moved dramatically upwards on the income scale, with substantial improvement in their overall economic performance.[5] More importantly, rapid and sustained growth in these countries was accompanied by a remarkable equity outcome, with a more equal distribution of income and rapid reduction in poverty.[6]

From the mid-1960s, an increasing number of studies probed these development successes, and equally the failures of the import-substituting countries. Two strands of the new literature are relevant here. First, there were studies that examined the comparative development experience, focusing primarily on the role of trade and industrial policy. The major multi-country studies in this group were directed by Little, Scitovsky and Scott (1970) at the Organisation for Economic Cooperation and Development (OECD), Balassa (1982) at the World Bank, Bhagwati (1978) and Krueger

[5] These four countries, which are popularly known as the four dragons, the four tigers, or the 'gang of four', were subsequently joined by Malaysia, Thailand, Indonesia, and China to form the country grouping of 'East Asian Miracle Economies' or High Performing Asian Economies' (HPAEs) (World Bank 1993).

[6] There is a vast literature on the East Asian growth and development experience. For a comprehensive survey, see World Bank (1993) and Booth (1999).

(1978) at the National Bureau of Economic Research, and Donges (1976) at the Kiel Institute of World Economics. Systematic empirical evidence of these studies created greater awareness of the economic wastefulness and irrationality of import-substitution regimes, and of the inherent growth conducive traits of export-oriented regimes. Secondly, the seminal works of Shaw (1973) and McKinnon (1973), which built on the early work of Gurley and Shaw (1955), spawned a large empirical literature that unveiled the growth retarding effects of financial repression. While the interplay between the two branches of development literature left much to be desired (McKinnon 1979), both taken together provided a strong critique of the 'promotion of investment at any cost' and financial repressionist approaches to economic growth that held sway in the 1950s and 1960s.

The new literature on trade and industry policy came up with strong empirical evidence that rapid investment expansion does not necessarily bring about a favourable growth outcome. The literature revealed many instances of rapid investment growth that were reflected in a mere increase in the incremental capital-output ratio with little impact on the rate of growth. There was also ample evidence that in most countries the employment outcome of investment-centred growth was dismal as the protectionist trade regimes induced a palpable shift in investment towards capital-intensive product lines (Krueger 1982; Little, Mazumdar, and Page 1987). The upshot was a growing recognition that it was at least as important, perhaps even more important, to stress the efficiency with which resources were used as it was to stress the level of investment.

The new finance literature argued that the Keynesian policy advocacy was not consistent with the salient features of financial relations in developing countries. In the typical developing economy where there is no robust market in stocks and bonds, bank loans and self-financing constitute the major sources of investible funds. Moreover, as portfolio choices are rather limited, the saving process in the economy tends to be highly 'money intensive'. Given the high money intensity of saving behaviour, low deposit rates of interest produce a bias in favour of current consumption and against future consumption leading to lower aggregate saving and investment levels as compared to socially optimal levels. In the light of these peculiarities of domestic financial relations, it was argued that financial repression retards economic growth through its adverse consequences for capital accumulation in the economy.[7]

Shaw's (1973) exposition of the adverse impact of low interest rates on

[7] In addition to adversely influencing the level of investment, financial repression may also impede efficiency of investment through a variety of avenues (for a survey, see Fry 1995: ch. 3).

investment is rooted in the debt-intermediation process. Low real deposit rates discourage financial savings and thus reduce the flow of loanable funds through the banking system to productive investment (Shaw's 'debt-intermediation view'). An additional linkage between savings and investment was suggested by McKinnon on the basis of possible complementarity of money and capital (McKinnon 1973). In an economy with a rudimentary capital market, self-financing is a major source of investment funds. Given the fact that investment projects are lumpy, investors must accumulate funds in the form of deposits until the required principal is reached. This process of self-finance within enterprises is impaired by financial repression because low real yield on deposits increases the cost of accumulating the necessary money balances in preparation for making future investments. Thus, the more attractive the returns on deposits, the more willing investors are to engage in the accumulation process (McKinnon's 'complementarity hypothesis').

The McKinnon–Shaw view of the danger of financial repression has, however, been strongly criticized by the neo-structuralist development economists and post-Keynesians. The neo-structuralist development economists (for example, van Wijnbergen 1982; Taylor 1983, 1988) put forward two main counter arguments. The first argument, widely known as the 'financial crowding out argument', points to the possibility of high interest rates on bank deposits generating a portfolio shift towards that asset and away from other assets in the household asset portfolio, instead of generating a net increase in total savings. While substitution is possible between bank deposits and various forms of other assets, the neo-structuralists place particular emphasis on the substitution between bank deposits and claims in the unorganized money market (UMM). The claims in the UMM, by their very nature, are not subject to reserve requirements. By contrast, reserve requirements constitute a leakage in the financial intermediation done through commercial banks. Given this difference, so the argument goes, an increase in real interest rate on bank deposits may reduce the overall degree of financial intermediation in the economy. Put simply, if saving is directed to the formal money market from the UMM as interest rates rise, the total supply of credit to the private sector may be reduced because banks are subject to reserve requirements while the UMM is not. The second argument is that even if the crowding out effect is unimportant and the availability of funds increases, the newly generated savings would not necessarily be transformed 'without hitches' into new capital formation. This is because the high interest rate policy itself would have led to a collapse of effective demand through increased saving propensities and/or cost-push contractionary effect on output and demand. As firms struggle or fail under these pressures, banks might end up with excess liquidity. To the extent that investment demand is related to the existing degree of capacity utilization, higher interest rates will reduce investment and capital accumulation.

The post-Keynesians (for example, Thirlwall 1976; Davidson 1986; Dutt 1991) also emphasize the cost-push (contractionary) effects of high interest rates which may retard (rather than promote) capital formation. In addition, they take issue with the McKinnon–Shaw proposition on the link between financial saving, bank lending, and investment. The basic (implicit) assumption of the McKinnon–Shaw model relating to this linkage seems to be that banks are used only as savings depositories, so that the supply of loans is dependent on the deposits held by the banks. The post-Keynesians argue that this one way linkage between financial savings and bank lending becomes less relevant in the determination of investment when one recognizes the capacity of the banking system to create credit, which in many ways is the most important task of banks in the process of economic development. In a context where loans given by banks end up being deposited in banks, so they argue, it is not the amount of deposits that determines loans, but the amount of loans that determines deposits. If the banks can create credit without having to rely on initial deposits, an increase in financial saving through higher real deposit rates makes no difference to the amount of total credit given to the private sector. Thus, as Keynes (1936) put it '(since) the banks hold the key position in the transition from a lower to a higher scale of activity ... the investment market can ... never become congested through shortage of saving'.

These contending perspectives are not immune to criticism, however. As regards the financial crowding out hypothesis, the mere existence of a sizeable UMM in the typical developing economy does not necessarily imply significant crowding-out following reforms in the organized money market (OMM). The crowding-out effect would be significant only if the UMM is closely linked with the OMM so that in the households' portfolio, bank deposits are a better substitute for UMM claims than cash or other assets and if it is 'competitive and agile' (Taylor 1983). The available evidence on the structure and working of informal credit arrangements in many developing countries, however, suggest that such characterization of the UMM is a highly questionable description of reality for the typical developing economy (Owen and Solis–Fallas 1989; Athukorala and Rajapatirana 1993). Moreover, it is important to note that McKinnon and Shaw were, in fact, aware of the possible contraction of UMM funds following an interest rate reform (Shaw 1973: p. 137; McKinnon 1973: p. 60). They, however, considered this to be a desirable outcome on efficiency grounds. That is, a given quantity of saving mobilized via the formal financial sector may be more productive than the same quantity of savings mobilized through informal channels.[8]

The post-Keynesian view that the investment market can never become congested implicitly assumes a well-developed financial system where banks have the ability to lend by creating deposits on the basis of prior lending. Such a characterization is not consistent with financial systems in many developing countries. In a context where banking habits are still at a formative stage, loans extended to finance investment projects, in effect, leak out of the financial intermediation process very quickly. If financial markets are underdeveloped, and bank liquidity preference is high, banks will not necessarily lend more; and even if they do, they will probably lend short-term rather than long-term. Furthermore, in the absence of near-money assets in the financial system, central banks in developing countries have a greater ability to control money supply (and thus, bank lending) than central banks in developed countries.

Despite counter arguments by economists of Keynesian persuasion, the McKinnon–Shaw case for ending financial repression, together with outward-orientation in trade and industry policy regimes soon became the new orthodoxy of economic policy reforms in developing countries. In response to this shift in conventional wisdom, an increasing number of developing countries began to unwind import-substitution cum financial repression policy regimes from the late 1970s, mostly as part of the IMF–World Bank sponsored liberalization/stabilization programmes.

NEW GROWTH ECONOMICS AND THE RENEWED EMPHASIS ON INVESTMENT

There has been a renewed interest in issues of capital accumulation and growth since the late 1980s. By this time, a number of comparative studies of post-World War II economic performance had alluded to a widening divergence in performance among high-performing countries, casting doubts on the predictive power of the neoclassical (Solow–Swan) growth model.[9] This set the stage for the emergence of the new growth theory, starting with the seminal work of Lucas (1988) and Romer (1986). Inspired by the new growth theory and aided by the availability of the Summers–Heston data

[8] Because the supply of credit in the UMMs is limited, money lenders in these markets operate on a small scale and usually charge high interest rates. Consequently, borrowers use these funds mostly for short-term projects and for activities where the potential competition for funding is low.

[9] For a comprehensive survey of this literature, see Maddison (1994).

set, there has been an outpouring of empirical work aimed at explaining the post-war growth experience.[10]

The empirical literature has largely taken the form of multi-country cross-sectional analyses. But a number of studies have also attempted to shed light on the debate through re-examination of the post-war development experience of the East Asian newly industrialized countries (NICs). A striking commonality across most, if not all, cross-country growth studies is that the investment rate has turned out to be the most robust explicator of inter-country variation in growth rates. Also, the magnitude of the estimated coefficient reported in most studies is too large to be explained in terms of the Solow–Swan model. A number of studies (for example, De Long and Summers 1991, 1992, 1993; Jones 1994; Lee 1995) have taken a more disaggregated approach to examine the importance of investment in machinery and equipment, as against total investment, in the growth process. A consensus has emerged that accumulation of machinery and equipment is much more important than accumulation of total capital per se in achieving rapid growth.

In addition to these cross-sectional studies, a number of studies have attempted to shed light on the new growth debate through historical case studies of the East Asian high-performing economies. The findings of these studies have by and large corroborated the findings from cross-sectional studies: efficiency of resource use (as measured by total factor productivity (TFP) growth) has played a minor role compared to physical investment (and the increase in the quality and quantity of the labour force) in driving East Asian growth (Young 1995; Rodrik 1956; Collins and Bosworth 1996).

CONCLUSIONS AND IMPLICATIONS

What are the implications of these findings for development policy? To the development economists in the 'revisionist' school of thought, the uniformly strong relationship between investment and growth rates is a strong reconfirmation of the old view that in the long run, investment is key to

[10] New growth theory has been instrumental in motivating new growth empirics. But it is important to note that the empirical studies are not an attempt to directly implement the new growth theoretic models. Rather the regression specifications have been carried out in an *ad hoc* fashion, drawing upon the older neoclassical model extended to incorporate various policy variables, accumulation of human capital, and other related variables suggested by the new theory (see Temple 1999 for a comprehensive survey). Attempts bordering on 'fishing for' statistically significant variables purely guided by data availability are also not uncommon. This has led to the criticism that the inferences drawn from the new growth empirics are 'fragile' (Levine and Renelt 1992).

economic performance (Helleiner 1994; Patnaik and Chandrasekhar 1996; Rodrik 1956, 1999). Drawing upon this empirical evidence, they argue that the neoclassical assault against the 'capital fundamentalism' of the 1950s and 1960s that led to favouring efficiency over capital accumulation was simply a false assignment of the causes of economic failure. The poor economic performance of many import-substitution economies, compared to the East Asian NICs, was not because of inefficiency in the use of resources nurtured by the protectionist regime, but because of other policy errors.[11] By contrast, so the revisionists argue, governments in East Asia complemented their outward orientation with sound macroeconomic policies and a coherent investment strategy that raised the private return to capital. These governments went considerably beyond simply removing obstacles to private investment; they directly promoted capital formation through subsidies and other means of direct intervention. On these grounds, Rodrik (1999: p. 16) even came up with the dramatic inference that 'an increase in investment, for whatever reason, tends to spur growth'.

But this interpretation amounts to an attempt to swing the pendulum too far back, which may run the risk of opening up new avenues for costly dirigisme. In a careful reading of the relevant literature, one does not find support for the view that the neoclassical resurgence from the 1970s resulted in dropping the investment ratio from the growth debate in favour of efficiency considerations. The development economists of neoclassical persuasion have continued to consider capital accumulation as a key variable in the growth process. They differ from the pioneers of development economics only in the emphasis on both resource accumulation and efficiency of resource use as key determinants of growth (Krueger 1980; Srinivasan 1999; Srinivasan and Bhagwati 1999). Put simply, what neoclassical growth economics simply postulates is that 'the level of investment and its efficiency are the approximate causes of growth, and that the policy regime (particularly the degree of openness to foreign trade and policy-induced distortions in the working of the price mechanism) is the primary determinant of the efficiency of investment' (Lal and Myint 1996: p. 3).

The main implication of this discussion for growth empirics is that both investment rate and a variable/s to capture the nature of the policy regime (preferably the latter interactively with the former) should be included as right-hand variables in the regression specification. Positive and statistically significant coefficients on both variables are the result postulated by the neo-classical development economists. By contrast, the 'capital fundamen-

[11] The major policy errors often highlighted in this debate relates to slippage in macroeconomic policy (Helleiner 1994; Rodrik 1995).

talism' postulates a positive and statistically significant coefficient only for the investment rate. Indeed, a major contribution of the new-wave empirical growth literature is to incorporate the differences in policy regimes and incentive structures in examining inter-country variations in growth performance. Unfortunately, the 'revisionist' economists who have attempted to resuscitate 'capital fundamentalism' have failed to draw upon this important development in the analysis of economic growth.

3

The Indian Policy Context

The economic policy of a nation is crucial in understanding its domestic saving and investment behaviour and the relationship between investment and growth. This is particularly true for a country like India where a highly interventionist government has followed a complex set of economic policies in a wide variety of areas and sectors since independence. Subsequent chapters examine which of these policies impacted on saving and investment behaviour and the mechanisms by which they did so. In order to set the stage for this analysis, it is necessary to understand policy trends and changes in emphasis placed on different elements of the overall policy regime over time. Towards this end, this chapter provides an introduction to the macroeconomic, trade, industrial, and financial sector policies prevailing in India since independence. The attempt here is not to give a comprehensive account of Indian economic policies, but simply to highlight the features of the policy regime that could be argued to have had an impact on saving and investment behaviour in India.[1]

Macroeconomic Policy

One of the key features of India's post-independence economic policy until the mid-1970s was the strong emphasis on maintaining a conservative stance with respect to monetary and fiscal policy. Unlike many other

[1] There is a vast literature on Indian policy reforms. For useful overviews, with extensive listing of the related literature see Bhagwati (1993), Joshi and Little (1996), and Srinivasan (2000). Key references on particular areas of reform are Reserve Bank of India (1985) and Joshi and Little (1994) for macroeconomics; Bhagwati and Desai (1970), Bhagwati and Srinivasan (1975), World Bank (1989), Aksoy (1992), and Pursell (1992) for trade; Ahluwalia (1985, 1991), Marathe (1989), and Mohan and Aggarwal (1990) for industry; and Ministry of Finance (1991), Sen and Vaidya (1997), Rangarajan (1998), and Hanson and Kathuria (1999) for finance.

developing countries, the Indian government kept a tight reign on the budget deficit and its monetization during this period. From the mid-1970s, there was however, a gradual erosion of fiscal conservatism resulting in a steady increase in the fiscal deficit (Fig. 3.1). This remarkable shift in fiscal policy stance can be traced to the changing political economy of the country, as socio-economic groups (such as public sector workers, small-scale industrialists and medium and large farmers) that were dormant in the past began to be increasingly assertive and asked for a greater share of government subsidies. At the same time, with the weakening of political power at the centre, the Indian state became increasingly populist as it resorted to settle the claims of various pressure-groups through the budgetary process.[2] The increasing fiscal deficits of the central government were an important contributing factor behind the severe balance-of-payment crisis of 1991. Since 1991, the Indian government has attempted to keep the fiscal deficit under control, with some degree of success.

The expansionary fiscal policies coupled with the limited measures to liberalize the economy in the mid-1980s (we describe these measures later in the chapter) contributed to a discernible increase in output (GDP)

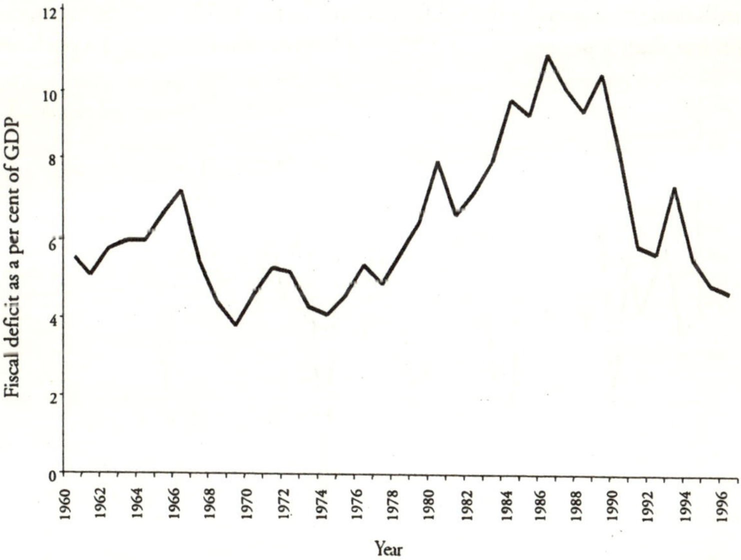

Figure 3.1: The Fiscal Deficit (as a per cent of GDP)

Source: Government of India, *Economic Survey*, various issues.

[2] Kohli (1991) calls these developments in India's political economy as its 'growing crisis of governability'.

growth in the economy from the early 1980s. This growth momentum, however, turned out to be unsustainable as the widening budget deficit and rapid increase in imports unmatched by export growth soon began to be reflected in a widening current account deficit. Despite rapid increase in inward remittances by expatriate Indians, the widening current account deficit began to reflect a rapid erosion in the nation's external reserve position. The situation was aggravated by the abrupt fall in remittance inflows and oil price increases caused by the Gulf War leading to the mid-1991 balance of payments crisis. The crisis led to a temporary decline in GDP growth in 1991 and 1992 and proved to be the harbinger of a significant structural adjustment-cum-liberalization reform implemented under the supervision of the International Monetary Fund (IMF).

Since then, there has been a rebound of the economy, with annual GDP growth rates comparable to or even higher than those of the 1980s (see Fig. 3.2). The average annual GDP growth rate during 1993–6 was 7 per cent, compared to 5.5 per cent for the 1980s.

As a consequence of expansionary macroeconomic policy, the rate of inflation witnessed an upsurge in the 1980s (see Fig. 3.3). The annual rate of inflation (measured by the GDP deflator) in the 1980s was 6 per cent, up from less than 3 per cent in the 1970s. Inflation peaked at over 10 per cent

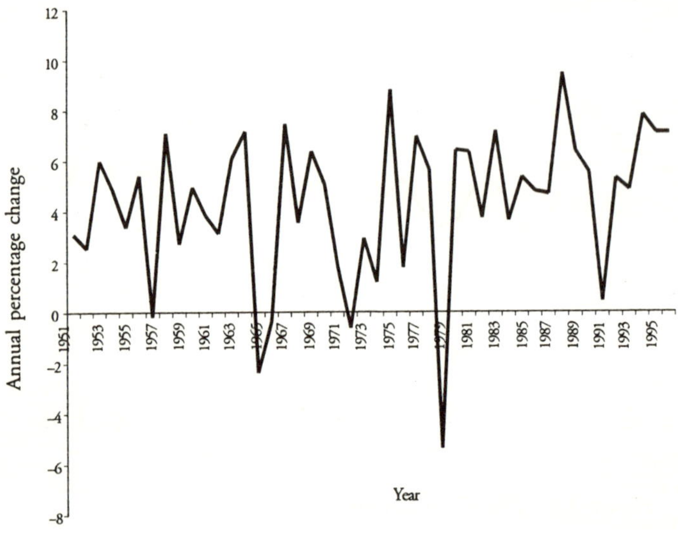

Figure 3.2: Growth of GDP

Source: Government of India, *Economic Survey*, various issues.

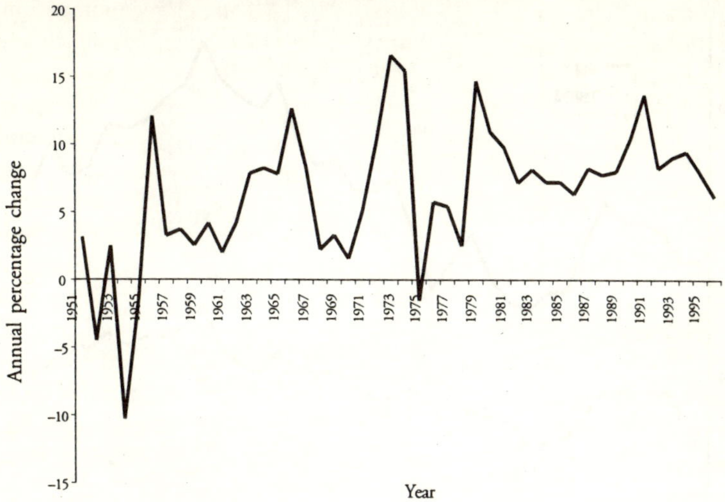

Figure 3.3: Rate of Inflation

Source: Government of India, *Economic Survey*, various issues.

during the 1991 crisis, but has subsequently come down, falling below 8 per cent since 1995. This was primarily the result of monetary tightening, but also of a freeze on all administered prices, including prices of food and fuel. Despite declared policy commitments, the government has not yet been able to achieve fiscal consolidation, which is required for successfully combining sustained rapid growth with low inflation. The very small improvement in the fiscal deficit since 1991 has been achieved by a fall in public investment, rather than through broadening the revenue base or pruning current expenditure. The loss in control over Indian public finances has led to a shift in the composition of central government expenditures from investment to consumption (the latter being mostly the salary bill of government employees and subsidies) (Mundle and Rao 1997). This is clearly evident from the steady decline in public investment as a ratio of GDP since the mid-1980s (see Fig. 3.4). Continued reliance on tight monetary policy on inflationary consideration at a time when the budget deficit is running high could thwart long run growth through continuing high interest rates. Moreover the reliance on cuts in public investment expenditure for want of reducing budget deficit essentially involves a costly compromise on infrastructure development needed for rapid growth under the market-oriented policy reforms (Joshi and Little 1997; Joshi 1998).

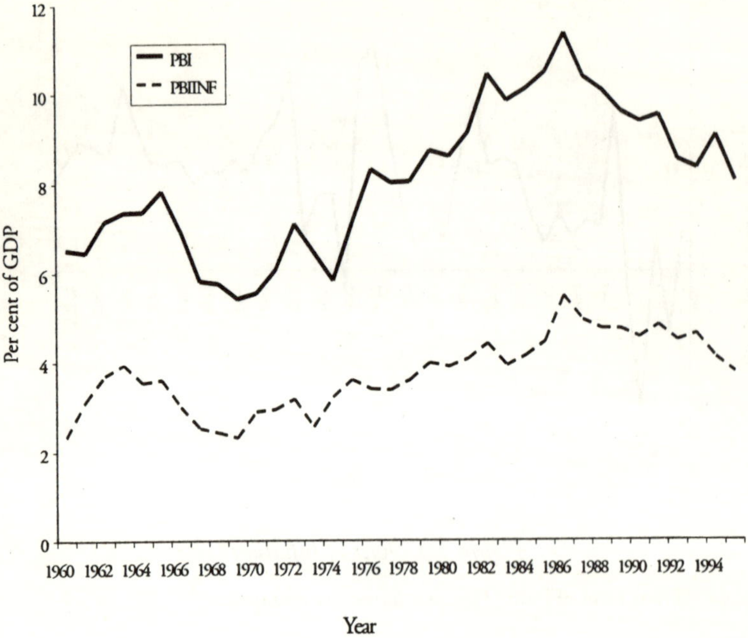

Figure 3.4: Public Investment, Total (PBI) and in Infrastructure (PBIINF) as per cent of GDP

Source: CSO, *National Accounts Statistics*, various issues.

Given that economic growth has been in the past greatly dependent on the provision of good quality infrastructure by the state (Ahluwalia 1985, 1991; Bardhan 1998), the fact that the fall in total public investment has been paralleled by a fall in public investment in infrastructure is of great concern.[3]

TRADE POLICY

From the mid-1950s till the late 1970s, India had a highly restrictive trade regime. Nearly all imports were subject to discretionary import licensing or were channellized by government monopoly trading organizations. The only exceptions were commodities listed in the Open General License

[3] Public infrastructural investment is defined to be gross domestic capital formation by the public sector in electricity, gas, water supply, transport, storage, and communications.

(OGL) category. Capital goods were divided into a restricted category and the OGL category. While import licenses were required for restricted capital goods, those in the OGL could be imported without a license subject to several conditions. The most important of these were that the importing firm had to be the actual user of the equipment and could not sell the latter for five years without the permission of the licensing authorities and that the resulting change in capacity must be compatible with the capacity approved by the industrial licensing authorities. Intermediate goods were divided into the banned, restricted, and limited permissible categories plus an OGL category. As these names suggest, the first three lists were in order of import licensing stringency. OGL imports of intermediate goods were also governed by the 'actual user' condition. The import of consumer goods were, however, banned (except those which were considered essential and could only be imported by the designated government channellizing agencies).

Move Towards Gradual Liberalization

Beginning with the export–import policy of 1977, there was a slow but sustained relaxation of import controls. Several capital goods, which until then remained under stringent import licensing, were steadily shifted to the OGL category. The number of capital goods on the OGL list increased from 79 in 1976 to 1170 in April 1988. These changes were made with the intention of allowing domestic industries to modernize, and the OGL status was usually accompanied by reduced customs tariff rates. Moreover, during the 1980s the import licensing of capital goods in the restricted list were administered with less stringency (Pursell 1992). As a consequence, the import penetration ratio in the capital goods sector increased from 11 per cent in 1976 to 18 per cent in 1985 (Goldar and Renganathan 1990). In the case of intermediate goods too, there was a steady shift of items from the restricted and limited permissible categories to the OGL category. However, in the case of both capital and intermediate goods, in most cases these goods were placed in the OGL list if they were not being domestically produced. Thus, import liberalization during this period may not have led to immediate direct competition to established producers of intermediate and capital goods in India (though in several instances, the goods that were allowed to be imported were imperfect substitutes of domestically produced goods) (World Bank 1989; Aksoy 1992). Furthermore, the average effective tariff rate for capital goods increased from 37 per cent in 1973 to 63 per cent in 1988. Also, consumer goods remained in the banned list for the entire duration of the 1970s and 1980s.

Like imports, exports were also subject to an elaborate licensing regime.

There were goods whose export was not allowed , goods whose exports were considered on a case-by-case basis, goods whose export was allowed within an export quota announced and allocated each year, goods whose export was channellized, and goods on the OGL list that could be exported subject to prescribed conditions. The aim of this licensing system was essentially threefold: first, to ensure that an 'essential' commodity was not exported when domestic demand was greater than domestic supply; second, to guard against adverse price movements in those international markets in which India was a key player; and third, to restrict the exports of intermediates in favour of "high-value-added" downstream products (Agrawal et al. 1995). Furthermore, there were a large number of export incentives for manufactured goods. Special import licenses allowed exporters to import raw materials more easily. The Cash Compensatory Support Scheme (which was introduced in 1964) provided cash assistance to exporters in respect of certain items. This was intended to compensate exporters for indirect taxes (most importantly, sales tax) on inputs imported or domestically produced. The Duty Exemption Scheme (introduced in 1976) granted customs duty exemption to registered exporters for imports of specified raw materials against an advance license for the manufacture of specified export products and imposed upon the exporters an export obligation in return.

The pace of the trade reforms, in particular the shift from quantitative import controls to a protective system based on tariffs, initiated in the mid-1970s were considerably quickened by the new government (led by Rajiv Gandhi) that came into power in November 1985. Also, beginning in the mid-1980s, there was a renewed emphasis by the new administration on export promotion. The number and value of incentives offered to exporters were increased and their administration streamlined. The allotment of Replenishment (REP) licences—tradeable import entitlements awarded to exporters on a product-specific basis—became increasingly generous (Agrawal et al. 1995). Export licensing was also not generally implemented in a manner that that could become a significant deterrent to exports. At the same time, the exchange rate became an important tool of export promotion and there was a steady devaluation of the Indian rupee during this period (see Fig. 3.5). The latter may have counteracted the decrease in protection brought about by the liberalization of import controls in the Indian manufacturing sector.

Reforms in the 1990s

In 1991, as a part of the structural adjustment programme, quotas on the imports of most machinery and equipment and manufactured intermediate goods were removed. REP licences were abolished and a large part of the

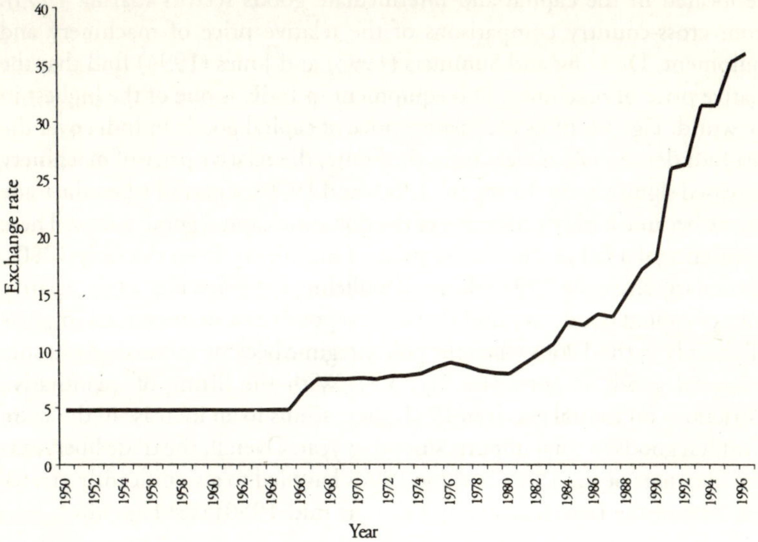

Figure 3.5: The Nominal Exchange Rate (Rupees per US Dollar)

Source: Government of India, *Economic Survey*, various issues.

import licensing system was replaced by tradeable import entitlements (named 'Eximscrips') linked to export earnings. Furthermore, the actual user criterion for the imports of capital and intermediate goods was removed. There was also a significant cut in tariff rates, with the peak tariff rate reduced from 300 per cent to 150 per cent and the peak duty on capital goods cut to 80 per cent. There was, however, little change in trade policy with respect to consumer goods, which remained in the negative (banned) list. By the late 1990s, consumer goods industries, which continued to benefit from these continuing import bans, accounted for over 40 per cent of domestic manufacturing value added (Joshi and Little 1997).

One aspect of Indian trade policy that may have been particularly detrimental to capital accumulation has been the high relative price of capital goods (this issue is explored in greater detail in Chapter 6). The high level of customs tariffs and taxes levied on imported capital goods has led to the domestic capital goods industry supplying the rest of the industrial sector at prices generally higher than international prices for comparable capital goods (Ettori 1990). The high level of prices in the capital goods sector compared to international norms may also be due to the high degree of inefficiency prevailing among public sector enterprises, most of which are located in the capital and intermediate goods sectors (Sarma 1995). From cross-country comparisons of the relative price of machinery and equipment, De Long and Summers (1993) and Jones (1994) find that the relative price of machinery and equipment in India is one of the highest in the world. Fig. 3.6 plots the relative price of capital goods in India over the past four decades. As is clear from the figure, the relative price of machinery increased significantly during the 1960s and 1970s, a period when the trade regime became highly protective of the domestic capital goods sector. There is evidence of a fall in the relative price of machinery from the early 1980s, particularly since the 1991 reforms. Paralleling the behaviour of the relative price of capital goods, we find that capital goods as a share of total imports fell sharply in the 1960s when the policy regime became increasingly hostile to capital goods imports (see Fig. 3.7). With the lifting of quantitative restrictions on capital goods in 1991, there seems to an increase in the share of capital goods in total imports since that year. Overall, the trade liberalization measures of the 1980s and the 1990s have led to a significantly greater openness of the Indian economy since the mid-1980s (see Fig. 3.8).[4]

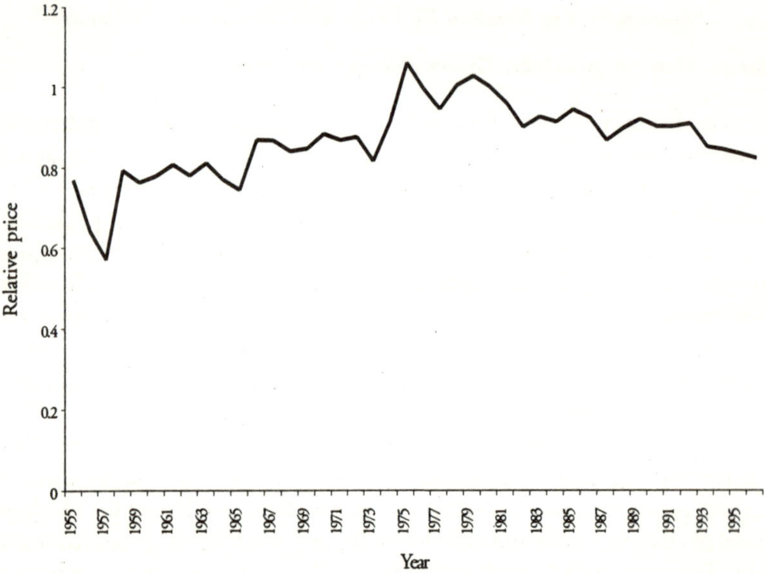

Figure 3.6: Relative Price of Capital Goods

Source: CSO, *National Accounts Statistics*, various issues.

[4] Openness, as is conventionally defined, is the ratio of exports plus imports to GDP.

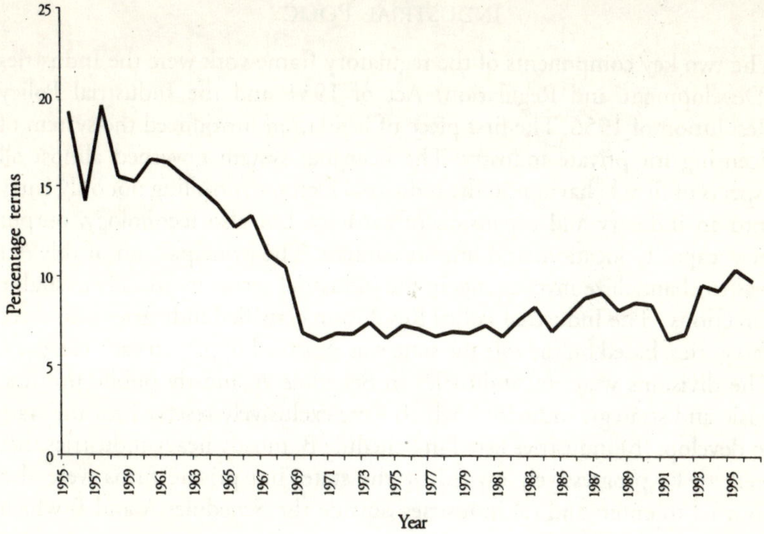

Figure 3.7: Share of Capital Goods in Total Imports

Source: Government of India, *Economic Survey*, various issues.

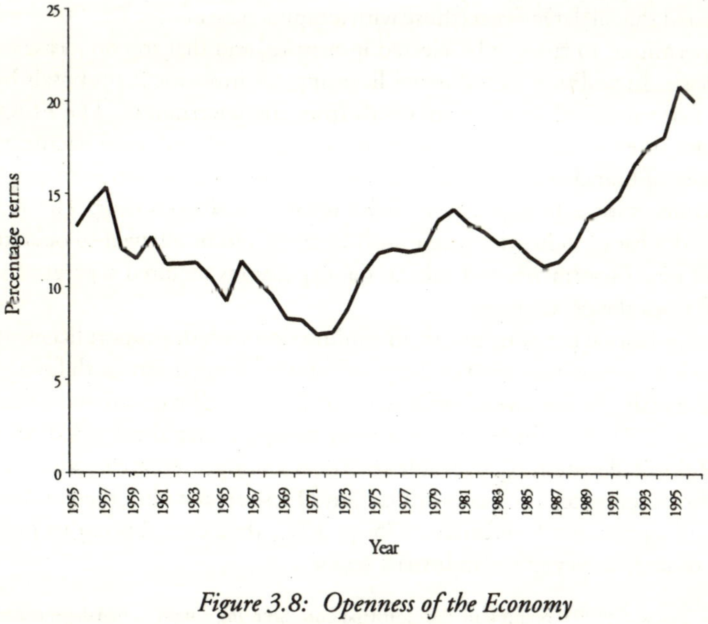

Figure 3.8: Openness of the Economy

Source: Government of India, *Economic Survey*, various issues.

INDUSTRIAL POLICY

The two key components of the regulatory framework were the Industries (Development and Regulation) Act of 1951 and the Industrial Policy Resolution of 1956. The first piece of legislation introduced the system of licensing for private industry. The licensing system governed almost all aspects of firm behaviour in the industrial sector, controlling not only entry into an industry and expansion of capacity, but also technology, output mix, capacity location, and import content. The principal aim of this Act was to channellize investments in the industrial sector in 'socially desirable directions'. The Industrial Policy Resolution classified industries into three categories, based on the role the state was expected to play in each category. The divisions were: (a) industries in Schedule A, mostly public utilities, basic and strategic industries, which were exclusively reserved for the state to develop; (b) industries listed in Schedule B, mostly heavy industries that were to be progressively owned by the state, but private firms were also allowed to enter; and (c) industries outside the Schedules A and B which were open to private firms.

The system of controls was reinforced in the 1970s with the introduction of the Monopolies and Restrictive Trade Practices (MRTP) Act in 1970 and the Foreign Exchange Regulation Act (FERA) in 1973. The MRTP Act stipulated that all large firms (those with a capital base of over Rs 200 lakhs) were permitted to enter only selected industries, and that too on a case by case basis. In addition to industrial licensing, all investment proposals by these firms required separate approvals from the government. The FERA provided the regulatory framework for commercial and manufacturing activities of branches of foreign companies in India and Indian joint-stock companies with a foreign equity holding of over 40 per cent. The Act specified a list of industries where such firms would be allowed to operate and all new investments and substantial expansions required separate approval from the government.

The industrial licensing system in conjunction with the import licensing regime led to the elimination of the possibility of competition, both foreign and domestic, 'in any meaningful sense of the term' (Bhagwati and Desai 1970: p. 272). As it became increasingly complex over time, it led to 'a wasteful misallocation of investible resources among alternative industries and also accentuated the under-utilization of resources within these industries' (Bhagwati and Srinivasan 1975, p. 191), thus contributing to high levels of inefficiency in the industrial sector.[5]

[5] As Bhagwati (1993) points out, 'the industrial-cum-licensing system ... had degenerated into a series of arbitrary, indeed inherently arbitrary, decisions where, for instance, one activity

In the mid-1980s, there were some half-hearted liberalization measures such as the dilution of licensing requirements as regards entry and expansion of capacity. The list of industries open to large firms was also extended and the asset threshold above which firms were subject to monopoly regulation raised. Substantial deregulation occurred in 1991, with the industrial licensing system abolished altogether, except for a select list of environmentally sensitive industries (Mookherjee 1995). Sections of the MRTP Act that restricted growth or merger of large business houses were eliminated. The list of industries reserved for the public sector was reduced from seventeen to six and private investment actively solicited in the infrastructural sector. Foreign ownership up to 51 per cent is now 'automatically' approved for a wide range of industries deemed to be of national importance. For the first time in the post-war period, proposals up to 100 per cent foreign ownership are now considered by the Foreign Investment Promotion Board. Clearly, the new policy regime provides a far more conducive environment for private sector firms to diversify and grow. However, certain aspects of the old regulatory framework remain in place, in particular, labour laws that prohibit firms from firing workers who have been in employment with the firm for more than one year, and bankruptcy procedures that do not allow firms to liquidate their assets easily. Moreover, the continued importance of public industry, especially its dominance of the non-tradeable goods and infrastructure sectors, continues to remain a major constraint on private sector growth.

FINANCIAL SECTOR POLICY

In the 1950s and 1960s, the Indian financial sector operated in a fairly liberal environment. This period saw the consolidation of the Reserve Bank of India (RBI) in its role as the agency in charge of the supervision and control of banks. An important feature of the banking sector during the period 1951–68 was that a large proportion of bank credit went to the industrial sector, and within it, to the large borrowers, with the agricultural sector getting a little over 2 per cent of bank credit. Thus, there was a growing realization among Indian policy makers that there was a need for extensive social control of the Indian banking system. In July 1969, as a consequence, 14 of the largest commercial banks were nationalized.

The evolution of the Indian financial sector beginning from 1969 can be divided into three distinct sub-periods: first, a period of increasing financial

---

would be chosen over another simply because the administering bureaucrats were so empowered, and indeed obligated, to choose' (p. 50).

repression from the early 1970s to the mid-1980s; second, a period of mild reforms till 1991; and finally, from 1991, a period of an increasingly liberalized financial sector. In the first period, the bank nationalization of 1969 was followed by the nationalization of six more Indian commercial banks in 1980. Banks were increasingly pressurized to lend to the priority sector, comprising agriculture and allied activities, small-scale industry, retail trade, transport operators, professionals, and craftsmen. While this meant that more credit was available to small-scale firms, medium and large firms may have received a decreasing share of bank credit in the process. At the same time, there was an increasing recourse to the banking sector via the statutory liquidity ratio to finance the ever widening budget deficits of the central government in the 1970s and the 1980s, possibly crowding out bank financing of private investment. While the commercial banks essentially provided short term credit to the manufacturing sector, long term loans were provided by all-India development banks like Industrial Development Bank of India and Industrial Credit and Investment Corporation of India. These term-lending institutions depended a lot on the government for resources (usually subsidized heavily) and their allocation of long term loans to firms was strictly monitored by the government according to plan priorities. The government also controlled the stock markets with respect to pricing, quantum, and timing of new issues.

While social control of the banking sector may have led to increasing inefficiency in the financial intermediation process (see Ministry of Finance 1991), there was significant growth in the commercial banking system in the country both in geographical coverage and amount of resources mobilized. This was in great part due a strictly enforced branch licensing policy followed by the RBI. Under this policy, the RBI restricted banks from opening branches in urban and metropolitan areas. Instead, the thrust of branch expansion was mostly to the 'under-banked' districts in rural and semi-urban areas. This led to an increase in bank deposits as a percentage of national income from 15.3 in 1969 to 51.8 in 1994. Furthermore, in contrast to the experience with financial repression in other developing countries, the real rate of return on bank deposits has been positive all through (except during the oil price shocks of 1973 and 1979 and the high inflation period of 1990; see Fig. 3.9). Primarily due to the branch licensing and real interest rate policies, there was a significant financial deepening in the Indian economy in the 1970s, as is evident from a sharply rising M3/GDP ratio during this period (see Fig. 3.10).

In the second period, from the mid-1980s, there was a gradual set of reforms in the money markets with little or no change in policies relating to the provision of credit to firms in the industrial sector. Some attempts were

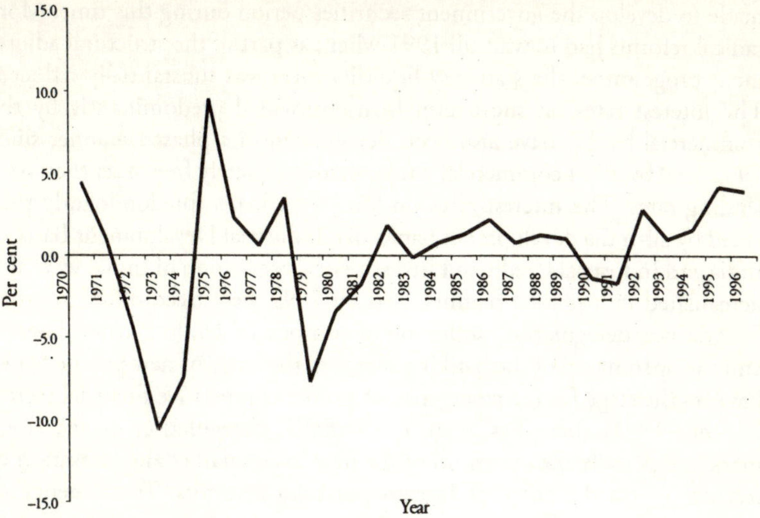

Figure 3.9: The Real Deposit Rate

Source: RBI, *Reports on Currency and Finance*, various issues.

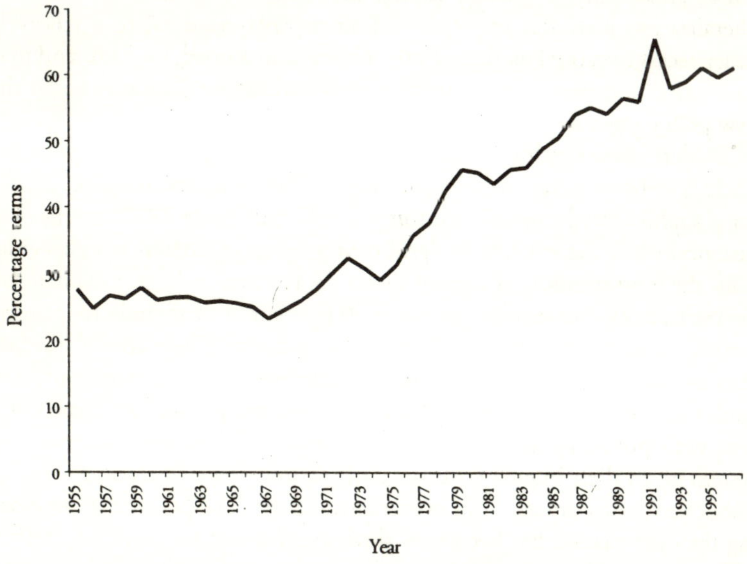

Figure 3.10: Financial Deepening (M3/GDP)

Source: Government of India, *Economic Survey*, various issues.

made to develop the government securities period during this time. More radical reforms had to wait till 1991 when, as part of the structural adjustment programme, the statutory liquidity ratio was substantially reduced. The interest rates on short-term loans (provided predominantly by the commercial banks) have also been deregulated in a phased manner since 1992, and by 1994 commercial banks were completely free to set their own lending rates. The interest rates on long-term loans (predominantly provided by all-India development banks like Industrial Development Bank of India and Industrial Credit and Investment Corporation of India) were also deregulated in a phased manner, and by 1992 were freed of all controls. Interest rate deregulation, softening of consortium lending arrangements, and the opening up of the banking sector to the entry of new private banks have set the stage for the emergence of a more competitive financial sector.

Since 1991, there has been a substantial deregulation of the stock market, especially the operation of the new issues market and relaxation of restrictions on the entry of foreign portfolio investors. Transparency of stock trading practices has improved as a result of the introduction of screen-based trading and the establishment of the National Stock Exchange that compete with the Bombay Stock Exchange, the premier exchange in the country. Indian firms with good track records have been allowed to issue bonds and equity in foreign capital markets. On balance, the financial liberalization measures implemented since 1991 have led to a relatively easier access to capital markets, both at home and abroad, for firms and may have eased borrowing constraints on their investment decisions under the new policy regime.

Despite these significant moves towards redressing financial repression, 'there is still a long way to go in creating an efficient financial sector suitable for a sophisticated modern economy' (Joshi and Little 1997, p. 16). For instance, while there has been significant progress in interest rate deregulation, the long-standing system of direct credit remains largely unchanged. Formally, banks are required to direct 40 per cent of their credit to priority sectors , notably agriculture and small-scale industry. There are still binding restrictions on new banks opening branches and on the operation of non-bank financial intermediaries. Although, in theory, private banks can compete with public banks, in practice the latter still dominate the banking system given their branch coverage and customer base (including captive public sector customers) built over many decades. The progress in developing the debt market has been very slow; the demand for corporate debt is still constrained by the portfolio restrictions imposed by the government on domestic insurance and provident fund institutions as well as on foreign institutional investors.

CONCLUSIONS

The evolution of economic policies in India in the post-independence period can be classified into three phases. The first phase was one of control and command, which stretched from the mid-1950s to the early 1980s. The second phase from the early 1980s to the early 1990s was a period of slow and uneven reform, with the liberalization measures occurring mostly in the trade and industrial sector. The third phase from 1991 to the present was one of rapid and radical reforms, with the reforms encompassing almost every aspect of the policy regime.

Several of the policy changes discussed in the chapter have significant implications for saving and investment behaviour and on the relationship between investment and growth. The complexity of the Indian policy regime and the occasional shifts in economic policy provides a challenge for the applied economist in delineating the links between policy variables and the behaviour of saving, investment, and output growth in the Indian context. This will be our task in the chapters that follow.

4

Saving and Investment in India: Trends and Patterns

This chapter surveys investment and saving performance in India during the post-independence period in order to set the stage for the empirical analysis in the ensuing chapters. Apart from delineating the overall trends, particular attention is placed on specific episodes of upswings and dips in saving/investment behaviour. India's saving/investment performance is compared with that of other developing countries. The methodology of estimating saving and investment in India and the key limitations of the data are discussed in Appendix 1.

TRENDS IN SAVING AND INVESTMENT IN INDIA

There has been a consistent increase in saving and investment rates in India through the post-independence period, though with considerable fluctuations from year to year (see Fig. 4.1). The gross domestic saving rate increased from about 10 per cent in the early 1950s to 17 per cent in the early 1970s, and then to over 25 per cent by the mid-1990s.[1] The investment rate increased from 11 per cent in the early 1950s to around 19 per cent in the early 1970s, and then to 26 per cent by the mid-1990s. Both the saving and investment rates exhibited significant cyclical behaviour, with the saving rate more volatile than the investment rate. The coefficient of variation over the period 1950–96 was 0.29 for the saving rate as compared to 0.25 for the investment rate.

[1] Note that the concept of gross domestic saving in Indian national accounts corresponds to what is commonly termed as gross national saving, as the former includes current transfers from Indian emigrants and net factor income from abroad.

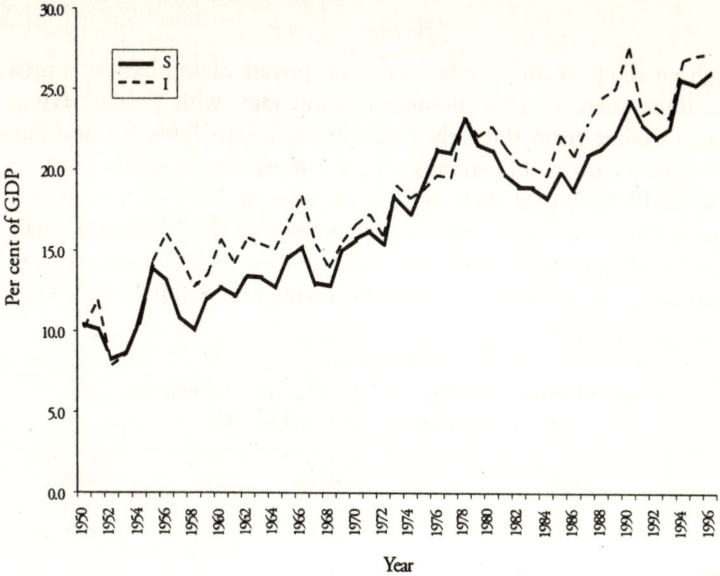

Figure 4.1: Saving and Investment Rates

Notes: S is Gross Domestic Saving (GDS) and I is Gross Domestic Capital Formation (GDCF). The GDCF series used is adjusted for errors and omissions.

Source: Government of India, *Economic Survey*, various issues.

Domestic investment in India has been predominantly financed through domestic saving. Foreign capital inflows (or foreign saving, which represents the difference between domestic investment and saving) have been less than 2 per cent of GDP during much of the period under consideration. The inflow of foreign aid to India (on a per capita basis) has been low throughout, ranking India virtually at the bottom of the list of aid recipients. This mostly reflects the fact that the economy is so large that only a dramatic influx could possibly make the inflow large relative to the vast population. The role of foreign direct investment has been even less important. This reflects the restrictive capital account regime and the unwillingness of the Indian government to invite foreign investment uncritically. India also experienced significant outflow of capital from the old industries, particularly tea, in the immediate post-independence period until about the early 1960s. Moreover, given the sheer size of the economy, the annual inflows of FDI relative to national income looks small in an international comparison (Bhagwati and Srinivasan 1975: p. 6).

Saving

Throughout the post-independence period, private saving has accounted for the lion's share of total domestic saving rate, with public savings showing a decline from the early 1980s onwards (see Table 4.1 and Fig. 4.2). The private saving rate increased from 8.6 per cent in 1950–5 to 17.3 per cent in 1970–5, and then to 22.4 per cent in 1991–6. The annual increase in the private saving rate was much faster in the 1950s and 1960s compared to the period from the late 1960s to early 1980s. From then on, there has been a significant increase in the saving rate well into the 1990s.

TABLE 4.1
Gross Domestic Savings (GDS) and its Components as a Percentage of GDP, 1950–96

Years	*GDS*	*Public*	*Private*
1950–5	10.3	1.7	8.6
1956–60	11.7	1.9	9.8
1961–5	13.2	3.1	10.1
1966–70	14.3	2.4	12.0
1971–5	17.3	3.2	14.0
1976–80	21.6	4.3	17.3
1981–5	19.1	3.6	15.5
1986–90	21.5	1.9	19.6
1991–6	24.1	1.7	22.4

Source: CSO, *National Accounts Statistics*, various issues.

Within private saving, household saving has continued to remain by far the most important component. Its share in total private saving declined marginally over the years, from over 88 per cent in the early 1950s to 84 per cent in the mid-1990s, reflecting the increase in corporate saving. Although corporate saving as a share of GDP has recorded almost a fourfold increase (from 1 per cent to 3.6 per cent) over this period (see Fig. 4.3), it still accounts for only 16 per cent of total private saving by the mid-1990s.

The share of financial saving in total household savings increased from 22 per cent in the early 1950s to 54 per cent in the mid-1990s (see Table 4.2). As a ratio of GDP, household financial saving increased steadily from

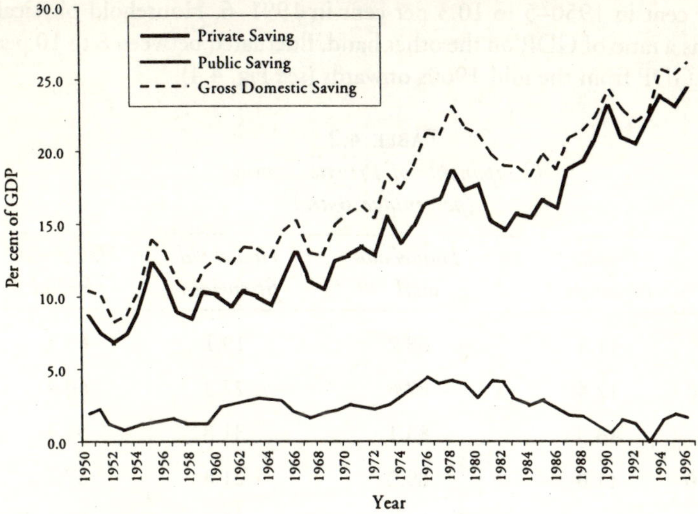

Figure 4.2: Gross Domestic Saving and its Components as a Percentage of GDP

Source: CSO, *National Accounts Statistics*, various issues.

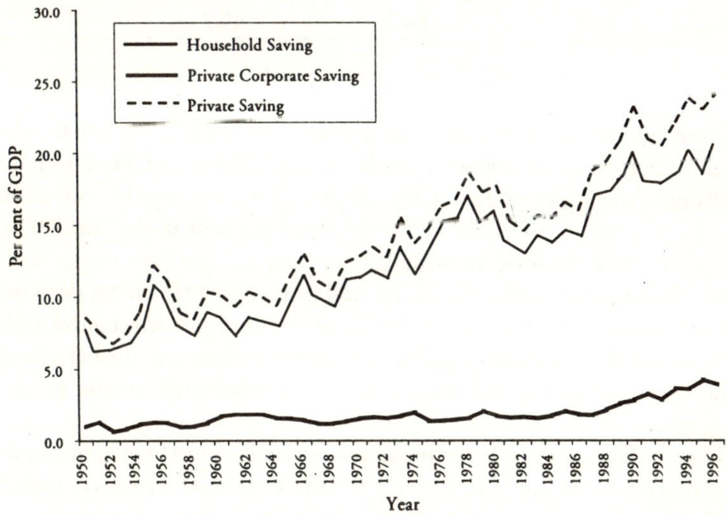

Figure 4.3: Private Saving and its Components as a Percentage of GDP

Source: CSO, *National Accounts Statistics*, various issues.

1.6 per cent in 1950–5 to 10.3 per cent in 1991–6. Household physical saving as a ratio of GDP, on the other hand, fluctuated between 8 to 10 per cent of GDP from the mid-1960s onwards (see Fig. 4.4).

TABLE 4.2
Components of Private Savings
(percentage share)

Years	*Private corporate*	*Household-total*	*Household-financial*	*Household-physical*
1950–5	11.8	88.2	19.1	69.1
1956–60	12.4	87.6	27.3	60.4
1961–5	16.9	83.1	31.8	51.2
1966–70	11.0	89.0	21.8	67.2
1971–5	11.7	88.3	30.7	57.6
1976–80	9.3	90.7	34.5	56.2
1981–5	10.9	89.1	44.4	44.7
1986–90	11.2	88.8	41.3	47.6
1991–6	15.8	84.2	45.7	38.4

Source: CSO, *National Accounts Statistics*, various issues.

Given the strong performance of private saving since the 1970s, the overall saving rate in India would have been much higher had it not been for the dismal showing in public saving. Public saving rate steadily increased from 1.7 per cent in the early 1950s to over 4 per cent in the late 1970s. From then on, it declined persistently, reaching 1.7 per cent in the mid-1990s. The share of public saving in total gross domestic saving declined from about 20 per cent in the late 1970s to a mere 7 per cent by the mid-1990s. Given the low share of public saving in overall saving, the behaviour of the aggregate saving rate continued to be dominated by the private saving rate.[2]

When public saving is decomposed into its main components, one finds that much of the fall in public saving since the 1980s could be attributed to the sharp deterioration in the saving of the government administration

[2] The correlation coefficient between gross domestic saving and private saving is 0.98 while that between gross domestic saving and public saving is 0.23.

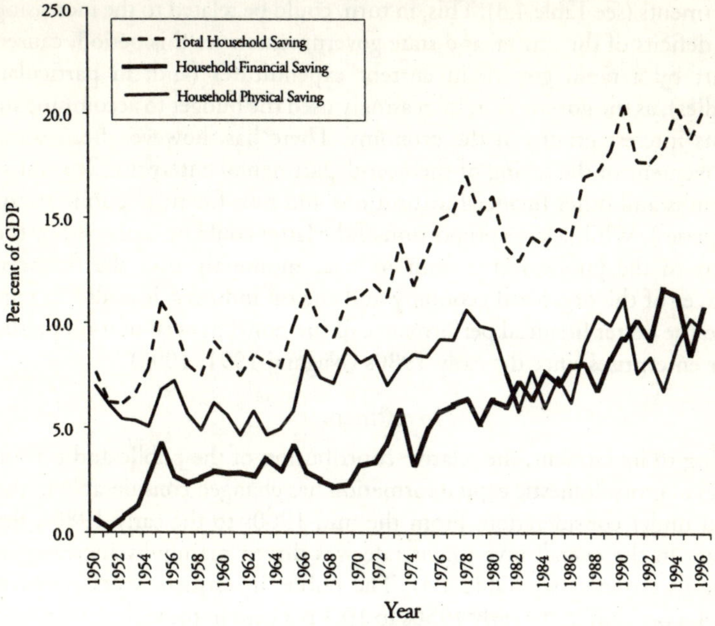

Figure 4.4: Household Saving and its Components as a Percentage of GDP

Source: CSO, *National Accounts Statistics*, various issues.

TABLE 4.3
Public Saving and its Components as a Percentage of GDP

Years	*Government administration*	*Departmental enterprises*	*Non-departmental enterprises*	*Total public sector*
1971–5	1.7	0.5	1.0	3.2
1976–80	2.3	0.6	1.4	4.3
1981–5	0.9	0.3	2.4	3.6
1986–90	–1.9	0.6	3.2	1.9
1991–6	–2.4	0.9	3.2	1.7

Source: CSO, *National Accounts Statistics*, various issues.

departments (see Table 4.3). This, in turn, could be related to the increasing fiscal deficits of the central and state governments over this period, caused in part by a rapid growth in current expenditures (and, in particular, subsidies), as the government increasingly used the budget to accommodate various interest groups in the economy. There has, however, been some improvement in the saving of the non-departmental enterprises (comprising banks and other financial institutions and non-financial public sector enterprises). While a large proportion of the latter could be explained by the returns to the public sector from its near monopoly over the financial resources of the organized economy and the oil industry, it is also in part due to the better financial performance of the non-financial non-oil public sector enterprises since the early 1980s (Nagaraj 1991, 1993).

Investment

Turning to investment, the relative contribution of the public and private sectors to gross domestic capital formation has changed considerably in the period under consideration. From the mid-1960s to the early 1980s, the increase in the overall investment rate was driven mainly by increases in public investment (see Table 4.4). The public investment rate improved from 3.4 per cent in the early 1950s to 10.7 per cent in the early 1980s, and to a doubling of the investment rate from 10.7 per cent in 1950--5 to 22.5

TABLE 4.4

Gross Domestic Capital Formation and its Components as a Percentage of GDP, 1950–96

Years	*Public*	*Private*	*GDCF*
1950–5	3.4	7.3	10.7
1956–60	6.2	8.5	14.7
1961–5	7.8	8.7	16.5
1966–70	6.4	10.1	16.5
1971–5	7.9	11.0	18.9
1976–80	9.3	12.0	21.3
1981–5	10.7	11.8	22.5
1986–90	10.2	13.6	23.8
1991–6	8.5	15.8	24.3

Source: CSO, *National Accounts Statistics*, various issues.

per cent in 1981–5. However, the rise in the investment rate from the mid-1980s onwards can be attributed mostly to the increase in private investment, in face of a steady decline in public investment (see Fig. 4.5). The public investment rate fell by two percentage points to 8.5 per cent in 1991–6, while the private investment rate increased by four percentage points to 15.8 per cent in the same period. The net effect of this on the aggregate investment rate was an overall increase of 1.8 percentage points to 24.3 per cent in 1991–6.

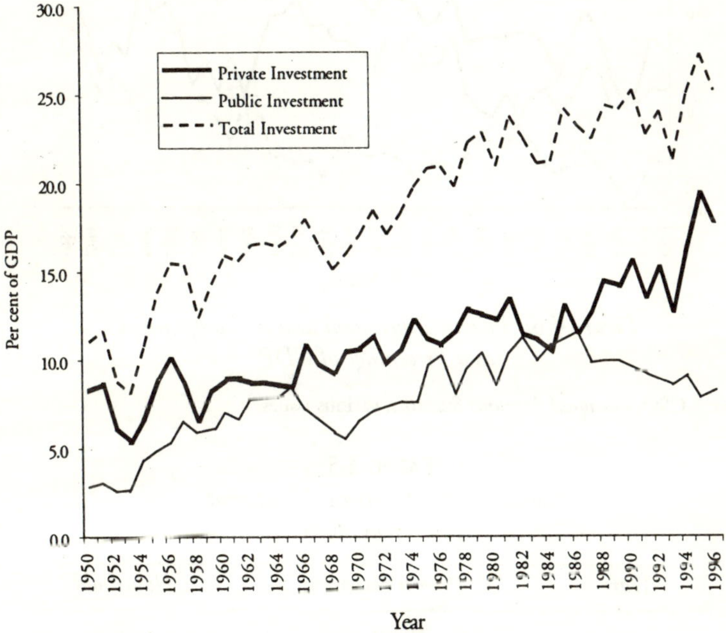

Figure 4.5: Total Investment and its Components as a Percentage of GDP

Source: CSO, *National Accounts Statistics*, various issues.

The increase in private investment in the 1980s and 1990s has mostly come from a rapid rise in private corporate investment, particularly in the 1990s (see Fig. 4.6). The share of corporate investment in total private investment, which varied in the range of 20 to 30 per cent during the first three decades of the post-independence period, increased to over 45 per cent in the 1990s (see Table 4.5). As a share of GDP, private corporate

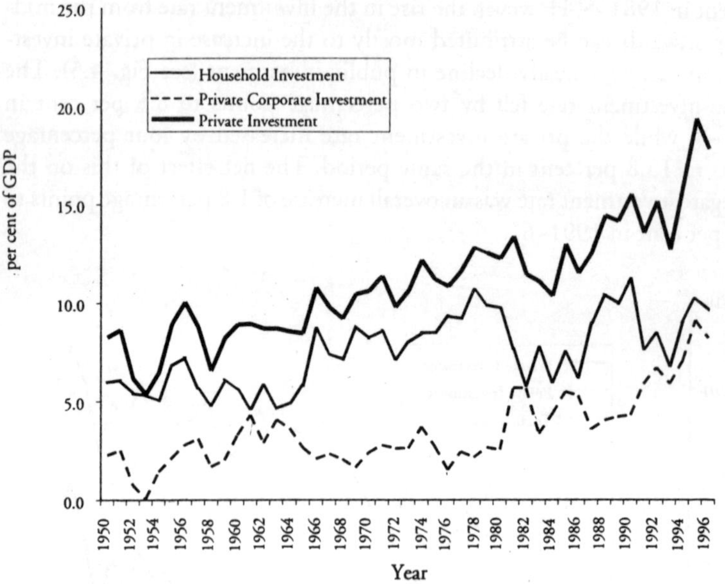

Figure 4.6: Private Investment and its Components as a Percentage of GDP

Source: CSO, *National Accounts Statistics*, various issues.

TABLE 4.5
Components of Private Investment
(percentage share)

Years	*Private corporate*	*Household*
1950–5	20.9	79.1
1956–60	30.4	69.6
1961–5	40.4	59.6
1966–70	20.7	79.3
1971–5	26.2	73.8
1976–80	18.8	81.2
1981–5	41.5	58.5
1986–90	31.5	68.5
1991–6	45.3	54.7

Source: CSO, *National Accounts Statistics*, various issues.

investment increased from 4.3 per cent in the second half of the 1980s to 7.1 per cent by the mid-1990s. Household investment, on the other hand, fell from 9.3 per cent of GDP to 8.5 per cent between these two periods. The sources of rapid rise in private corporate investment in the 1990s will be examined in Chapter 6.

SPECIAL EPISODES OF SAVING AND INVESTMENT BEHAVIOUR

Two specific episodes of saving/investment behaviour in India, which represented a significant departure from the overall trends, have generated a considerable discussion and debate on the underlying causes (Datta Roy Choudhuri and Bagchi 1990; Shetty 1990; EPWRF 1995; Athukorala and Sen 1995). The first episode was in the early 1980s when saving and investment rates fell sharply after almost two decades of sustained growth from the late 1960s (see Fig. 4.2). The gross domestic saving rate fell from 21.2 per cent of GDP in 1980 to 19 per cent in 1982 and remained depressed at around 18–19 per cent of GDP in the years 1983–6 (see Table 4.6). The aggregate investment rate fell from 23.8 per cent of GDP in 1981 to 21.1 per cent in 1983, before recovering to 24.2 per cent in 1985 (see Table 4.7). The fall in the saving/investment rates was particularly puzzling, given the high rates of economic growth witnessed in the same period.[3]

The second episode was the decline in the saving and investment rates immediately after the initiation of the structural adjustment cum stabilization programme of 1991. In 1991, gross domestic saving and gross domestic capital formation fell by 1.5 and 2.5 percentage points of GDP respectively from their 1990 levels. Since the fall in the saving and investment rates took place in the aftermath of the 1991 reforms, the decline in saving and investment was interpreted by some observers as an untoward consequence of the reform process (for example, EPW Research Foundation 1995; Patnaik and Chandrasekhar 1998).

With respect to the first episode, it was generally considered at that time that the saving/investment decline was a reflection of an upward revision of the private corporate investment series by the RBI with no corresponding adjustment of total investment (which is independently measured using the commodity flow method; see Appendix 1) for the years 1981–4 (see CSO 1988; Datta Roy Choudhury 1988; Gothoskar 1988). As a consequence of this revision, the household investment/physical saving series was adjusted

[3] Roy and Sen (1991) argue that the apparent contradiction between falling or stagnant saving rates and high economic growth during this period can be explained by the finding that there have been changes in the composition of aggregate savings during this time, with more household saving moving to sectors and assets that involve lower capital–output ratios.

TABLE 4.6

Gross Domestic Saving and its Components as a Percentage of GDP, 1980–96

Year	*Household total saving*	*Household financial saving*	*Household physical saving*	*Private corporate saving*	*Private saving*	*Public saving*	*GDS*
1980	16.1	6.3	9.7	1.7	17.7	3.4	21.2
1981	13.7	6.0	7.7	1.6	15.2	4.5	19.8
1982	12.9	7.2	5.8	1.6	14.6	4.4	19.0
1983	14.1	6.4	7.7	1.5	15.7	3.3	18.9
1984	13.7	7.7	6.0	1.7	15.4	2.8	18.2
1985	14.6	7.1	7.5	2.0	16.6	3.2	19.8
1986	14.2	8.0	6.2	1.8	16.0	2.7	18.7
1987	17.0	8.0	8.9	1.7	18.7	2.2	20.9
1988	17.2	6.9	10.4	2.1	19.3	2.0	21.4
1989	18.2	8.3	9.9	2.6	20.8	1.6	22.4
1990	20.5	9.3	11.2	2.8	23.3	1.0	24.3
1991	17.7	10.1	7.7	3.2	21.0	1.9	22.9
1992	17.7	9.3	8.4	2.8	20.5	1.5	22.0
1993	18.5	11.7	6.8	3.6	22.1	0.6	22.7
1994	20.3	11.3	9.0	3.5	23.8	1.8	25.6
1995	18.8	8.6	10.3	4.2	23.0	2.3	25.3
1996	20.3	10.7	9.6	3.9	24.2	1.9	26.1

Source: CSO, *National Accounts Statistics*, various issues.

downward by as much as 2–3 percentage points of GDP. Given the methodology used in the calculation of gross domestic saving and adjusted gross domestic capital formation, this led to a downward revision of both the saving and investment rates. However, one finds that the household investment rate remained depressed even in the years following the revision to the private corporate investment series by the RBI (in particular, the years 1985 and 1986; see Table 4.7). It is, therefore, not clear whether the recorded fall in the saving and investment rates was spurious or a genuine decline brought about by adverse changes in the economic fundamentals.

As regards the second episode, there is evidence to suggest that the

TABLE 4.7
Gross Domestic Capital Formation (GDCF) and its Components as a Percentage of GDP 1980–96

Year	*Household investment*	*Private corporate investment*	*Private investment*	*Public investment*	*GDCF*
1980	9.7	2.5	12.3	8.7	20.9
1981	7.7	5.7	13.4	10.4	23.8
1982	5.8	5.7	11.4	11.1	22.5
1983	7.7	3.4	11.1	10.0	21.1
1984	6.0	4.4	10.3	10.8	21.2
1985	7.5	5.5	13.0	11.2	24.2
1986	6.2	5.3	11.5	11.7	23.2
1987	8.9	3.6	12.6	9.9	22.5
1988	10.4	4.0	14.4	9.9	24.4
1989	9.9	4.2	14.1	10.0	24.1
1990	11.2	4.3	15.5	9.7	25.2
1991	7.7	5.9	13.5	9.2	22.7
1992	8.4	6.7	15.1	8.9	24.0
1993	6.8	5.9	12.7	8.6	21.3
1994	9.0	7.1	16.0	9.0	25.1
1995	10.3	9.1	19.3	7.9	27.3
1996	9.6	8.2	17.8	7.4	25.2

Source: CSO, National Accounts Statistics, various issues.

estimates of savings and investment released by the CSO in the years immediately following the reforms may have been subject to significant measurement errors due to the failure of the estimation procedures developed during the pre-reform ('controlled') era to capture changes in economic behaviour brought about by the opening up of the economy as part of the 1991 reforms. This is most apparent when one compares estimates of the aggregate savings and investment rates for the years 1990–2 in the 1995 and the 1998 issues of the *National Accounts Statistics* (NAS) released by the CSO (see Table 4.8). The saving rate fell by 2.3 percentage points of GDP from 1990 to 1992 according to the 1998 NAS, as compared to an estimated fall of 3.7 percentage points according to the 1995 NAS. Similarly, the 1998 NAS estimate of the fall in the investment rate between 1990 and 1992 is 1.2 percentage points of GDP, as compared to the 1995 NAS estimate of 2.4 percentage points. Thus, the drop in the saving and investment rates between 1990 and 1992 were far less pronounced in the revised estimates reported in the 1998 NAS as compared to the original estimates reported in the 1995 NAS. It is possible that this inconsistency in estimates for the saving and investment rates in the period 1990–2 would have been due to measurement errors that were presumably more pronounced in the immediate post-reform period, reflecting structural changes in the economy brought about by reforms (Athukorala and Sen 1995).

TABLE 4.8
CSO Estimates of Saving and Investment Rates

Year	*Gross domestic saving as per cent of GDP*		*Gross investment as per cent of GDP*	
	1995	*1998*	*1995*	*1998*
1990	23.7	24.3	25.7	25.2
1991	23.1	22.9	22.9	22.7
1992	20.0	22.0	23.3	24.0

Source: Estimates as presented in the1995 and 1998 *National Accounts Statistics.*

INDIA'S COMPARATIVE SAVING AND INVESTMENT PERFORMANCE

In Tables 4.9 and 4.10, India's saving and investment performance during 1960–95 is compared with other developing countries for which data are readily available. It is evident that in the 1960s, India's saving performance was superior to that of many other developing countries. Interestingly, India's saving rate at that time (14.3 per cent) was much higher than that of Korea, Indonesia, and Singapore, and only slightly lower than that of Thailand. From about the early 1970s the increase in India's saving rate continued to lag behind that of all these 'High Performing Asian Economies' (HPAEs).[4] By the mid-1990s, India's saving rate (22 per cent) amounted to a little over a half of the average rate for the HPAEs. Among the South Asian countries, India's performance has continued to be impressive, apart from some notable catching-up by Sri Lanka, following the market-oriented policy reforms in the late 1970s. In Latin America, only two countries—Chile and Costa Rica—have maintained consistently superior saving records compared to India during this period. Countries like Brazil, Peru, Argentina, and Mexico, which had higher saving rates than India in the

TABLE 4.9

Gross Domestic Saving Rate for India and Selected Developing Countries, 1960–95

Countries	*1960–4*	*1965–9*	*1970–4*	*1975–9*	*1980–4*	*1985–9*	*1990–5*
South Asia							
India	14.3	15.0	17.4	20.8	19.3	20.8	21.8
Pakistan	10.5	11.8	8.7	7.3	7.9	9.6	15.8
Sri Lanka	11.9	10.4	13.5	13.8	13.7	11.9	14.6
Bangladesh	–	–	–	1.5	1.9	2.9	6.3
East Asia							
Taiwan	21.2	22.2	30.5	31.8	32.0	36.0	28.2
China	–	–	–	32.6	34.3	35.2	39.5
China:							
Hong Kong	20.9	25.8	29.3	32.3	31.7	35.0	34.1
Singapore	4.3	14.9	24.0	33.2	42.7	41.0	23.6
Korea, Rep. of	4.4	13.0	17.5	25.3	26.9	35.6	35.9
Thailand	16.4	21.3	22.6	21.9	23.8	29.1	35.6

(contd.)

[4] This nomenclature was first introduced in World Bank (1993) to refer to the four East Asian newly industrialized economies (South Korea, Taiwan, Hong Kong, and Singapore) and newcomers to export-oriented industrialization in the region, the so called second-tier exporting countries—China, Indonesia, Malaysia, Thailand, and the Philippines.

Table 4.9 (contd.)

Countries	*1960–4*	*1965–9*	*1970–4*	*1975–9*	*1980–4*	*1985–9*	*1990–5*
Indonesia	10.0	5.6	20.7	28.1	31.6	29.3	33.1
Malaysia	23.8	24.4	26.9	32.5	31.6	34.6	35.7
Latin America							
Paraguay	12.6	12.8	15.8	21.6	18.8	20.6	12.0
Venezuela	35.2	33.7	39.6	36.0	27.4	23.9	22.5
Costa Rica	14.4	13.0	14.6	16.1	22.9	23.7	22.9
Brazil	19.8	20.3	20.1	21.5	20.9	25.5	22.3
Mexico	16.1	18.2	18.1	20.3	27.1	23.6	19.5
Peru	38.0	29.2	17.1	18.0	28.5	21.5	14.3
Colombia	16.8	17.5	18.2	20.6	17.7	23.6	19.4
Chile	15.2	20.0	16.3	17.3	14.3	25.3	28.4
Dominican Rep.	13.6	7.9	13.3	18.2	16.7	19.9	15.8
Argentina	22.1	23.7	23.7	30.6	23.5	21.2	17.3
Ecuador	10.9	12.3	18.8	23.0	23.6	20.0	22.7
Jamaica	26.0	28.1	21.5	15.0	14.0	19.7	16.5
Honduras	13.3	16.4	16.1	17.4	12.6	13.5	17.6
El Salvador	12.4	11.0	14.3	18.8	8.2	5.7	3.3
Panama	14.8	20.4	–	–	–	12.3	22.6
Uruguay	18.2	19.4	18.0	18.9	16.0	17.3	14.4
Bolivia	10.7	19.1	26.2	23.0	14.0	6.8	7.8
Guatemala	8.5	11.3	13.8	15.6	10.6	9.2	9.5
Nicaragua	15.1	15.8	16.5	15.5	6.3	4.6	–8.5
Haiti	5.2	3.1	9.0	7.3	6.2	4.9	–6.1

Note: – Data not available.
Source: Compiled from World Bank, *World Tables Database* and Republic of China, Council for Planning and Development, *Taiwan Statistical Data Book* (various issues)(for Taiwan).

1960s, ended up with lower or comparable rates in the mid-1990s. In general, India's saving performance has been consistently superior to that of the overall Latin American record from after about the first oil shock in the early 1970s. Beneath these general patterns, there are large, inter-country differences in saving rates, reflecting a variety of factors, presumably including differences in national cultures, demographic structure, taxation policies, and the overall macroeconomic climate.[5]

The overall inter-country patterns in investment performance and India's relative investment performance are remarkably similar to the patterns observed above relating to saving performance. Generally, countries with increasing saving rates also have increasing investment rates, while those with declining saving rates have slipped down in the investment ranking. These similarities are consistent with the Feldstein–Horioka proposition that, as against the popular perception about rapid globalization of capital, domestic investment is fundamentally determined by domestic saving (Feldstein and Horioka 1980). This is because, so argue Feldstein and Horioka, gross international flow of funds are often part of offsetting transactions that leaves no net transfer of capital from one country to another. Even though most of the legal barriers to capital mobility across these countries no longer exist, capital markets in these countries remain essentially segmented along national lines. Capital may be free to move internationally, but its owners and managers prefer to keep almost all of each nation's savings at home (Feldstein 1995). The Feldstein–Horioka proposition is based on the experiences of the OECD countries. Presumably, it is even more relevant for developing countries where capital markets remained relatively underdeveloped and far less integrated with OECD capital markets. Moreover, there are significant differences among developing countries with regard to the restrictiveness of the policy regimes relating to capital account transactions.

TABLE 4.10
Gross Domestic Investment Rate for India and Selected Developing Countries, 1960–95

Countries	*1960–4*	*1965–9*	*1970–4*	*1975–9*	*1980–4*	*1985–9*	*1990–5*
South Asia							
India	16.4	16.7	18.1	21.3	22.1	23.6	23.5
Pakistan	17.8	17.6	14.4	17.7	18.7	18.6	19.5
Sri Lanka	–	–	16.5	18.4	29.4	22.8	24.5
Bangladesh	9.8	11.7	8.1	10.1	14.3	12.7	13.8
East Asia							
Taiwan	15.6	20.2	24.4	27.7	25.7	19.8	27.5

(contd.)

[5] For studies that attempt to explain the difference in saving/investment rates across countries, see Edwards (1996) and Loayza et al. (1998, 2000).

Table 4.10 (contd.)

Countries	*1960–4*	*1965–9*	*1970–4*	*1975–9*	*1980–4*	*1985–9*	*1990–5*
China	–	–	–	32.5	33.8	36.9	38.2
Hong Kong	29.5	23.4	23.2	27.4	30.6	25.4	29.6
Singapore	15.3	24.2	41.1	39.9	47.4	38.3	36.4
Korea, Rep. of	14.2	23.5	25.2	29.3	29.9	30.6	36.8
Thailand	17.9	23.5	25.0	26.6	29.0	29.9	41.4
Indonesia	10.2	9.3	19.3	24.3	27.3	27.7	31.9
Malaysia	19.0	19.6	24.9	26.0	34.8	26.2	36.5
Latin America							
Paraguay	14.0	16.0	16.9	25.8	26.6	24.1	19.5
Venezuela	22.2	26.5	31.1	37.8	21.6	20.9	16.7
Costa Rica	18.3	19.4	23.5	23.7	25.4	25.8	27.1
Brazil	19.9	19.8	22.3	23.5	20.0	21.6	20.6
Mexico	18.3	20.2	20.2	22.4	23.6	20.3	22.1
Peru	39.5	31.7	19.0	21.4	28.4	20.9	17.5
Colombia	17.8	18.3	19.5	17.9	19.8	19.8	18.8
Chile	17.4	18.7	17.3	18.4	17.2	21.3	26.7
Dominican Rep.	13.7	15.1	20.4	23.6	22.2	25.0	20.2
Argentina	23.0	22.2	23.1	29.0	22.1	17.7	17.0
Ecuador	13.4	16.6	20.7	26.2	21.9	20.8	19.9
Jamaica	28.0	31.1	29.4	18.1	20.5	22.6	19.7
Honduras	14.4	17.8	19.8	22.9	18.2	17.7	25.6
El Salvador	14.2	14.0	16.8	21.9	12.9	12.9	17.4
Panama	18.5	21.5	–	–	–	5.5	21.9
Uruguay	19.6	15.7	18.6	21.6	17.0	12.3	13.2
Bolivia	17.9	22.9	25.6	27.3	11.7	10.7	14.5
Guatemala	10.4	12.8	14.3	19.6	13.9	12.6	16.1
Nicaragua	17.0	20.5	20.9	14.8	20.8	22.6	18.7
Haiti	8.5	7.1	13.8	16.3	17.0	14.6	6.5

Note: – Data not available.

Source: Compiled from World Bank, *World Tables Database* and Republic of China, Council for Planning and Development, *Taiwan Statistical Data Book* (various issues)(for Taiwan).

Behind this overall similarity between saving and investment patterns, significant differences can be observed across countries in terms of the degree of reliance on net foreign capital inflows (foreign saving) for domestic capital formation (recall that for each country, the difference between investment and saving rates for each year represent net foreign capital inflow as a share of GDP). For instance, in India, the difference has varied in the narrow range of 0.7 to 2.1 percentage points through the period under study. Interestingly, there has not been any noticeable increase in the share of net foreign capital inflow in the domestic investment rate. By contrast, for most countries in Latin America as well as for Bangladesh and Pakistan the magnitude of the difference between the two ratios are much larger, ranging from about 5 to 10 percentage points of GDP.

In sum, in all the countries considered here, domestic investment is predominantly determined by domestic saving. The relationship between the two ratios is particularly strong for India, reflecting the restrictive capital account regime (which has changed only marginally even after the 1991 policy reforms).

CONCLUSIONS

There has been an overall increase in saving and investment rates in India through the post-independence period, though with considerable fluctuations from year to year, from less than 10 per cent to over 25 per cent. Domestic investment has been predominantly financed through domestic saving. The contribution of foreign capital inflows (or foreign saving, which represents the difference between domestic investment and saving) has remained less than 5 per cent throughout the period.

Private saving accounted for over 90 per cent of total domestic saving rate throughout, with public saving rate declining persistently from the early 1980s. Much of the fall in public saving since has emanated from deterioration in the fiscal position of the government administrative departments. Despite the rapid growth of corporate saving over the past two decades, household saving continued to account for over four-fifths of total private saving.

The relative contributions of the public and private sectors to gross domestic capital formation have changed considerably over the years. From the mid-1960s to the early 1980s, public investment accounted for much of the increase in the total investment. From then on, private investment has dominated overall investment trends in the economy. The increase in private investment in the last two decades has come mostly from a rapid rise in private corporate investment, whose share in total investment increased from 30 per cent to over 45 per cent during these two decades.

In an international comparison, in the early 1960s India had high saving and investment rates, as compared to many other countries, including the present day high-performing East Asian economies. From about the early 1970s, India has continuously lagged behind the latter countries. However, India's saving and investment performance has continued to remain impressive among developing countries in South Asia and, to a lesser extent, among those in Latin America. Overall saving and investment patterns across countries are consistent with the famous Feldstein–Horioka proposition that, as against the popular perception about rapid globalization of capital, domestic investment has continued to be determined overwhelmingly by domestic saving. Among the countries covered in the comparison, India has one of the lowest degree of reliance on net foreign capital inflows for financing domestic capital formation.

5

The Determinants of Saving

The purpose of this chapter is to examine the determinants of the saving rate in India. The framework for our analysis is derived from the life-cycle model that has been the standard theory for the explanation of changes in private saving over time and across countries. The attractiveness of the life-cycle model for our analysis lies both in its elegant formulation of the effect of growth and demographic changes on saving, and the flexibility provided for incorporating other relevant theoretical considerations to form an integrated analytical framework, without changing the basic structure of the model.

The rest of the chapter is divided into four sections. The next section contains the analytical framework, drawing on the life-cycle model of saving and consumption. The next two sections discuss the models and the database to be used in the empirical analysis. The final section presents the results.

THE ANALYTICAL FRAMEWORK

This section begins with the basic, stripped-down version of the life-cycle model (LCM), and considers modifications/extensions to reflect both recent developments in consumption theory and the structural features that are prevalent in developing countries.[1]

The Life-cycle Model

In the life-cycle model, accumulation for retirement is the prime motive for saving. The model is built around the consumption/saving behaviour of a

[1] For details on the life-cycle model and its advantages over other approaches, see Modigliani (1986), Gersovitz (1988), and Deaton (1989).

representative agent who is assumed to maximize the present value of lifetime utility, subject to a budget constraint. The budget constraint is equal to the current net worth plus the present value of expected labour income over the remaining working life of the agent. Under the simplifying assumptions of perfect capital markets and perfect foresight of the agent about the 'true' income generation process, the model predicts that consumption in a particular period depends on expectations about life time income (*not* on the income in that period, as postulated by the Keynesian model). As income tends to fluctuate systematically over the course of a person's life, saving behaviour is crucially determined by one's stage in the life cycle (Modigliani 1986).[2] Individuals smoothen consumption over their life times, and are consequently, net savers during their working years and dis-savers during retirement.

When the model is extended to the national level, the major determinants of the saving rate (over time in a given country or across countries) are the rate of growth of per capita income, and the age structure of the population. With respect to the rate of growth of per capita income, *GY*, the simplest version of the life-cycle model predicts that an increase in the latter will unambiguously increase the aggregate saving rate, because it increases the lifetime resources (and saving) of younger-age groups relative to older-age groups. However, when wealth is introduced as an additional explanatory variable, the LCM yields ambiguous predictions about the relationship between saving and growth. For example, young people may have low current income but high lifetime wealth, and may therefore borrow to finance current consumption. If they borrow enough, then at sufficiently high rates of economic growth, their lifetime wealth will be high enough relative to that of their elders so that further increases in the rate of growth will decrease the aggregate saving rate. Whether higher growth increases or reduces the saving rate depends on whether the age profile of saving is negatively correlated with age, which is an empirical matter (Deaton and Paxson 2000).

The age structure of the population is uniquely related to population growth, *GPOP*, under the assumption of 'balanced population growth' (Modigliani 1986). This is because an increase in population growth rate caused by an increase in age-specific fertility rates increases the number of savers relative to the number of dis-savers. This implies that if all the individual households in two given economies have the same saving profile over their life cycles, the economy with the faster population growth may show a higher aggregate saving rate.

[2] See Hadjimatheou (1987) for a succinct formal presentation of the basic model.

Relaxation of the assumption of 'balanced population growth', however, complicates the postulated link between demographic factors and saving in the LCM model. As already noted, in the simple two-period formulation of the life cycle model, an increase in population growth rate increases the number of active workers (savers) relative to the number of the retired (dissavers), and therefore increases the aggregate saving rate. This formulation ignores childhood dependency: it assumes that 'workers spring from the womb, tools in hand, and immediately begin to accumulating wealth for their retirement' (Deaton 1992; p. 48). In reality, an increase in the population growth rate increases the number of economically active individuals relative to the retired, but may be accompanied by an increase in the share of the young in the population. Because both the young and the retired (the 'dependent generation') consume more than they can earn, the net effect on aggregate saving of population growth is theoretically ambiguous. Moreover, a given change in the degree of childhood dependence may not have the same impact of saving compared to that brought about by a similar change in aged dependence. This is because the young do not consume independently of the family (Gersovitz 1988; p. 405). With economies of scale in family consumption, large families can provide a child with the same welfare with a less than proportionate increase in expenditure compared to a small family. As well, when they decide to have large families, parents may choose to decrease their consumption, may increase their work time (or effort), or increase their saving in advance of births. These considerations call for the inclusion of aged-dependence and young-dependence as separate explanatory variables (in place of population growth) in saving analysis.

The other determinants of private saving suggested by the LCM is the real interest rate on bank deposits (*RID*), wealth (*W*), and social security payments (and other government transfers to households by the government). The net effect of the interest rate on saving/consumption is unclear in the model. A higher interest rate increases the present price of consumption relative to the future price (the substitution effect), and thus provides an incentive to increase saving. However, if the household is a net lender, the interest rate rise also raises lifetime income, and thus tends to increase consumption and decrease saving (the income effect). Thus, saving responds positively to rises in the interest rate only if the substitution effect is stronger than the income effect. In the case of a typical developing economy, it could be argued that the impact of a change in real interest rate on saving is expected to be positive (McKinnon 1973; Shaw 1973). The underlying reasoning is the following. In the typical developing economy where the portfolio choices are rather limited, the saving process tends to be highly *money intensive*. Given this peculiarity of saving behaviour, plus the fact that the bulk of saving comes from small savers, the substitution effect generally tends to be much larger than the income effect of an interest rate change.

Wealth is postulated to have a negative effect on household saving. Accumulated wealth lessens a household's dependence on current income sources, because households can draw on accumulated assets to maintain their consumption levels. The availability of social security and retirement pension also impacts on saving through changing the household's perceived lifetime income. The smaller coverage of the social security system in a country is postulated to provide an added incentive for thrift and saving (Feldstein 1974; Modigliani and Sterling 1983).

Extensions and Modifications

The formulation of the basic life-cycle model raises a number of issues. The first issue is to do with the key premise of the life-cycle hypothesis that the saving rate is related to the growth of per capita income, *not* the level of per capita income. The absence of a link between current saving and current income in the LCM theory of consumption is an implication of the assumption that individuals are forward-looking, and therefore, base their saving decisions on lifetime income rather than current income. However, the validity of this premise is greatly in doubt for low-income countries such as India. As Modigliani (1993: p. 210) himself notes,

> For at least that portion of the population that lives at, or near, the starvation level, may find it impossible or too burdensome to set aside resources now in order to provide for later consumption. People in that predicament may tend to live more from hand-to-mouth, skipping retirement or being supported by the extended family. It is thus conceivable that, for a sufficiently low value of per capita income, ... the saving–income ratio for given growth would ... tend to rise with income.

In our empirical specification, we use *both* the level and the growth of per capita income as explanatory variables for the saving rate.[3]

A second consideration is to do with the hypothesis of perfect capital markets on which the postulated link between income growth and saving rate is based. Households can effectively smoothen consumption over the lifetime only if they can freely borrow and lend within the limits of their lifetime budget constraint (they can borrow against their future income). To the extent that households are liquidity constrained,[4] that is, they are

[3] The link between consumption and the level of income was made by Keynes in *The General Theory* through the innovation of the consumption function and is usually referred to as the 'absolute income hypothesis'. Hussein and Thirlwall (1999) find strong support for this hypothesis using panel data for 62 countries for the period 1967–95.

[4] Liquidity constraint may arise from a number of market imperfections such as the

unable to borrow freely against future income, their consumption behaviour might indeed be linked to current income rather than to lifetime income (Zeldes 1989; Deaton 1991).

Quite apart from forcing households to maintain consumption at current income levels, the borrowing constraint can in fact convert a negative saver into a positive saver (Gersovitz 1988). This is because households are forced to save more at present in order to undertake lumpy (indivisible) expenditure plans in the future, in the absence of access to adequate borrowing. The result is a positive relationship between the degree of capital market imperfection and the private saving rate. For instance, with little or no consumer credit available, consumers are forced to save the full amount if they want to buy a house or make other large purchases such as consumer durables. In the same manner, there can also be 'investment promoted saving' (Liu and Woo 1994), when households are motivated to accumulate saving to undertake future investment projects, in the absence of access to institutional credit.[5] Interestingly, these influences on saving behaviour imply that following financial liberalization, the national saving rate of a country can decline as young consumers move from being credit constrained under the financially repressed regime to smooth their consumption under the liberalized regime (De Melo and Tybout 1986; Jappeli and Pagano 1989; Bayoumi 1993; Warman and Thirlwall 1994; Bandiera et al. 2000). To capture the possible impact of borrowing constraint on saving behaviour, total lending to the household sector by banks, financial institutions, and the government relative to income (*BOR*) is included as an additional determinant of the saving rate. The impact of the financial liberalization process beginning in 1991 is captured both by the real interest rate variable (*RID*) and the variable measuring borrowing constraints (*BOR*).

A third issue relates to the implicit assumption of the LCM that the consumer knows future income streams with certainty. This assumption may be valid for households in developed countries who save in large part to accumulate wealth. In contrast, income prospects are much more uncertain for most households in developing countries so that saving for these households is not only about accumulation but also about consumption smoothing

under-developed nature of the financial system, inability of borrowers to come up with acceptable collaterals, and various government interventions, including restrictions on consumer credit imposed by the government as part of its saving promotion campaign (Stiglitz and Uy 1996).

[5] On these grounds, some analysts (for example, Stiglitz and Uy 1996) have identified financial restraint (mainly constraints on consumer credit and the discouragement of the development of mortgage markets) as a possible reason for the high saving rates in the East Asian countries, particularly in Korea and Taiwan.

in the face of volatile incomes. Uncertainty of future income streams is particularly true for rural households in developing countries, who are likely to face large weather-related shocks to their incomes. Thus, the precautionary motive can also be an important consideration behind saving (Deaton 1989; Kimball 1990; Hubbard, Skinner and Zeldes 1994). This precautionary view of saving points to the need for an appropriate measure of macroeconomic uncertainty as an explanatory variable, in addition to the conventional life cycle variables, in saving analysis. As is standard in the literature, we capture uncertainty in the economic environment by the inflation rate (*INF*) (Fischer 1993), with the expectation that the inflation rate and saving will be positively related.[6]

The fourth issue stems from the finding of recent empirical studies that consumption does not adjust immediately in response to current 'news' about lifetime resources (Van de Stadt et al. 1985; Carroll and Weil 1994; Deaton and Paxson 1994). The relatively slow adjustment of consumption to changes in expected future income implies that habits play an important part in determining consumption and that the consumer's past consumption influences the utility yielded by present consumption (Abel 1990).[7] In our econometric methodology, we incorporate habit formation in consumption by the inclusion of appropriate lags of the dependent variable in regression estimation.

The fifth issue relates to the effect of terms of trade changes on saving behaviour. In theory, terms of trade changes are already a part of GDP. However, in practice, the price deflators used in national income accounting generally allow for changes in *the general level of prices* and fail to capture *price-induced structural effects* on the level and growth of real income such as those due to changes in the terms of trade. Thus, changes in the terms of trade can be expected to have an additional effect to that of changes in GDP on saving (Ady 1976). Several empirical studies have also documented the significant impact that terms of trade movements have on the saving rate (Masson, Bayoumi and Samiei 1995; Dayal–Ghulati and Thimann 1997; Haque, Pesaran and Sharma 1999). We include the terms of trade (*TOT*) to

[6] The inclusion of the inflation rate can also be justified on the grounds that the LCM model assumes inflation neutrality, the absence of money illusion or the real balance effect. There are, however, good reasons for doubting the validity of this assumption. Furthermore, quite apart from its influence on real returns to saving, inflation may influence saving through its impact on real wealth. If consumers attempt to maintain a target rate of consumption to wealth or of liquid assets to income, saving will rise with anticipated inflation (Deaton 1977).

[7] Habit persistence in consumption may be seen as an implication of the 'relative income hypothesis' of Duesenberry (1962) who argued that the consumption expenditures of an individual would be influenced both by the individual's own past consumption and the average standard of living of others in the individual's social class.

capture the impact of real income losses or gains brought about by changes in the former. When we assume forward-looking consumption smoothing behaviour on the part of private agents in the face of volatile and unpredictable income, the sign can go either way, depending on whether movements in *TOT* are perceived to be temporary or permanent (Frankel and Razin 1992). A terms of trade deterioration that is perceived to be temporary may lead to an increase in absorption (that is, an increase in expenditure measured in terms of domestic goods) as consumers attempt to offset the decrease in purchasing power of domestic goods so as to keep real expenditure constant. In other words, deterioration of the terms of trade induces domestic residents to reduce their saving in order to sustain their real standard of living. By the same reasoning, households may increase saving when faced with lower future real income as a result of a long-run terms of trade deterioration.

A final consideration relates to the interaction of private saving with public saving, *PUBSAV*. The statistical relationship between public saving and private saving is at the centre of the debate on the possible impact of the fiscal policy stance on national saving rate (Corbo and Schmidt–Hebbel 1991; Lopez, Schmidt–Hebbel and Serven 2000). While the government can choose the level of its own saving directly, a change in this variable need not imply a one-for-one change in national saving. This is because households (and firms) may respond in such a way as to offset the government action, at least to some extent. At the extreme case, the Ricardian Equivalence proposition of Barro (1974) postulates that a government issue of bonds to finance its dis-saving results in an equal increase in private saving, because the private sector saves in anticipation of a future increase in taxes to service the bonds (Bernheim 1987). This view presupposes that public saving is a perfect substitute for private saving.[8] On the other hand, when governments shift funds from consumption to particular types of investment, such as infrastructure, that the private sector is unlike to undertake, the return to, and the volume of, private saving may increase.

Four more variables are chosen in the light of the Indian debate on the determination of domestic saving. These are inward remittances by expatriate Indians relative to income (*TRN*), the share of agriculture in GDP (*AGS*), a dummy variable to capture the dip in the household saving rate for the years 1981–4 (*D81–84*), and the population per bank branch ('bank density') (*BDN*). Since the mid-1970s, there has been a significant increase in inward remittances by expatriate Indians, mostly the Indian workers who

[8] The Ricardian equivalence proposition assumes perfect capital markets and the absence of uncertainty. If either assumption does not hold, then private and public saving may not be perfect substitutes.

migrated to the Gulf countries in response to the oil boom.[9] As it is unrealistic to assume that they are current transfers intended solely for consumption, remittances can be considered a positive influence on domestic saving (Joshi and Little 1994).[10] Quite apart from this general impact, some studies have treated remittances as a special influence on financial saving (RBI 1982: Appendix V1; EPWRF 1995). The theory behind this relationship has not been explicitly stated, but the underlying assumption seems to be that, as the bulk of remittances is transferred through banking channels, these tend to raise the money holdings of households. However, as Rakshit (1983) forcefully argues, 'the fact that [remittances] initially raise money balances is of no importance in explaining why households find it advantageous to hold a large fraction of their saving in the form of currency and bank deposits' (p. 761). Thus, *a priori*, it is not possible to state whether a higher inflow of remittances will lead to higher or lower saving.

In the debate on the causes of the rapid increase in the saving rate in India in the second half of the 1970s (the high saving phase of the Indian economy), one of the underlying causes considered was the significant decline in the share of agriculture in total GDP, partly as a result of a significant worsening of the internal terms of trade and partly as an outcome of the ongoing process of structural transformation in the economy (Rakshit 1983; RBI 1982; Joshi and Little 1994). This view was based on the hypothesis that agricultural households have a greater marginal propensity to consume compared to non-agricultural (mostly urban) households; a hypothesis which has not yet been supported by firm statistical evidence. In fact, the permanent income hypothesis (which postulates a higher marginal propensity to save out of transitory income) would lead one to expect the marginal propensity to save to be higher for agricultural households than for non-agricultural households.

As discussed in Chapter 4, there was a dip in the domestic saving rate in the years 1981–4, presumably reflecting a downward revision of the household saving series by the Central Statistical Organisation (CSO) due to a change in the estimation procedure for the latter. We introduce a dummy variable for these four years in the saving function (*D81*–84) in order to test whether the changes in the CSO's estimates of household saving are

[9] According to the Indian balance of payments records, private transfers (which predominantly consist of remittances) increased from 0.2 per cent of GDP in the early 1970s to 1.5 per cent of GDP in the early 1990s.

[10] In this connection, it is important to note that, according to the method of estimation of household saving in India, the contribution of migrant transfers (or for that matter, any other form of income transfers from the rest of the world such as interest and dividend transfers) are captured in reported saving estimates in India (see Joshi and Little 1994).

significant in explaining the fall in the saving rate over and above the influence of economic fundamentals captured by the other variables in the saving function.

A notable development in the Indian financial system following the nationalization of commercial banks in 1969 has been the rapid expansion of bank branches in the country (Sen and Vaidya 1997). Population per bank branch declined persistently from over 90,000 in the mid-1950s to around 14,000 in the early 1990s. The rapid expansion of bank branches would have contributed to an increase in saving in the economy, both by improving the accessibility to banking facilities of the general public and by reducing the cost of banking transactions (through reduced transport cost) (Thirlwall 1974; Joshi and Little 1994). As Lewis (1955: p. 229) remarks, 'if they [savings institutions] are pushed right under the individual's nose ... people save more than if the nearest savings institution is some distance away'. Thus, a negative relationship can be assumed between population per bank branch (bank density) and household financial saving. However, whether increased financial intermediation itself significantly raises the overall propensity to save depends also on the degree of substitution between financial saving and other items in the household asset portfolio. Thus, the expected sign of this relationship in private and total saving functions is ambiguous.

THE EMPIRICAL MODELS

The theory that we have discussed in the previous section essentially focuses on private saving. However, in our empirical analysis, we consider both the private saving and national saving. This we do for the sake of completeness and also to facilitate comparisons with other studies, which have mostly focused on national saving.[11] It should also be noted that the framework is developed first for individuals in the economy, and then applied to households. Therefore, it could be argued from a theoretical standpoint that the most appropriate dependent variable for empirical analysis is household saving, and *not* private saving (since private saving comprises both household and corporate saving). However, the conventional view on this is that, since business firms are owned by households, the overall level of private saving is still basically determined by household saving behaviour (Modigliani

[11] The implicit assumption in these studies is that public saving is determined by the variables that drive private saving and is consistent with the lack of an established theory of public saving. Such an assumption may not be inappropriate in the Indian context, given that public saving comprises a small proportion of total saving and is falling steadily over time in the past two decades (see Chapter 4).

1970). Thus, if firms save more, households may save less, because they will regard the firms as doing the saving for them (that is, in their expenditure decisions, households 'pierce the corporate veil').

Thus, the specification of the private saving function is as follows:

SPRV = f[GY, GPOP, RID, W, LY, BOR, INF, TOT, SPB, TRN, AGS, D81–84, BDN] (5.1a)

For national saving, we use the following specification:

SNAT = f[GY, GPOP, RID, W, LY, BOR, INF, TOT, TRN, AGS, D81–84, BDN] (5.1b)

Note that the only difference between the two equations is the appearance of public saving as an explanatory variable in the private saving function. We have also omitted aged- and young-dependence and social security payments in the final specification of the saving functions as time-series data for these variables are not available for India.

Dependent variables:

SPRV Private saving rate, defined as the ratio of household plus corporate saving to Gross National Disposable Income (GNDI), which is GNP plus unrequited current transfers from abroad;

SNAT Gross domestic saving as a ratio of GNDI.

Independent variables:

(The signs expected for the regression coefficients are given in parentheses)

GY (+ or –) Rate of growth of real per capita GNDI;

GPOP (+) Rate of growth of the population;

RID (+ or –) Equals i – *INF*, where *i* is the nominal interest rate on bank deposits and *INF* is the inflation rate;

W (–) Real wealth, proxied by the ratio of money stock (M3) to GNDI;

LY (+) Real per capita GNDI;

BOR (+) Total lending to household sector by domestic sources as a ratio of GNDI;

INF (+) The rate of inflation;

TOT (+ or –) Equals PX/PM, where PX and PM are the price of exports and imports respectively,

SPB (+ or –) Public saving as a ratio of GNDI;

AGS (+ or –) Share of agriculture in total GDP;

TRN (+ or –) Remittances by Indian expatriates relative to GNDI;

D81–84 (–) An intercept dummy variable to capture the change in estimation procedures for household saving by the CSO for the years 1981–4, (1 for years 1981 through 1984 and zero otherwise), and

BDN (–) Population per bank branch ('bank density').

DATA AND THE ESTIMATION PROCEDURE

Equations (5.1a) and (5.1b) are estimated over the sample period from 1955 to 1996 using annual data.[12] The variables *LY* and *BDN* are measured in natural logarithms; all other variables are relative to GNDI (except of course *TOT* and *D81–84*). Data sources are listed and methods of data transformation adopted are discussed in Appendix 3.

We began the estimation process by examining the time-series properties of the data, using the standard Dicky–Fuller procedure (as described in Appendix 2): The test results (presented in Table 5.1) suggested that the variables do not have the same order of integration; *SPRV*, *GPOP*, *W*, *LY*, *BOR*, *SPB*, *TRN*, and *BDN* are found to be integrated of order one (I(1)), while *GY*, *RID*, *INF*, and *AGS* belong to the I(0) category. As explained in Appendix 2, we therefore opt to use the general to specific modelling procedure of Hendry, which minimizes the possibility of estimating spurious relations while retaining long-run information.

TABLE 5.1
Tests for Unit Roots of Variables Used in the Saving Function[1]

Data series	*ADF test of H_0:I(1) versus H_1:I(0)*[2]	*Whether I(1) or I(0)?*
SPRV	–3.18 (0)	I(1)
SNAT	–2.85 (0)	I(1)
GY	–5.67 (0)[3]	I(0)
GPOP	–0.07 (2)	I(1)
RID	–4.33 (0)[3]	I(0)

(contd.)

[12] Note that the sample period for the estimation of the investment function in Chapter 6 differs from that for the saving function. This is due to the unavailability of data on *W* for 1954.

Table 5.1 (contd.)

Data series	*ADF test of* H_0*:I(1) versus* H_1*:I(0)*[2]	*Whether I(1) or I(0)?*
W	–2.66 (0)	I(1)
LY	0.47 (0)	I(1)
BOR	–3.01 (0)	I(1)
INF	–4.21(0)[3]	I(0)
TOT	–2.74 (0)	I(1)
SPB	–1.96 (0)	I(1)
TRN	–2.12 (0)	I(1)
AGS	–4.83 (0)[3]	I(0)
BDN	–0.79 (1)	I(1)

Notes:

(1) Except in the cases of GY, GPOP, RID, INF and TOT, all the tests were conducted 'with trend' to allow for the possibility that, for most economic time-series, the usual competing alternative to the presence of a unit root is a deterministic linear trend. The critical value at the 5 per cent level is 3.52.

(2) Figures in parentheses indicate the order of augmentation required to obtain residual whiteness.

(3) Rejection of null hypothesis.

RESULTS

Regression estimates for private and national saving are given in Tables 5.3 and 5.4. To facilitate the interpretation of the results, a summary of the variables and used in the regressions is presented in Table 5.2.

Private Saving

The variables *GPOP, W, BOR, AGS,* and *D81–84* had statistically insignificant coefficients in all experimental runs and were therefore dropped from the final equation.[13] An additional variable which we call 'the crisis dummy' (*CRD*) (which takes value 1 for 1991 and 1992 and zero for the other years) has been added to account for the 'unexplained dip' in the saving rate during the balance of payments crisis in the early 1990s. The final parsimonious

[13] We used one-period lagged *W* given the possible multicollinearity between *SPRV* and *W*.

TABLE 5.2
Summary Data on Variables Used in the Econometric Analysis of Saving

Variables	*1955–9*	*1960–9*	*1970–9*	*1980–4*	*1985–90*	*1991–6*
Dependent Variable						
SPRV (%)	10.0	10.7	15.1	15.6	19.2	22.6
SNAT (%)	11.8	13.4	18.8	19.2	21.4	24.3
Explanatory Variables						
GY (%)	3.7	4.0	3.1	5.6	6.0	6.8
GPOP (%)	2.0	2.2	2.3	2.2	2.1	1.8
RID (%)	–1.6	–1.4	–1.4	–1.1	0.5	1.5
W (%)	27.1	25.5	34.4	46.3	54.2	60.3
LY	1468	1667	1899	2172	2592	3269
BOR (%)	0.8	1.1	1.7	2.4	2.6	2.1
INF (%)	4.2	6.3	8.1	9.0	8.3	9.5
TOT (%)	82.3	87.9	85.0	108.2	115.6	99.2
SPB (%)	1.71	2.73	3.71	3.65	2.14	1.68
TRN (%)	0.4	0.2	0.5	1.3	0.9	1.7
AGS (%)	45.9	39.3	35.4	30.1	27.3	24.1
BDN	890	734	307	168	142	145

Notes: LY is in constant (1981) Indian rupees; BDN is in thousands. Figures reported are annual averages for the given sub period.

Source and methods: Data sources and methods of data compilation are explained in *Appendix 3.*

estimated equation, together with a set of commonly used diagnostic statistics and long-run elasticities relating to the key explanatory variables (computed from the long-run (steady-state) solutions to the estimated equations), is given in Table 5.3. The equation is statistically significant at the one per cent level (in terms of the standard F test) and performs well by all diagnostic tests. In terms of the Chow test for parameter stability conducted by splitting the total sample period into 1955–79 and 1980–96 there is no evidence of parameter instability. On re-estimating for the sub-period 1956–90, all equations pass the Chow test of out-of-sample forecasting

TABLE 5.3
Determinants of the Private Saving Rate: Regression Results

$$\Delta SPRV_t = \underset{(0.92)}{0.12} + \underset{(1.93)^b}{0.11GY_t} + \underset{(2.77)^c}{0.14RID_{t-1}} + \underset{(2.95)^c}{0.07LY_{t-1}} + \underset{(4.44)^c}{0.27INF_t} - \underset{(1.43)^a}{0.02\Delta TOT_t}$$

$$\underset{(3.75)^c}{-0.07TOT_{t-1}} - \underset{(3.33)^c}{0.42SPB_t} - \underset{(1.37)^a}{0.73TRN_{t-1}} - \underset{(4.07)^c}{0.03BDN_{t-1}} - \underset{(2.77)^c}{0.02CRD} - \underset{(5.23)^c}{0.78SPRV_{t-1}}$$

$\bar{R}^2 = 0.63$	$F(11,30) = 7.47^c$	*S.E. of regression* = 0.008
$DW = 2.17$	$LM1 - \chi^2(1) = 1.07$	$LM2 - \chi^2(2) = 2.10$
$RESET - \chi^2 = 0.15$	$JBN - \chi^2(2) = 0.06$	

Long-run (steady-state) effect on saving rate:

Income growth	0.14[a]
Real interest rate (RID)	0.18[b]
Per capita income (LY)	0.09[c]
Inflation (INF)	0.35[c]
Terms of trade (TOT)	–0.09[c]
Public saving (SPB)	–0.53[c]
Remittances (TRN)	–0.93[a]
Bank density (BDN)	–0.04[c]

Notes: t-ratios of regression coefficients are given in brackets. Approximate critical values for the *t*-ratios are as follows: 10 per cent = 1.31 ([a]), 5 per cent = 1.69 ([b]) and 1 per cent = 2.44 ([c]). The test statistics are: *LM* = Lagrange multiplier test of residual serial correlation; *RESET* = Ramsey test for functional form mis-specification; *JBN* = Jarque-Bera test for the normality of residuals.

ability (Chow's prediction failure test) for the post reform period (1991–6). Apart from these tests, a residual correlogram of up to six years was estimated for each equation, with no evidence of significant serial correlation.

The result for the *RID* variable suggests that one percentage point increase in RID is associated with a 0.08 percentage point increase in the private saving rate. Considering the fact that during the study period, financial savings on average accounted for over 45 per cent of total private savings, there is no evidence of substitution of other assets for financial assets in response to changes in the real deposit rate. Overall, the Indian experience provides support for the McKinnon–Shaw proposition that, in an economy where the saving behaviour is highly intensive in money and near-money assets, high real interest rates promote private saving in the economy. As has been discussed in Chapter 3, unlike other developing countries, Indian policy makers ensured that the real interest rate on bank deposits remained positive for much of the period under consideration. This has clearly been an important factor behind the high saving rates witnessed in India in the post-independence period.

As postulated by the life-cycle model, the income growth variable (*GY*) is an important determinant of the private saving rate—the coefficient on *GY* is positively signed and is statistically significant at the 5 per cent level. An increase in the growth rate by one per cent leads to a long-run increase in the saving rate by 0.14 per cent. However, other variables suggested by extensions to the life-cycle model—*GPOP* and *W*—do not seem to be important in explaining the private saving rate in India.[14]

We find that the Keynesian 'absolute income hypothesis' holds for saving behaviour in India—the coefficient on *LY* is positive and statistically significant at the one per cent level, and suggests that a one per cent increase in per capita income leads to an increase in the private saving rate by 0.09 per cent. This provides support for the argument that for countries in the initial stages of development, the level of income is an important determinant of the capacity to save. In this respect, our results are consistent with other studies that examine the effect of the level of income on the saving rate, such as Modigliani (1993) and Hussein and Thirlwall (1999).

Among the remaining variables, *BDN* stands out as a highly significant variable in explaining variations in the private saving rate. A one per cent increase in bank density leads to a 0.04 per cent increase in the private saving rate. This result provides strong support for the view that the expansion of banking facilities since the 1970s seems to have contributed significantly to the improvement in the saving propensity in the economy. There is no evidence to suggest that the expansion of bank branches generated greater financial savings in the form of bank deposits at the expense of the accumulation of other assets.

The coefficient of *TOT* is negative and statistically significant, suggesting that real income gains (losses) associated with terms of trade improvements lead to lower (higher) saving. Thus, Indian households seem to

[14] It should be noted that the lack of significance of *GPOP* may due to the weakness in the construction of the series in the Indian context and the lack of year-to-year variability in the data. In the case of *W* too, money stock as a ratio of income may be a poor proxy of total private wealth.

consider terms of trade movements as permanent shocks. The coefficient on *TRN* is negative, but attains significance only at the 10 per cent level, providing some, albeit weak, statistical support for the view that migrant remittances hinder domestic saving performance. We also find that macroeconomic uncertainty, as captured by the inflation rate, has a positive effect on the private saving rate. This provides support for the precautionary motive for saving, which argues that individuals save more in the face of increased uncertainty in the economic environment.

There is evidence that public saving is a substitute for private saving in the Indian context, although not to the fullest extent suggested by the Ricardian equivalence hypothesis. The results suggest that a one percentage point increase in the public saving ratio is associated with a 0.53 percentage point reduction in the private saving rate. Thus, an improvement in public saving resulting from a shift in income from the private sector to the government (say, through an increase in income tax) will contribute to an increase in total domestic saving. However, there is no support for full Ricardian equivalence, which predicts full counterbalancing of public saving by private dis-saving; the coefficient attached to *SPB* is well below unity.

As noted, *AGS* failed to attain statistical significance in all saving functions. Thus, there is no empirical support for the view that the decline in the share of agriculture in domestic production (and the accompanying increased urbanization of the economy) has contributed to the growth in private saving. Furthermore, the coefficient on *BOR* failed to attain statistical significance, suggesting that the borrowing constraint is not a significant explicator of saving net of the other factors captured in our regression specification.[15]

The lack of the significance of the dummy variable *D81–84* provides some support for the view that the dip in the saving rate in the years 1981–4 may not necessarily be due to measurement errors in the saving rate emanating from the change in the estimation procedure for those years due to revision in the saving data by the Reserve Bank of India (RBI), and could be related to economic fundamentals (see the discussion in Chapter 4). We also do not find strong evidence of inertia in the private saving rate (as predicted by the habit formation perspective on consumption), with long-run responses of the saving rate to its key determinants not considerably higher than the short-run ones.

[15] As the variables measuring borrowing constraints (total household financial liabilities relative to income), the growth rate of output and the private saving rate may be simultaneously determined, we re-estimated the saving function using two-stage least squares instead of OLS and instrumenting *BOR* and *GY* by their lags, with no change in the results.

National Saving

The final parsimonious estimated equation, together with a set of commonly used diagnostic statistics and long-run elasticities, is given in Table 5.4. The results are broadly similar, both in terms of goodness of fit and the other statistical properties of the estimated equation, to the regression estimates for private saving. Moreover, there is no statistically significant difference between the coefficients of the variables of interest in the estimated equations for private and national saving.[16] This is consistent with our prior expectations, given the dominance of private saving in national saving in India (see Chapter 4).

TABLE 5.4
Determinants of the National Saving Rate: Regression Results

$$\Delta SNAT_t = \underset{(1.78)^a}{-0.17} + \underset{(0.91)}{0.05GY_t} + \underset{(2.17)^b}{0.08RID_{t-1}} + \underset{(3.68)^b}{0.08LY_{t-1}} - \underset{(1.63)^b}{0.03\Delta TOT_t}$$

$$\underset{(3.41)^c}{-0.07TOT_{t-1}} - \underset{(1.83)^b}{1.08TRN_{t-1}} - \underset{(3.65)^c}{0.03BDN_{t-1}} - \underset{(2.56)^c}{0.02CRD} - \underset{(4.57)^c}{0.70SNAT_{t-1}}$$

$\bar{R}^2 = 0.49$	$F(9,32) = 5.38^c$	*S.E. of regression* = 0.010
$DW = 2.19$	$LM1 - \chi^2(1) = 2.20$	$LM2 - \chi^2(2) = 0.64$
$RESET - \chi^2 = 0.11$	$JBN - \chi^2(2) = 1.04$	

Long-run (steady-state) effect on saving rate:

Income growth	0.08
Real interest rate (RID)	0.12[a]
Per capita income (LY)	0.11[c]
Terms of trade (TOT)	–0.10[c]
Remittances (TRN)	–1.59[a]
Bank density (BDN)	–0.04[c]

Notes: t-ratios of regression coefficients are given in brackets. Approximate critical values for the *t*-ratios are as follows: 10 per cent = 1.31 ([a]), 5 per cent = 1.69 ([b]) and 1 per cent = 2.44 ([c]). The test statistics are: *LM* = Lagrange multiplier test of residual serial correlation; *RESET* = Ramsey test for functional form misspecification; *JBN* = Jarque-Bera test for the normality of residuals.

[16] The difference between each coefficient in the two estimated equations fall within one standard error band.

The main difference between the results for private and national saving is the lack of significance of the inflation rate in explaining variations in the latter. Given that we have already found that the inflation rate has a positive effect on private saving, it would appear that the Tanzi effect (which postulates a positive relationship between tax revenues and the inflation rate) does not hold in the Indian case.

Behaviour of Key Explanatory Variables

Combining the regression estimates for the private saving function with an analysis of the behaviour of the key explanatory variables allow us to understand the reasons for the rapid rise in the national saving rate in India since the mid-1950s. Plots of per capita income, the terms of trade, remittances, and bank density are provided in Figs 5.1, 5.2, 5.3, and 5.4 respectively, with the plots of the real interest rate on bank deposits, the inflation rate, and private and public saving rates provided in Figs 3.9, 3.3 (in Chapter 3), and 4.2 (in Chapter 4), respectively. It is clear from the figures that the relative importance of the key explanatory variables in

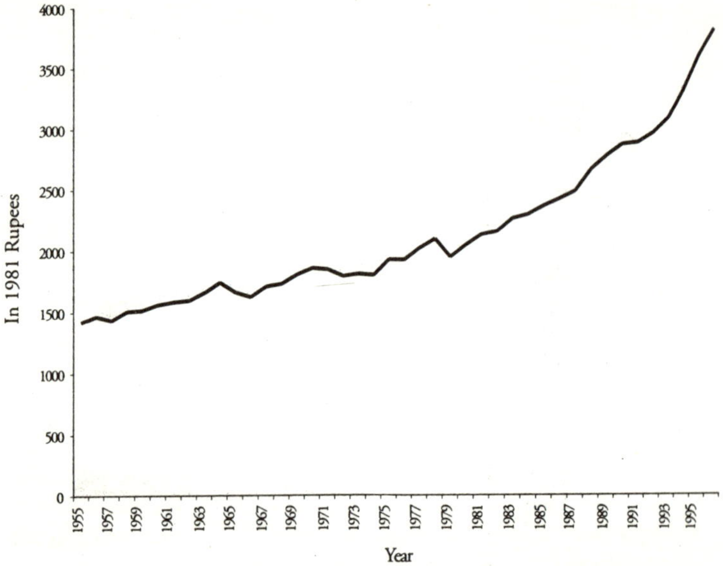

Figure 5.1: Behaviour of Per Capita Gross National Disposable Income (LY), 1955–96

Source: Author's calculations, from CSO, *National Accounts Statistics*, various issues.

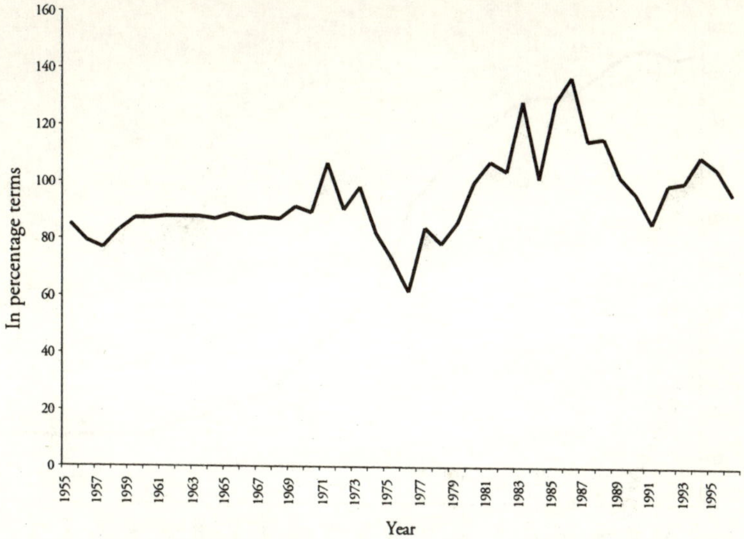

Figure 5.2: Behaviour of Terms of Trade (TOT), 1955–96

Source: Author's calculations, from IMF, *International Financial Statistics Yearbook*, various issues.

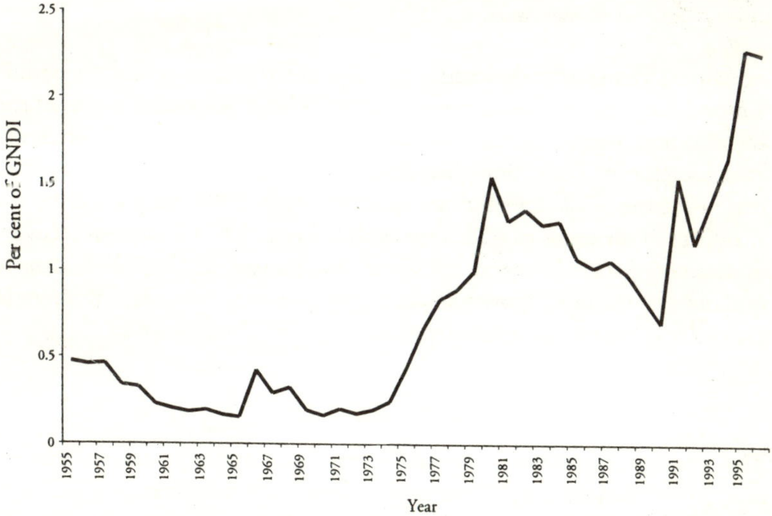

Figure 5.3: Behaviour of Net Current Private Transfers (TRN), 1955–96

Source: Author's calculations, from Reserve Bank of India, *Reports on Currency and Finance*, various issues.

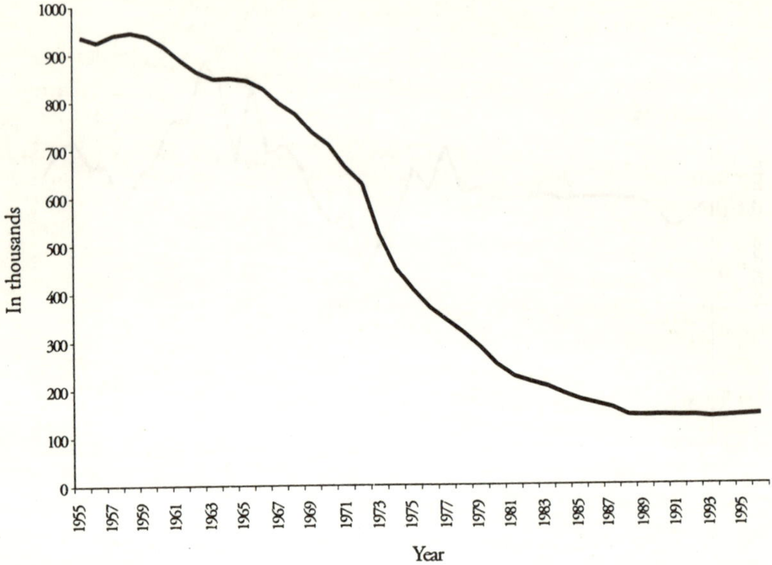

Figure 5.4: Behaviour of Bank Density (BDN), 1955–96

Source: Author's calculations, from Reserve Bank of India, *Reports on Currency and Finance*, various issues.

explaining changes in the saving rate has differed from period to period. Thus, the increase in the saving rate in the 1970s in the face of stagnant real incomes and negative real interest rates could be attributed to the phenomenal increase in bank branches amongst the population. One possible reason for the fall in the saving rate in the early 1980s appears to be the sharp rise in the terms of trade during this period. The subsequent recovery of the saving rate followed by significant growth in the 1990s can be explained by the rapid growth in per capita income and the improvement in the real interest rate on bank deposits.

CONCLUSIONS

The econometric evidence reported in this chapter point to the real interest rate, growth and the level of per capita income, spread of banking facilities, and the rate of inflation as statistically significant positive influences on domestic saving. Terms of trade changes and inward remittances by expatriate Indians seems to have a significant negative impact on the saving rate. There is also a clear role for fiscal policy in increasing total saving in the economy, with the private sector considering public saving as an imperfect substitute for its own saving. The result relating to the inflation rate needs to be qualified by referring to the fact that India has throughout been a low inflation country. What the result seems to suggest is that mild inflation is conducive for private saving.

In Chapter 4 it was observed that India's saving rate has continued to remain high by the average developing country standards. The regression results reported in this chapter help in understanding this superior saving performance. While the general economic performance (measured in terms of both income growth and the level of per capita income) has been a significant determinant of saving performance, the Indian economy has managed to maintain the saving rate at a level beyond what is permitted by economic performance alone through a progressively important role played by financial intermediation. Throughout the period under study up to 1991, the nominal interest rate was an administered price, changed at infrequent intervals. However, there were no persistent adverse movement in real deposit rates; macroeconomic policy had an anti-inflationary stance and sharply negative real deposit rates were not allowed to persist for long. At the same time, and perhaps more importantly, the spread of banking facilities played a useful supplementary role in increasing private (and hence total) saving through a persistent reduction in bank density in the country.

6

The Determinants of Investment

Aggregate investment is composed of public and private investment. Public investment is generally considered to be exogenously determined by political and institutional factors, rather than by economic variables. In this chapter, we examine the determinants of private investment in India over the past four decades.

There are a sizeable number of studies on the determinants of private investment in India and other developing countries.[1] These studies, however, suffer from a number of methodological flaws. First, whereas the theory of investment is about the investment behaviour of the *firm* (business fixed investment[2]), the commonly used dependent variable is total private investment, which includes *both* business fixed and residential investment. Total private investment is, however, a poor proxy for business fixed investment because there are fundamental differences between residential investment and business fixed investment, in terms of the underlying determinants. When a firm invests in a machine or in building a factory, it adds to its existing stock of capital. The additional capital will then be used with other factors of production to produce goods and services for sale. In deciding how much more capital to use in production (and therefore, how much to invest), the firm balances the contribution the additional capital makes to its revenues against the cost of using more capital. Therefore, variables such as expected sales that affect revenues and the interest rate, or the relative price of new capital goods that affect costs, would play an important role in determining business fixed investment.

[1]See Rama (1993) and Agenor and Montiel (1996: pp. 84–8) for surveys and references for developing countries, and Goldar (1997) for India.

[2] That is, business investment in equipment and structures.

In contrast, residential investment is an investment by households in an asset (that is, in a form of holding wealth), and is therefore determined by the relative attractiveness of housing as an asset as compared to other assets such as stocks, bonds, gold, and silver. Factors that may affect residential investment are households' wealth, interest rates, the average level of rents prevailing in the economy in that period, and the capital gains expected in purchasing a house in that period and selling it at a later period. Clearly, while there is some overlap in the set of variables that determine business fixed and residential investment, there are several variables that are important determinants of business fixed investment but are not so for residential investment (and vice versa).

A second limitation of existing studies on investment in developing countries is that many of these studies have employed *ad hoc* investment functions formulated largely to suit the nature of readily available data, rather than derived systematically from a formal model of investment behaviour. Consequently, none of the studies have appropriately captured the effect of the user cost of capital on private capital formation, a key link between financial markets and real economic activity in any industrial-country macroeconomic model. The effect of the level of existing capital stock on investment, another key postulate of the received theory of investment, has also been largely ignored.

This chapter examines the determinants of investment in India using a formal model of business investment. The model is derived from the neoclassical theory of business fixed investment, with appropriate adoption to reflect structural features specific to investment behaviour in India and other developing countries. In the Indian context, business fixed investment would include investment in equipment and structures both by the private corporate sector and by unincorporated enterprises in the household sector. In theory, the same set of economic factors should drive investment decisions in the private sector, whether they are private corporate firms or unincorporated enterprises. However, the relative importance of these factors in determining the investment decisions of firms in the private corporate and household sectors may well differ, reflecting differences in the economic attributes and the policy environment.

The estimation of an investment function for the business sector in India is hindered by the absence of direct estimates of fixed investment made by firms in the household sector. Nor do the available investment data in India permit us to decompose household fixed investment into investment in equipment and structures made by firms in the household sector and residential investment (see Appendix 1). Given these data constraints, we obtain an indirect (proxy) estimate of business fixed investment, which we dub non-residential business fixed investment , by subtracting household investment in structures from total private fixed investment. An investment function is estimated for the non-residential business sector over the period 1954–96. For the reasons given above, a separate investment function is also estimated for the private corporate sector for the same period. The investment function used in the empirical analysis is derived from the neoclassical model of investment, with appropriate modifications to suit the structural features of the typical developing economy.

The specification of the investment function is discussed in detail in the next section, with emphasis on the salient features of the neoclassical model of investment and the modifications made. The following section presents the estimated investment functions for non-residential business and private corporate investment, and discusses the implications of the results. One striking feature of investment behaviour noted in Chapter 4 was the high rate of growth of private corporate investment in the post-1991 period. In the final section, we attempt to shed light on this phenomenon using the estimated corporate investment function.

THE ANALYTICAL FRAMEWORK

The basic premise of the neoclassical investment model is that firms 'maximize utility of a consumption stream subject to a production function relating the flow of output to the flows of labor and capital services' (Jorgenson 1967: p. 136).[3] The firm supplies capital services to itself through the acquisition of investment goods. The demand for capital is therefore a derived demand and is assumed to positively depend on expected output and negatively depend on the expected rental cost of capital. Assuming constant elasticity of substitution (σ) between capital and variable inputs, we observe the following relation between desired capital stock (K^*), the expected level of output (Y) and the expected rental cost of capital (C):

$$K_t^* = \alpha Y_t C_t^{-\sigma} \tag{6.1}$$

where C_t is

$$C_t = PK_t[r_t - \pi_t^e + \delta]/P_t, \tag{6.2}$$

Here, α is the distribution parameter, PK is the price of capital goods, P the output price level, r the nominal bank lending rate, π^e the expected inflation

[3] For a comprehensive survey of the theoretical literature on the modelling of business fixed investment, see Chirinko (1993).

rate of capital goods and δ the rate of capital depreciation.[4] If there are costs to adjusting the capital stock and gestation lags in the adjustment process, then firms gradually respond to changes in the desired capital stock. Equation (6.1) highlights the dependence of the desired capital stock on a quantity variable (Y) and a set of price variables (PK and r).

To derive the investment function, we divide total (gross) investment into net and replacement components. Net investment (I_t^n) is determined by a distributed lag on new orders, which equal in a given period the change in the desired capital stock:

$$I_t^n = \sum_{t=0}^{J} \beta_j \Delta K_{t-j}^* \tag{6.3}$$

where β represents the delivery lag distribution extending for J+1 periods. Replacement investment (I_t^r) is taken to be proportional to the capital stock available at the beginning of the period and adjusts instantaneously,

$$I_t^r = \delta K_{t-1} \tag{6.4}$$

Combining (6.1), (6.3), and (6.4) and appending a stochastic error (u_t), we obtain the neoclassical model of investment:

$$I_t = \delta K_{t-1} + \sum_{j=0}^{J} \alpha \beta j \Delta (Y_{t-j} \; C_{t-j}^{-\sigma}) + u_t \tag{6.5}$$

For estimation purposes, we approximate K^* linearly on the assumption that expectations of the output and rental cost terms are based on extrapolations of past values. This gives the following modified model:

$$I_t = \delta K_{t-1} + \sum_{j=0}^{J_1} \theta_{1j} \Delta Y_{t-j} - \sum_{j=0}^{J_2} \theta_{2j} \Delta C_{t-j} + u_t \tag{6.6}$$

where the distributed lag coefficients are an amalgam of the delivery lag, expectational and production parameters.

For the purpose of this study we augment this basic model by adding the following explanatory variables: credit availability (BC), uncertainty in the macroeconomic environment (proxied by the standard deviations of output (SY) and cost of capital (SC)), post-reform intercept dummy (PRD), and public investment (IPB). The rationale behind this augmentation is discussed below, focusing on each variable in turn.

The basic model is based on the assumption of perfect capital markets, which implies that the firms can borrow freely in order to implement their

[4] Investment tax credit, depreciation allowances, and corporate income tax are ignored for lack of data.

investment plans. The validity of this assumption in the context of developing countries can be questioned on the basis of the neo-liberal literature on financial repression due to McKinnon (1973) and Shaw (1973). These authors have forcefully argued that, in the typical developing country, the availability of loanable funds may influence investment behaviour independent of the cost of capital. This view suggests the inclusion of a credit constraint, proxied by real bank credit to the private sector (*BC*), as an additional explicator in the investment function (Solimano 1992). As discussed in Chapter 3, policies of financial repression were followed in India since the early 1970s to the early 1990s. The priority sector lending requirements and the use of the banking sector for deficit financing may have led to a rationing of credit from commercial banks to private firms in the manufacturing sector.

The use of *BC* as an explicator of investment can be further supported by drawing upon the recent theoretical literature on the implications of the 'finance constraint' for the firm's investment decisions.[5] According to this literature, external finance, if available at all, may be more costly than internal finance because of transactions costs, contract enforcement (agency cost) problems and asymmetric information. The argument rests on the distinction between insiders (the firm's owners/managers), who have full information about a particular firm's investment prospects, and outsiders who may correctly perceive the prospects for a population of firms but cannot distinguish the quality of individual firms. An empirical implication of the application of asymmetric information and agency cost issues to financial markets is that the availability of finance (in particular, bank credit) may constrain the investment decisions of certain firms (especially those which are smaller in size or younger in age).[6] One can reasonably argue that problems of asymmetric information and contract enforcement will be more severe in developing countries such as India where greater heterogeneity among firms exist, capital markets are quite segmented and there is a lack of a well developed system of property rights (Aivazian 1998).

The basic model also assumes that the investment decision is reversible (that is, invested capital can be sold easily to other users) and that each decision is an once and for all opportunity. A new view of investment has, however, stressed that many real-world investment decisions violate these assumptions and that irreversibility and the possibility of delay are important

[5] For useful surveys of this literature, see Gertler (1988) and Hubbard (1998).

[6] Empirical studies that have tested the 'finance constraint' using firm-level panel data include Fazzari, Hubbard and Petersen (1988), Devereux and Schianterelli (1990), and Hoshi, Kashyap and Scharfstein (1991). Recent studies on India are Athey and Laumas (1994), Eastwood and Kohli (1999), and Kumar, Sen and Vaidya (2001).

considerations in the investment decision (Pindyck 1991; Dixit and Pindyck 1994). Plant and equipment investment can be considered sunk costs if capital, once installed, is firm- or industry-specific and cannot be put to productive use in a different activity or if secondary markets are not efficient. The decision to undertake an irreversible investment in an uncertain environment can be viewed as involving the exercising of an option—the option to wait for new information that might affect the desirability and timing of the investment. The value of the lost option is a component of the opportunity cost of investment. According to the new view, this opportunity cost can be substantial in most circumstances and a higher degree of uncertainty about the future can have a significant negative effect on investment. Here, uncertainty can originate from two independent sources, namely macroeconomic environment and policy factors. The second source of uncertainty can be considered to be of more relevance in a reforming economy where entrepreneurs' willingness to invest in certain sectors (say, export-oriented activities) would depend on whether they perceive certain reforms (such as trade liberalization) to be credible and sustainable (Rodrik 1991; Ibarra 1995).

Empirical studies of the effect of macroeconomic conditions on investment have used a variety of measures of macroeconomic uncertainty (Ferderer 1993; Pindyck and Solimano 1993; Price 1995). In this study, we use the three-year moving average standard deviations of the change in output (*SY*) and the change in rental cost of capital (*SC*) as measures of the degree of uncertainty.[7] Capturing the impact of policy credibility on investment performance poses a more serious problem (Rodrik 1991). As seen in Chapter 3, the Indian government embarked in 1991 on a structural adjustment programme that was comprehensive in its coverage and far-reaching in its nature. In such a context, there are both conceptual and measurement problems in deciding on the relevant policy variable where credibility is the issue. Rather than focusing on a specific policy variable, we include an intercept dummy variable, *PRD*, which takes the value 1 for the post-reform years and zero otherwise, to test whether the structural adjustment policy reforms *per se* has influenced investment behaviour, over and above its impact operating through other variables explicitly allowed for in the regression specification.

Finally, we chose public sector fixed capital formation (*IPB*) as an explanatory variable for the following reasons. Public investment may affect

[7] For a variable x, the 3 year moving average is $y(t) = \Sigma x(t-j)/3$, where $j = 1, 2, 3$. The standard deviation of x at time t, sdx(t), then, is $sdx(t) = \sqrt{\dfrac{\sum_{j=1,\ldots,3} [x(t-j) - y(t)]^2}{3}}$

private investment both *via* supply and demand sides. On the supply side, the private sector relies on public investment for most of the infrastructure, because this is either a natural or a legal monopoly of the government. Thus public investment in infrastructure and private investment should be complementary (Blejer and Khan 1984). On the demand side, in theory, the relationship is ambiguous. If there is some slack in the economy one would expect a change in public investment to push private investment in the same direction. Otherwise, some private investment will probably have to be 'crowded out'. This ambiguity notwithstanding, given the dominant role played by the government in the provision of infrastructure and in key intermediate- and investment-goods producing industries in India, it is generally assumed that 'the stimulation effect of public investment on private investment tends to dominate any possible negative effect through competing for investible funds' (Bardhan 1998: p. 25).

With these additional variables and an intercept term, the investment function can be written as:

$$I_t = c + \delta K_{t-1} + \sum_{j=0}^{J} \theta_{1j} \Delta Y_{t-j} - \sum_{j=0}^{J} \theta_{2j} \Delta C_{t-j} + \theta_3 BC_t + \theta_4 PBI_t - \theta_5 SY_t - \theta_6 SC_t + u_t \quad (6.7)$$

Before turning to the estimation of the model, one additional methodological issue needs to be addressed. This has to do with the well-known 'Lucas Critique' of reduced-form models (Lucas 1976). As we have already noted, the coefficients of eqn 6.7 are a combination of both expectational and structural (technology) parameters and are, therefore, not invariant to changes in policy regimes. Following the Lucas Critique, one can argue that the preferred route to the modelling of dynamic models is the estimation of stochastic first order conditions for optimal choice by rational, forward-looking representative agents (the 'Euler Equation' approach). The Lucas Critique seems particularly relevant in our case; with the sharp changes in policy that occurred in the Indian economy in 1991, parameter instability of a reduced form model (such as eqn 6.7) between the pre- and post-reform periods is a distinct possibility. Should this be the case, the use of an empirical model estimated for the pre-reform period to make post-reform inferences is problematic.

In this study our preferred strategy is to use a data-based approach to guard against the possibility of parameter instability, namely to employ a recursive estimation technique to check for possible structural instability of the empirical model. The choice of this approach is based on two considerations. Firstly, the presence of credit constraints on the firm's investment demand implies that at any point in time, there will be some firms which are credit constrained and some which are not. The Euler equation approach invariably precludes this possibility. The preferred modelling strategy from a time-series perspective is, therefore, to include a proxy for the credit constraint as an additional variable in the investment demand function.[8] Secondly, Oliner, Rudebusch and Sichel (1995, 1996) have found that traditional reduced-form investment models exhibit only modest amount of parameter non-constancy even in the presence of significant policy shifts, and that the 'empirical Euler equations appear to provide no improvement when judged by the metric of structural stability'. (Oliner, Rudebusch, and Sichel 1996: p. 311).

We will estimate investment functions separately for private corporate investment and non-residential business investment. For estimation purposes, equations for private corporate investment and non-residential business investment can be specified as follows:

$$ICP = f(KCP, DY, DCCP, IPB, BC, SY, SCCP, PRD) \quad (6.8a)$$

$$INRB = f(KNRB, DY, DCNRB, IPB, BC, SY, SCPV, PRD) \quad (6.8b)$$

where:

ICP	Real fixed investment, private corporate sector;
INRB	Real fixed investment, non-residential business sector;
KCP	Real capital stock, private corporate sector;
KNRB	Real capital stock, non-residential business sector;
DY	Change in real GDP;
DCCP	Change in the cost of capital, private corporate sector;
DCNRB	Change in the cost of capital, non-residential business sector;
IPB	Real fixed investment, public sector;
BC	Real bank credit to the private sector;
SY	3 year moving average of the standard deviation of Y;
SCCP	3 year moving average of the standard deviation of *CCP*;
SCNRB	3 year moving average of the standard deviation of *CNRB*;
PRD	Post-reform dummy, value of 1 for years 1991–6, 0 otherwise.

[8] The analogue to this in the time-series consumption function literature is the modelling of current consumption as a function of past period's consumption and current income (popularized by Campbell and Mankiw 1987). Such a formulation is justified on the grounds that the Rational Expectations–Permanent Income Hypothesis may apply to some individuals but not to others (who may, for example, be liquidity constrained).

RESULTS

Equations (6.8a) and (6.8b) are estimated over the sample period 1954 to 1996 using annual data. All variables, except *SY*, *SCCP*, *SCNRB*, *CCP*, and *CNRB* (which are measured in proportional form), and of course *PRD*, are measured in natural logarithms. Data sources are listed and methods of data transformation adopted are discussed in Appendix 3. A summary of the variables used in the regressions is presented in Table 6.1.

TABLE 6.1
*Summary Data on Variables Used in the Econometric Analysis of Investment**

Variables	*1954–9*	*1960–9*	*1970–9*	*1980–4*	*1985–90*	*1991–6*
Dependent variable						
ICP	121	187	191	540	764	2150
INRB	285	409	562	950	1599	3079
Explanatory variables						
KCP	612	1426	1964	3077	5246	10,699
KNRB	6128	8453	13,265	17,778	21,217	29,298
BC	61	122	329	563	687	897
Y	5918	8089	11,445	15,207	20,616	28,230
IPB	352	635	879	1442	1913	2204
CCP(%)	8.6	6.4	9.9	13.9	15.7	13.8
CNRB(%)	0.01	–0.1	6.6	12.0	12.8	11.7
SY(%)	1.4**	1.5	1.7	1.3	0.6	1.4
SCCP(%)	1.5**	0.8	1.0	1.6	2.0	0.8
SCNRB(%)	2.8**	0.9	1.6	1.7	1.7	1.1

Notes: * Value series are in billions of Indian rupees at constant (1981) prices. Figures reported are annual averages for the given sub-period.
** For the period 1957–9 only.

Source and methods: Data sources and methods of data compilation are explained in Appendix 3.

We begin the estimation process by testing the time series properties of the data. The results for the ADF test (presented in Table 6.2) suggests that the variables do not have the same order of integration; *ICP*, *INRB*, *KCP*, *KNRB*, and *IPB* are found to be I(1) variables while *DCCP*, *DCNRB*, *DY*,

BC, SY, SCCP, and *SCNRB* belong to the I(0) category. As in the previous chapter, we opt to use the general to specific modelling procedure (as described in Appendix 2), which serves to minimize the possibility of estimating spurious relations while retaining long-run information.

TABLE 6.2
Tests for Unit Roots of Variables Used in the Investment Function[1]

Data series	*ADF test of H_0:I(1) versus H_1:I(0)*[2]	*Whether I(1) or I(0)?*
ICP	–1.70 (0)	I(1)
INRB	–1.59 (1)	I(1)
KCP	–1.72 (1)	I(1)
KNRB	9.20 (0)	I(1)
DY	–6.76 (0)[3]	I(1)
DCCP	–5.72 (0)[3]	I(0)
DCNRB	–7.21 (3)[3]	I(0)
BC	–5.72 (0)[3]	I(0)
IPB	–2.77 (1)	I(1)
SY	–6.14 (0)[3]	I(0)
SCCP	–6.93 (0)[3]	I(0)
SCNRB	–6.21(0)[3]	I(0)

Notes:

(1) Except in the cases of DY, DCCP, DCNRB, SY, SCCP and SCNRB, all the tests were conducted 'with trend' to allow for the possibility that, for most economic time-series, the usual competing alternative to the presence of a unit root is a deterministic linear trend. The critical value at the 5 per cent level is 3.52.

(2) Figures in parentheses indicate the order of augmentation required to obtain residual whiteness.

(3) Rejection of null hypothesis.

The use of the ordinary least squares (OLS) method to estimate equations (6.8a) and (6.8b) can yield biased coefficient estimates because autonomous shocks to the error term (such as a shock to technology or to demand) may be correlated with the change in output (*DY*), as a profit-maximizing firm decides on the combination of capital, other factors of production, and output simultaneously. To guard against the potential simultaneity bias, the equation was using two-stage least squares (2SLS). The growth rates of real agricultural output and real government consumption and the lagged dependent variable were used as instruments for *DY*. We first present the results for private corporate investment.

Private Corporate Investment

The final parsimonious estimated equation, together with a set of commonly used diagnostic statistics, are reported in Table 6.3. The equation is statistically significant at the one per cent level (in terms of the standard F test) and it performs well by all diagnostic tests. Apart from these tests, a

TABLE 6.3
Determinants of Private Corporate Investment: Regression Results

$$\Delta ICP_t = \underset{(1.62)}{-1.28} + \underset{(1.76)^{a}}{0.13\Delta BC_{t-1}} + \underset{(2.06)^{b}}{2.98DY_t} - \underset{(2.14)^{c}}{3.89DCCP_t} + \underset{(1.53)}{0.68\Delta IPB_t} + \underset{(3.33)^{c}}{1.06IPB_{t-1}}$$

$$\underset{(2.01)^{b}}{-0.50KCP_{t-1}} + \underset{(3.71)^{c}}{0.75PRD} - \underset{(3.41)^{c}}{0.45ICP_{t-1}}$$

$\bar{R}^2 = 0.30$	$F(8,32) = 3.18^{c}$	*S.E. of regression* = 0.10
$DW = 2.19$	$LM1 - \chi^2(1) = 1.03$	$LM2 - \chi^2(2) = 0.17$
$RESET - \chi^2 = 0.01$	$JBN - \chi^2(2) = 2.60$	$SPEC - \chi^2(2) = 3.46$

Long-run (steady-state) Investment Elasticity:

Income (DY)	6.64^{b}
Cost of Capital (DCCP)	-8.69^{b}
Public Investment (IPB)	2.36^{a}
Capital Stock (KCP)	-1.11^{a}

Notes: t-ratios of regression coefficients are given in brackets. Approximate critical values for the *t*-ratios are as follows: 10 per cent = 1.31 ([a]), 5 per cent = 1.69 ([b]), and 1 percent = 2.44 ([c]). The test statistics are: *LM* = Lagrange multiplier test of residual serial correlation; *RESET* = Ramsey test for functional form mis-specification; *JBN* = Jarque-Bera test for the normality of residuals; *SPEC* = Sargan's test for the correct specification of instruments.

residual correlogram of up to six years was estimated for each equation, with no evidence of significant serial correlation. To determine whether the parameters of the equation were constant over the post-reform period, the equation was re-estimated using recursive 2SLS. By plotting the recursive estimates of the coefficients of the key explanatory variables in the equation—$DCCP_t$, DY_t, ΔIPB_t, IPB_{t-1}, and ΔBC_{t-1}—we found no evidence of structural instability in the parameter estimates.[9] Thus, the coefficient estimates can be used with confidence for making inferences about the impact of policy reforms on investment behaviour.

The results support the hypothesis that business investment in a given year is negatively affected by the size of the initial capital stock; the coefficient on *KCP* is statistically significant at the one per cent level and suggests a long-run investment elasticity of –1.11 with respect to *KCP*. The coefficient on change in rental cost of capital (*DCCP*) is statistically significant with the postulated (negative) sign. A one percentage point rise in the rate of increase in real rental cost of capital is associated with a 8.69 per cent decline in corporate investment in the long run.[10] The standard accelerator mechanism is important in explaining corporate investment behaviour; the coefficient on the income variable (*DY*) is positive and statistically significant at the 5 per cent level. It suggests that one per cent increase in income is associated with a 6.64 per cent increase in business investment in the long run.

There is evidence of a significant positive short run effect of bank credit (*BC*) on private investment. An increase in real bank credit by one per cent is associated with a 0.13 per cent increase in annual increase in corporate investment. However, the coefficient on the lagged level term of *BC* turned out to be statistically insignificant with erratic sign changes in various experimental runs (and therefore was omitted in the reported regression). This implies that the availability of bank credit is not important in determining the long-run (steady-state) level of investment.

The results for the public investment variable provide support for the proposition that, in the Indian economy, public investment has a strong complementarity relationship with corporate investment. The impact (short-run) and steady-state elasticities of corporate investment with respect to public investment are 0.68 and 2.36 respectively.

In the experimental runs, the variables representing uncertainty in the

[9] Graphs are not reported due to space constraints. They are available from the authors on request.

[10] This apparently large elasticity coefficient does not seem unrealistic given the fact that the value of *DCCP* has varied with a narrow margin (between –2.5 per cent to 3.2 per cent) during the study period.

macroeconomic environment (*SY* and *SCCP*) consistently had statistically insignificant coefficients with some sign reversal. These variables were, therefore, dropped in the final equation. The absence of a statistically significant impact of *SY* and *SCCP* on investment in the Indian case may perhaps reflect the fact that, unlike most other developing countries, India has had a stable macroeconomic environment for most of the time period under consideration (Joshi and Little 1994).

The positive and significant coefficient attached to the post-reform dummy (*PRD*) can be interpreted to imply a favourable perception on the part of entrepreneurs on the credibility and sustainability of the reform process, which has led to an increase in corporate investment. We defer further discussion of the post-reform dummy to the next section where we discuss the effect of the structural adjustment programme (SAP) on corporate investment in more detail. We next present the results for non-residential business investment.

Non-residential Business Investment

We report the final parsimonious estimated equation (along with the diagnostic statistics) in Table 6.4. As in the case of private corporate investment, we estimated a residual correlogram of up to six years with no evidence of significant serial correlation. Also, to determine whether the parameters of the equation were constant over the post-reform period, the equation was re-estimated using recursive 2SLS with no evidence of structural instability in the parameter estimates. Here again, the coefficient estimates can be used with confidence for making inferences about the impact of policy reforms on investment behaviour.

We find that the equation is statistically significant at the one per cent level and that the results are stronger for non-residential business sector investment than that for private corporate investment (as indicated by a higher adjusted R-square). It is interesting to note that several variables that we have found to be important in explaining private corporate investment are not statistically significant in the regression for non-residential business investment. The most striking omission is the cost of capital, which as we have seen earlier, is highly significant in the regression for private corporate investment. Furthermore, the post-reform dummy is not significant at conventional levels of significance. This implies that the 1991 reforms do not seem to have a perceptible effect on non-residential business investment (in contrast to private corporate investment). The support for an accelerator mechanism is far weaker for non-residential business investment; the coefficient on the income variable (*DY*), while positive, is not statistically significant.

TABLE 6.4
Determinants of Non-residential Business Investment in India: Regression Results

$$\Delta INRB_t = -15.1 + 0.17BC_{t-1} + 0.86DY_{t-1} - 0.29IPB_{t-1} + 1.42\Delta KNRB_{t-1} + 0.69INRB_{t-1}$$
$$(4.47)^c \quad (1.76)^c \quad (1.23) \quad (2.10)^a \quad (4.40)^c \quad (4.83)^c$$

$$-0.50KCP_{t-1} + 0.75PRD - 0.45ICP_{t-1}$$
$$(2.01)^b \quad (3.71)^c \quad (3.41)^c$$

$R^2 = 0.39$	$F(5,35) = 6.02^c$	*S.E. of regression* = 0.13
$DW = 1.76$	$LM1 - \chi^2(1) = 0.55$	$LM2 - \chi^2(2) = 0.69$
$RESET - \chi^2 = 7.30^a$	$JBN - \chi^2(2) = 0.17$	

Long-run (steady-state) Investment Elasticity:

Income (DY)	1.24
Bank Credit (BC)	0.25^c
Public investment (IPB)	0.41^b
Capital Stock (KNRB)	2.06^c

Notes: t-ratios of regression coefficients are given in brackets. Approximate critical values for the *t*-ratios are as follows: 10 percent = 1.69 (^{a}), 5 per cent = 2.04 (^{b}), and 1 per cent = 2.75 (^{c}). The test statistics are: *LM* = Lagrange multiplier test of residual serial correlation; *RESET* = Ramsey test for functional form mis-specification; *JBN* = Jarque-Bera test for the normality of residuals

As in the case with private corporate investment, we find evidence of a long-run positive effect of public investment on non-residential business investment. However, unlike the case of private corporate investment, there is evidence of both a short-run and long-run positive impact of bank credit on non-residential business investment. The larger impact of bank credit on non-residential business investment could be explained by the inclusion of unincorporated enterprises in the latter. In the presence of imperfect information in financial markets, there would be higher informational costs associated with firms in the household sector (which would be smaller in size and less established than private corporate firms), leading to greater finance constraints faced by these firms. Bank credit would, therefore, have a stronger impact on firms in the household sector than for those in the private corporate sector.[11] We find that a one per cent increase in bank credit

[11] Gertler and Gilchrist (1994) find that for the United States, contractionary monetary policy has a stronger negative effect on the investment activities of small firms as compared to

leads to a 0.25 per cent increase in non-residential business investment in the long run. Finally, as in the case with private corporate investment, the variables representing uncertainty in the macroeconomic environment (*SY* and *SCNRB*) had little explanatory power with respect to total private investment.

An econometric issue that arises in the case of the estimation of the investment function for the non-residential business sector is the measurement of the capital stock, *KNRB*. As we do not have data on capital stock for the private sector disaggregated by type of asset (so that we cannot obtain data on the stock of equipment held by households), we use total private capital stock as a proxy for the capital stock for the non-residential business sector. Clearly, there are significant measurement errors associated with the latter. This may explain why the capital stock variable is of the wrong sign—positive—in the regression, even though it is statistically significant. We have noted in the introduction to this chapter that there are also measurement problems with non-residential business investment, which is the dependent variable (since our measure of non-residential business investment omits investment in structures made by firms in the household sector). However, errors in the measurement of the dependent variable in the regression are not likely to lead to any bias or inconsistency in the coefficient estimates of the regression. On the other hand, measurement errors with one explanatory variable will lead to inconsistent estimates of *all* other explanatory variables, even those measured correctly (see Johnston 1991: p. 430). This implies that the results for non-residential business investment cannot be taken with as much confidence as that for private corporate investment.

Behaviour of Key Variables over Time

Figure 6.1 plots total non-residential business investment (*INRB*) and private corporate investment (*ICP*) over time.[12] While total non-residential business investment show a fairly smooth growth over the period 1954–96, private corporate investment seems to be more volatile. Interestingly, there seems to be an upsurge in both non-residential business investment and private corporate investment since the mid-1980s. The increase has been far more pronounced for private corporate investment, especially since 1991. We plot the behaviour of the key determinants of investment (as revealed by the regressions earlier) in Figs 6.2, 6.3, and 6.4. Mirroring the behaviour of

large firms. They attribute this to the greater prevalence of finance constraints among small firms and, thus, a higher dependence on bank credit.

[12] We plot logs of the respective variables instead of the raw data in Figures 6.1 to 6.5 for comparability and greater ease of viewing.

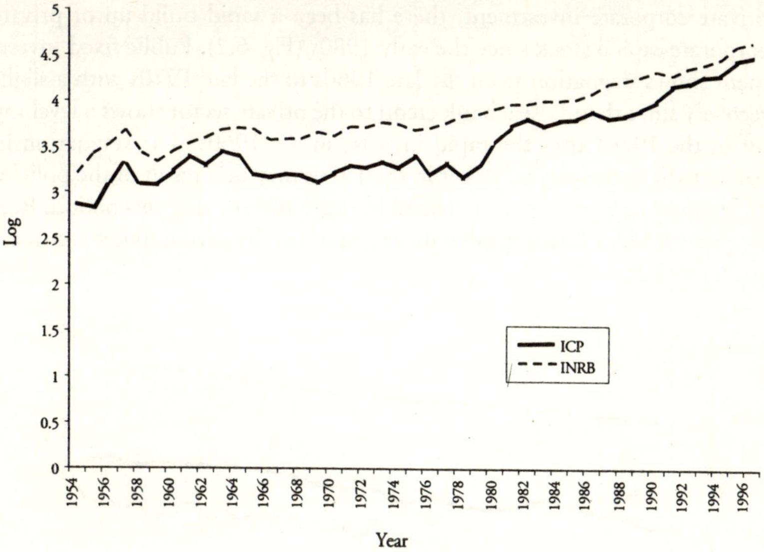

Figure 6.1: Behaviour of Private Corporate Investment (ICP) and Non-residential Business Investment (INRB), 1954–96

Source: CSO, *National Accounts Statistics*, various issues.

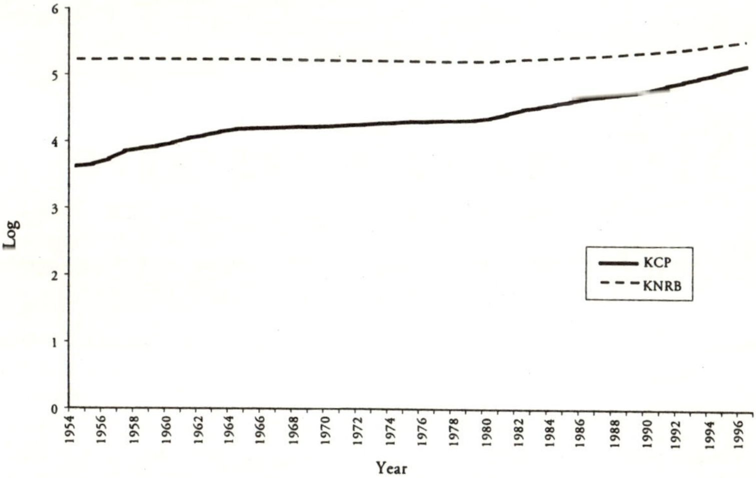

Figure 6.2: Behaviour of Capital Stocks for Private Corporate Sector (KCP) and Non-residential Business Sector (KNRB), 1954–96

Source: Authors' calculations from CSO, *National Accounts Statistics*, various issues.

private corporate investment, there has been a rapid build-up of private corporate capital stock since the early 1980s (Fig. 6.2). Public fixed investment shows stagnation from the late 1960s to the late 1970s with a slight recovery since then.[13] Real bank credit to the private sector shows a levelling off in the 1970s after the rapid increase in the 1960s. The stagnation in bank credit to the private sector in the 1970s may be a result of the policies of financial repression that increased in magnitude during this period. Real output exhibits a steady growth during much of the period under consideration (see Fig. 6.3).

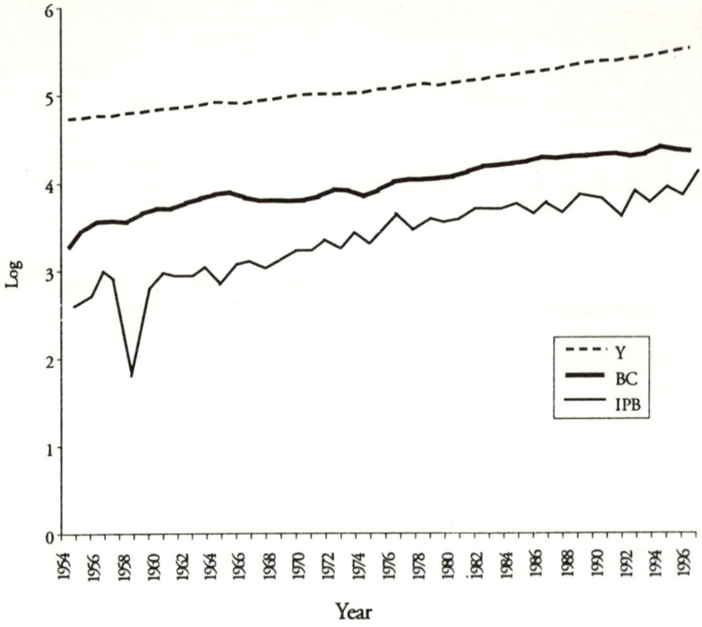

Figure 6.3: Behaviour of Real GDP (Y), Bank Credit to the Private Sector (BC), and Public Investment (IPB), 1954–96

Source: CSO, *National Accounts Statistics*, and IMF, *International Financial Statistics*, various issues.

The cost of capital both for the non-residential business and private corporate sectors has been quite volatile, in great part due to the high variability of the rate of inflation in capital goods prices (see Fig. 6.4). Both the series, however, show an increase in the 1980s followed by a sharp

[13] The stagnation of public investment in India from the mid-1960s onwards has also been observed by Patnaik and Rao (1977) and Srinivasan and Narayana (1994).

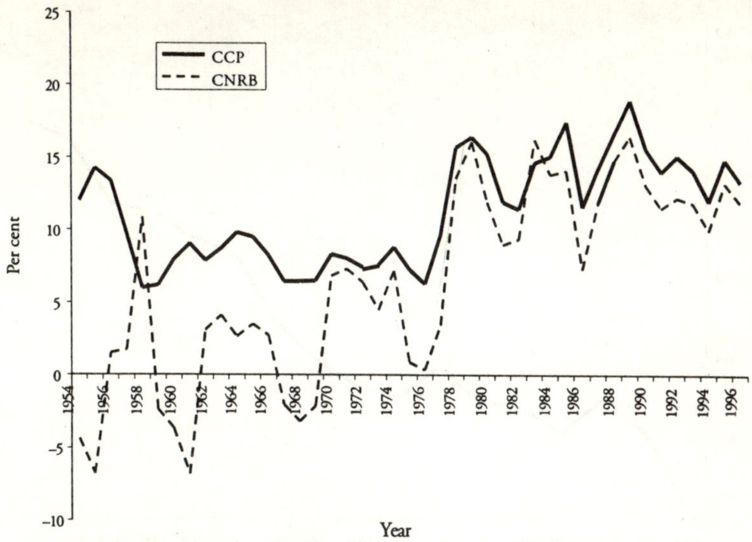

Figure 6.4: Behaviour of Cost of Capital to the Private Corporate Sector (CCP) and Non-residential Business Sector (CNRB), 1954–96

Source: Authors' calculations from CSO, *National Accounts Statistics*, various issues.

decline following the initiation of policy reforms in 1991. It is pertinent to examine possible reasons for this fall in the cost of capital and its implications for private corporate investment below.

THE 1991 REFORMS AND ITS EFFECT ON PRIVATE CORPORATE INVESTMENT

An important 'stylised fact' of private investment behaviour in developing countries is the negative impact that a stabilization cum structural adjustment programme (SAP) may have on private investment in the immediate post-reform years (see World Bank 1988; Harrigan and Mosley 1988; Greenaway and Morrissey 1992). As we have described in Chapter 3, in 1991, following a balance of payments crisis, the Indian government initiated a comprehensive stabilisation cum structural adjustment programme. In contrast to the evidence on the impact of SAPs on private investment from other developing countries, we noted a marked increase in private corporate investment in India in the post-reform period. Annual average corporate investment more than doubled between 1985–90 and 1991–6 as compared to 1985–90 (see Table 6.1). This increase is vividly shown by the mean-adjusted investment series plotted in Fig. 6.5.

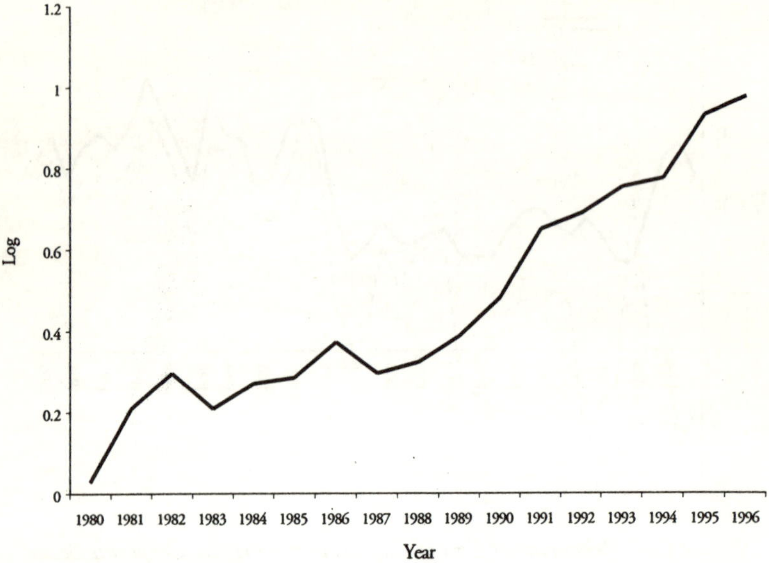

Figure 6.5: Private Corporate Investment (ICP), Mean-adjusted, 1980–96

Source: CSO, *National Accounts Statistics*, various issues.

What may explain this post-reform surge in private corporate investment? The estimated investment function for private corporate investment, when analysed in the context of data reported in Table 6.1, yield the following inferences.

The slowdown in the growth of real public sector investment (the average annual rate of growth in real public investment decreased from 6 per cent in 1980–90 to 3.8 per cent in 1991–4) and the decline in real bank credit (from an annual average level of Rs 687 billion during 1985–90 to Rs 651 billion during 1991–4)[14] during the *immediate* post-reform years seem to have had an adverse impact on corporate investment. However, these negative effects were more than offset by the positive effect of a recovery in economic activity (real GDP growth averaged 5 per cent in 1992–6, as compared to 0.4 per cent in 1991) and the decline in real rental cost of capital brought about by the policy reforms. The cost of capital index fell by 12 per cent between 1985–90 and 1991–6. An inspection of the composite data series of *CCP* (see Fig. 6.6) suggests that the dominant force behind this decline was a decline in the price of investment goods brought about by

[14] This was due to tight monetary policy that accompanied the reform package.

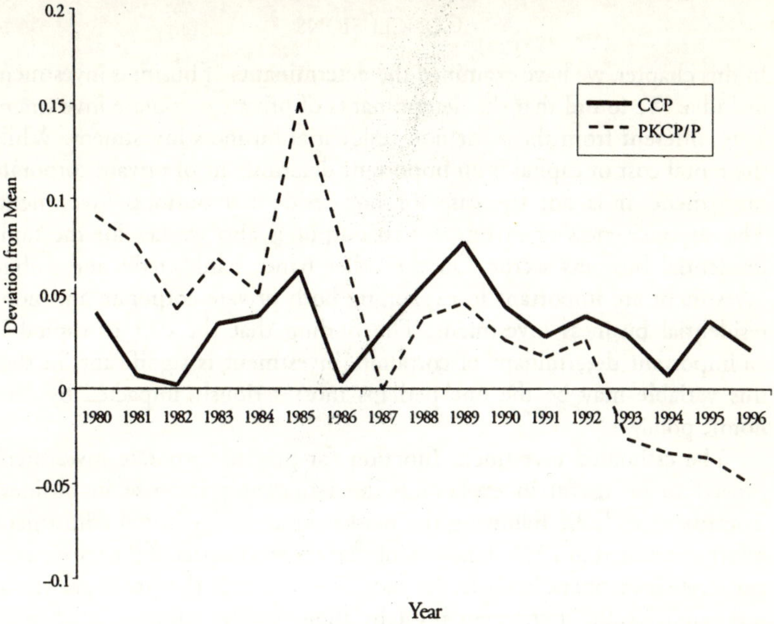

Figure 6.6: Behaviour of Cost of Capital (CCP) and the Relative Price of Capital Goods (PKCP/P) for the Private Corporate Sector, 1980–96

Source: Authors' calculations from CSO, *National Accounts Statistics*, various issues.

import liberalization.[15] Interestingly, the decline in the investment goods price was much larger in magnitude than the combined cost raising effects of currency depreciation and the increase in bank lending rates.

Added to these positive effects has been the general investment-enhancing impact of the new investment climate in the post reform era. The statistically significant positive coefficient on the post-reform dummy (*PRD*) in the estimated regression is consistent with the view that the reforms have had a positive impact on investment over and above their impact operating through the explanatory variables. It can be argued that the corporate sector may have considered the reforms to be credible for two reasons: firstly, the reforms measures were 'forceful and explicit', and secondly, the reform process 'moved over a number of areas, in rapid succession' (Bhagwati 1993: pp. 84, 85).

[15] The average nominal tariff rate on capital goods declined from 85 per cent in 1991 to 25 per cent in 1994.

CONCLUSIONS

In this chapter, we have examined the determinants of business investment in India. We found that the determinants of private corporate investment were different from those for non-residential business investment. While the rental cost of capital is an important determinant of private corporate investment, it is not the case for non-residential business investment. The responsiveness of investment to output is also weaker for the non-residential business sector. On the other hand, bank credit and public investment are important in explaining both private corporate and non-residential business investment. The finding that the cost of capital is an important determinant of corporate investment is significant, in that this variable may be the one perhaps most seriously impacted by economic policy.

The estimated investment function for private corporate investment proved to be useful in explaining the remarkable increase in business investment in India following the market-oriented structural adjustment reforms initiated in 1991. It is evident that the net impact of the reforms on corporate investment has been salutary. The decline in the rate of growth of real public sector investment brought about by the reform-related fiscal squeeze seems to have had a significant adverse impact on corporate investment. However, this adverse impact was outweighed by the salutary effects of the decline in real rental cost of capital brought about by the reform process, and favourable changes in investor perception in the aftermath of the reforms.

7

Investment and Growth

How important is investment in explaining economic growth? As discussed in Chapter 2, the early models of growth in the Harrod–Domar tradition considered the investment rate as the prime mover of economic growth. In the neoclassical growth theory developed in the 1950s, the investment rate was taken to be important in explaining the level of per capita income, but not the growth rate of per capita income. More recently, investment has regained importance as a key determinant of growth in the light of the new, but already mainstream, endogenous growth theory.

In this chapter, we will not attempt to examine which theory of growth is more appropriate in the Indian context. Such an attempt falls outside the scope of our study. Rather, we are interested in pursuing a more limited objective: to ascertain empirically the strength of the relationship between the investment rate and the growth rate in the Indian economy, with emphasis on the role of policy in mediating the postulated relationship.

To examine the link between investment and growth, we need to have a analytical framework which appropriately captures causality running from the former to the latter in an empirically testable manner. The framework we use is the *new view of economic growth* due to Scott (1989, 1992). As we explain in the next section, Scott's theory has certain features that make it more attractive for our purpose, from both theoretical and empirical points of view. In particular, it provides a clear theoretical case for using the *gross* investment rate, rather than the stock of capital, as the appropriate indicator of investment in explaining long-term growth. It also provides an explicit role for policy to influence, interactively with gross investment, the relationship between investment and growth. By contrast, the mainstream endogenous growth theory, in its various formulations, redefines technology (which is exogenous in the orthodox Solow–Swan model) as another form of endogenously determined reproducible capital (termed knowledge), to combine with traditional capital to form a composite capital input. The shortcoming of this theory from an empirical point of view is that knowledge is not-measurable. Moreover, it does not provide for an explicit role for policy.

This chapter is divided into six sections. Firstly, we compare Scott's model to other theories of growth, and highlight its main strengths relative to other frameworks. In the next two sections, we provide an exposition of the Scott model and then discuss the manner in which it can be implemented empirically. We then discuss the data and the econometric procedure used in the analysis. The final two sections present the empirical models and discuss the results.

THE ROLE OF INVESTMENT IN GROWTH: A SELECTIVE SURVEY

As we saw in Chapter 2, most growth theories allow for a role for the investment rate to impact on growth. In the orthodox neoclassical growth model pioneered by Swan (1956) and Solow (1956), change in the investment rate is important only in explaining the movement of the economy from one steady level of income to another. Change in the investment rate does not affect the long-run growth rate. Growth is mainly determined by two exogenous factors, namely growth of population and growth of productivity on the steady-state growth path. A movement from one-steady state growth to another propelled by increased investment can generate only transitional growth. But such transitional dynamics are postulated to explain only a small part of the observed growth experience.[1]

There have been some recent attempts to modify the Solow–Swan model with a view to improve its usefulness in explaining inter-country variations in growth (for example, Barro 1991; Mankiw, Romer and Weil 1992).[2] However, there is considerable controversy about the empirical relevance of these new formulations, and their ability to go beyond the issue of convergence and provide a fuller account of the determinants of long-term growth. For instance, in a recent comprehensive survey of the growth literature, Temple (1999: p. 151) infers,

> [It] would be a long way off the mark to assert that the new growth evidence only succeeds in demonstrating the explanatory power of the original neoclassical growth model. A wide variety of variables have been shown to affect growth over thirty year time spans, even through systematic differences in rates of efficiency growth across

[1] For a simple exposition of the neoclassical and the endogenous growth models, with emphasis on their key predictions, see Appendix 4.

[2] Mankiw (1995) provides a comprehensive survey of this literature.

countries. These differences are left unexplained by the Solow–Swan model, but are surely important in understanding the variation in experience over the last thirty years.

The growing awareness of the inadequacy of the Solow–Swan model and its recent reformulations in explaining the growth of nations sparked the emergence of new (endogenous) growth theories in the 1980s. While there have been a bewildering array of formulations, the purest of the endogenous growth models is one which redefines technology as another form of endogenously determined reproducible capital (termed 'knowledge'). The latter, combined with traditional capital, forms a composite capital input that exhibits constant returns, making growth endogenous (Romer 1986, Lucas 1988). Thus, in this theory, the investment rate has an explicit role in determining output growth interactively with knowledge. However, the problem with this theory from an empirical standpoint is that knowledge (or technology, as it is conventionally called) is not measurable. Given this difficulty, the bulk of evidence marshalled for testing the endogenous growth theory has simply focused on the issue of convergence of growth rates across nations (assuming technology is given) (Riedel 1996).

Under the assumption of given technology, the theory predicts that a permanent increase in the investment rate will lead to a permanent increase in the growth rate of output (Appendix 4). But the actual growth experiences of nations do not corroborate this postulate. As Jones (1995) argues, if the theory was correct, the large permanent movements in investment rates in the OECD countries should have led to permanent changes in the growth rates of these countries. However, the evidence only suggests that the permanent increases in investment rates in the OECD countries affected growth over a relatively short horizon of eight to ten years.

In our view, the key limitation of the endogenous growth theory in its empirical implementation is that it predicts a strong relationship between changes in the investment rate and the growth rate of output, while ignoring the role of policy in influencing the quality of investment. Given that knowledge (technology) is unmeasurable, it is dropped altogether from the estimating equation, leaving no room for policy to interact with investment through its quality in determining growth rate differentials.

Scott (1989) comes up with a new model of endogenous growth, which, unlike the mainstream endogenous models, combines technological change and related policy factors in a directly testable form. The Scott model is rooted in the empirical observation that investment and technological change are part and parcel of the same thing, and thus investment measured in 'gross term' (that is, without netting for depreciation) captures both investment (capital formation) and technological effort. In the model, economic growth is determined simply by three variables, the gross investment rate, the efficiency of investment and the growth rate of the quality-adjusted labour force. This theory, therefore, allows the investment rate to impact on long-term growth, as in the endogenous growth theories, but unlike the latter, qualifies the relationship between investment and growth by taking into account the efficiency of investment. More importantly, it allows for policy to impact on the relationship between investment and growth by affecting the efficiency of investment. We turn now to an exposition of Scott's theory.

SCOTT'S NEW VIEW OF ECONOMIC GROWTH[3]

Scott (1989) develops and presents his *new view of economic growth* as a reaction to the traditional growth empirics rooted in the neoclassical growth theory. There are two assumptions that underpin this literature. Firstly, there is the view that the growth of output can be decomposed in two distinct and separable components—the growth in factor inputs and the growth of technical change. This view is known as growth accounting and it begins by postulating a production function such as

$$Y = AK^{\alpha}L^{1-\alpha} \tag{7.1}$$

where K and L are capital and labour inputs and A is the Hicks-neutral productivity term. Taking logs and differentiating this production function, one obtains the following formula:

$$\frac{\dot{Y}}{Y} = \alpha\frac{\dot{K}}{K} + (1-\alpha)\frac{\dot{L}}{L} + \frac{\dot{A}}{A} \tag{7.2}$$

This equation says that output growth is equal to a weighted average of capital and labour growth plus the growth rate of A. The last term, A/A, is commonly referred to as total factor productivity growth and is taken to be the 'unexplained' residual in the growth accounting exercise. Thus, underlying this view is the assumption that 'the proximate causes of economic growth can be usefully analysed with the help of a production function' (Scott 1992: p. 622).[4]

The second assumption is diminishing returns to capital. It is this

[3] In his 1989 book, Scott provides a detailed exposition of his theory of economic growth and the differences between his theory and other perspectives on growth. For shorter accounts of Scott's theory, see Scott (1992) and Lal and Myint (1996: pp. 86–92).

[4] The origin of growth-accounting exercises goes back to Solow (1957). Growth accounting exercises using eqn (7.2) have been performed for several countries by Denison (1962).

assumption that is central to the prediction of the neoclassical growth models that changes in the investment rate do not have any long-term impact on the growth of output.[5]

Scott (1989) begins with a critique of these two assumptions. With respect to growth accounting, he takes issue with the practice of measuring total factor productivity growth separately from the growth in capital stock. In Scott's view, growth comes about by firms changing the way they do things, and that invariably involves a cost. The cost of changing economic arrangements, in terms of consumption foregone, is investment. Technological change is just one of the ways in which economic arrangements are changed and, like all others, involves a cost, or, in other words, investment. Thus, technical change and investment are for practical purposes inseparable.[6] Moreover, given the fact that technical change generally comes mostly by adapting existing techniques rather than investing *de novo*, measuring the change in capital stock as gross investment minus depreciation is unwarranted. This practice essentially implies that each rupee's worth of depreciation subtracts as much from output as each rupee of gross investment adds to it. However, if depreciation is mostly obsolescence (that is, a change in relative prices reduce the value of the capital), then it does not directly reduce output at all, but merely transfers income from the owners of the machine to the workers as part of the ongoing process of technical change. Thus, Scott (1989: p. 92) argues,

> for all practical purposes, depreciation in a progressive economy should be regarded as essentially a transfer of income from capitalists to workers. The latter benefit from rising wage rates, which result in appreciation, which is omitted from the conventional accounts. Were it included, it would offset depreciation on capital assets. It would then be clear that net investment for society as a whole is (approximately) equal to *gross* investment as conventionally measured, and not to gross investment minus depreciation.

If obsolescence were an unimportant part of depreciation, or if depreciation were small, it would not greatly matter if one uses gross investment or net investment (that is, gross investment net of depreciation) to obtain changes in capital stock. Scott (1992) argues, however, that just the opposite is true and that the contribution of capital to output growth is two or three times as big if gross investment is used to measure changes in capital stock rather than net investment. This difference, so argues Scott, is enough to eliminate

[5] See Appendix 4 for a fuller discussion of this assumption and its implications.

[6] To support this view, Scott (1991b: p. 11) cites Schmookler (1966) who reports that the stimulus for almost some 934 inventions he studied was 'a technical problem or opportunity conceived by the investor in economic terms [and thus] inventions are motivated and caused by similar factors to those which cause investment, that is, by their expected profitability'.

the famous unexplained residual in growth accounting, that is total factor productivity growth.

In sum, the fundamental problem of growth accounting is that it takes capital stock (measured in net terms) to explain both the level of output and its rate of change. However, the change in output is primarily caused by gross investment and, therefore, 'it is simpler to relate investment to changes in output directly. rather than making investment increase the capital stock which then increases output' (Scott 1992: p. 624).

Secondly, as regards the traditional growth theoretic assumption of diminishing returns to capital, Scott notes that the actual evidence on the returns to capital suggests the opposite: returns to capital increase as the stock of cumulative investment increases. The proponents of traditional growth theory have in fact noted this 'stylized fact'. But they have simply treated this as a reflection of an outward shift of the production function (due to technological progress), rather than a sign of increasing return to investment. Given the inseparability of investment and technical progress, Scott treats this as a very arbitrary practice. He argues that the more appropriate approach to growth empirics is to treat growth due to capital growth and technical progress as both the result of investment. Thus, Scott defines investment to be the 'cost of change, and so will cover all activities associated with growth'. In Scott's view, 'investment should be defined as the cost (in terms of consumption foregone) of changing, hopefully of improving, economic arrangements' (Scott 1992: p. 625). As he argues (Scott 1989: p. 331):

> Incurring capital expenditure leads to a rearrangement of the things of this world. It does not lead to there being any more of some substance capital. There is then simply change which is due to investment, and to population growth. We cannot separate change which is more capital from change which is technical progress. We must abandon the attempts to distinguish between movements along a production function whose arguments are labour, land and all capital, and a shift in that function due to technological progress.

Underlying this view is the premise that there are no diminishing returns to capital stock (measured as the sum of all past gross investment), which has solid empirical foundation. Since current investment changes economic arrangements, it also creates and reveals new investment opportunities. Thus, there are externalities to the act of investment.[7] Scott identifies two such externalities, namely the learning externality and the market externality. The former is the creation of investment opportunities for other firms

[7] The view that there are externalities to investment is also found in Arrow (1962), and more recently, in Romer (1986, 1990).

when one firm invests at a faster rate. The latter is the possibility that, in the presence of imperfect markets, if all firms were to expand their investment together, all these firms would find their demand curves shifting faster to the right, and thus, all firms in the economy would benefit from a coordinated increase in investment.[8] The presence of externalities to investment implies that the marginal return to new investment will not decline, and may even increase. Scott (1989: p. 150–1) states that,

> A firm ... in equilibrium growth is then continually changing its organization, at a cost that is its investment expenditure. It is continually confronted by investment opportunities from which it selects only some. It makes two decisions: how much to invest (i.e. the rate of investment) and which projects to invest in. These decisions are interdependent, and both are taken with the same objective in view, maximization of the firm's value to its owners. Undertaking investments alters the investment opportunities, not just by removing some, but also by creating others. The firm is always selecting the best opportunities it is aware of, but undertaking in investments makes it aware of new opportunities since it learns by experience and by investing. Some of its investment consists of the cost of searching for opportunities. This is the case for research and development expenditures, which must be widely interpreted to include market research, investigation of new sources of supply, hire of business consultants and efficiency experts, etc. But almost any investment expenditure, by changing the world, enables something new to be learned. There is therefore no new reason why investment opportunities should become exhausted.

Therefore, Scott argues that the process of economic growth is best depicted by a set of inexhaustible investment opportunities, which is like a cake that is being continually remade, instead of the conventional production function, as is done in neoclassical growth theory. He does allude to the possibility that the average quality of investment may not stay constant. As investment proceeds, and the country catches up with new opportunities (in particular those associated with economic opening), wage rates will bid up and eventually the set of opportunities can become finite. Also, persistent increase in the rate of investment can lead to worsening of average quality, leading to the shrinking of the set of opportunities. But based on empirical regularities, Scott considers that, as a working hypothesis, an inexhaustible constant set of investment opportunities seems plausible.[9]

On the basis of above considerations, Scott comes up with the following simple linear equation to explain growth:

[8] This notion is similar to the argument put forward by Murphy, Shleifer and Vishny (1989) that lack of investment coordination could lead to a smaller market and, hence, lower economic growth.

[9] He writes, 'My own investigations suggest a movement in one direction only—happily that of expansion' (Scott 1989: p. 162).

$$g = \alpha Qs + \beta g_L \quad (7.3)$$

where

g growth rate of output;

Q an index of the quality (or efficiency) of investment;

s investment rate;

g_L growth rate of the quality-adjusted labour force; and

α and β are constants.

In contrast, neoclassical growth theory would predict that the growth rate of output would be determined by the exogenous rate of growth of technical change and the growth of the labour force. That is, in the neoclassical model, growth could be expressed as:

$$g = \alpha + \beta g_L \quad (7.4)$$

The key difference between eqns (7.3) and (7.4) is the absence of the investment rate (and the quality of investment) in the latter equation.

The mainstream endogenous growth theory, unlike the neoclassical model, allows for the investment rate to determine economic growth. However, it differs from the Scott model in that there is no explicit role for efficiency of investment and the underlying policy. In the Scott model, policy can influence growth by impacting on both the volume and the quality of investment. The most important role for policy, according to Scott, is to provide for 'a framework of institutions in which individuals are free to undertake socially profitable investments, and rewarded for doing so. It requires efficient markets and efficient managers and workers, and rapid imitation and learning from others. Education, training and good communication are clearly important, as are contacts with other countries—hence openness in foreign trade and willingness to admit foreign investment' (Scott 1989: p. 630). Thus, the role of policy is to provide for a facilitating environment for *good quality* investment to take place.

APPLICATION OF THE SCOTT MODEL

As discussed, Scott's theory postulates that the growth rate of output is a function of merely three variables—the rate of investment, the efficiency of investment, and the growth of quality-adjusted labour force. While the theory is simple, its empirical implementation is not that straightforward. We discuss three issues that arise in the empirical implementation of the model.

Output and Investment

Given that theory is framed in terms of an array of investment choices faced by profit-maximizing enterprises and individuals, in empirical implementation growth needs to be measured relating to the non-residential business sector rather than the whole economy. In other words, the relevant concept of output is not the conventionally measured Gross Domestic Product (GDP) but GDP of the non-residential business sector. The latter would exclude government administration, defence, and housing from the conventional GDP estimates. Consistent with this, the investment rate is measured for the non-residential business sector. Note that what is relevant here is gross investment, not net investment.

Quality-adjusted Labour Force

The variable g_L measures the contribution of the labour input to economic growth. It would be misleading to take g_L as being the growth in the total number of workers, as there may be an increase in the educational attainment of the labour force over time. We thus obtain the growth in quality-adjusted labour force by applying the following formula:

$$QLF = (1 + LF^{*}SS)LF \tag{7.5}$$

where QLF is total quality-adjusted labour force, LF is the total labour force, and SS is the ratio of the labour force that has achieved secondary education and more (for further details, see Scott 1989). Thus, g_l is simply the change in QLF.

The Efficiency of Investment

Perhaps the most difficult variable to measure is the efficiency of investment. Relating to what determines the quality of investment (Q), Scott (1989: p. 177) writes:

> The knowledge, intelligence, originality, commonsense, and effort of business, inventors, and scientists are highly relevant, as are the economic institutions that influence their perception and choices, including the degree of competition, taxes and subsidies, the credit system, and product and factor markets generally.

Guided by both these considerations and the Indian policy context, we consider the following variables:

Openness of the Trade Regime

This is a particularly important variable impacting on changing investment quality in the Indian context, given the extremely protectionist regime that prevailed for much of the period in question and liberalization initiatives from the early 1980s. There has been significant amount of debate in India on whether the high incremental capital–output ratios or slow growth in total factor productivity growth (both signs of the inefficiency of investment) observed in the past could be attributed to the inward-looking trade policies.[10]

Measuring openness has remained a problematic issue in the literature, however, and most of the measures commonly used are often not strongly correlated with each other (Pritchett 1996). Guided by recent empirical literature of openness and growth, we use three different separate measures of openness.

The first measure is the conventional definition of openness: the ratio of exports plus imports to GDP (*OPEN*).

The second measure is the ratio of imported capital goods to total investment (*MSI*). This measure captures the notion that the efficiency of investment would depend in part on the quality and range of capital goods and that imported capital goods can be considered to have a higher productivity to domestically produced capital goods (this could be partly due to the fact that the capital goods available in world markets reflect state-of-the-art research and development and technology and partly because the domestic capital goods have operated under significant protection, as in India). Such a notion that imported capital goods are important in determining the efficiency of investment is also found in the endogenous growth theories of Romer (1987, 1992), Grossman and Helpman (1991), Rivera–Batiz and Romer (1991), and Lee (1995). In these theories, the availability of specialized intermediate and capital inputs to domestic producers are essential to economic growth and a trade regime that allows domestic firms ease of access to such goods in the world market can greatly increase the efficiency of investment. Given the tight import restrictions on capital goods in India, the variable *MSI* can be said to capture the openness of the trade regime with respect to capital goods imports. As we have seen in Chapter 3, there is evidence of an increase in the ratio of imported capital goods to total investment from the mid-1980s, when import restrictions on capital goods gradually became weaker. In the empirical section, we would like to examine whether these changes in trade policy led to an increase in the efficiency of investment.

The third measure is the share of manufacturing exports to the total output of the manufacturing sector (*SMX*). This is a proxy for the degree of

[10] For a discussion on why the incremental capital–output ratio has been observed to be so high in India, see Rangarajan (1994). Several studies have documented slow total factor productivity growth in India in the 1960s and 1970s, and an improvement in TFPG after the partial deregulation of 1985. See Ahluwalia (1985, 1991) and Srivastava (1996).

anti-export bias of the policy regime affecting the manufacturing sector.[11] The greater the degree of export-orientation of firms in the manufacturing sector, the greater is the possibility of learning and knowledge slipovers to these firms, and thus, the higher the quality of investment (Rodrik 1995a, Edwards 1998). This has been found to be an important source in the success of the East Asian economies (World Bank 1993).

Macroeconomic Instability

Several studies in the growth literature have shown that macroeconomic instability, as evident by a high inflation rate, can have a deleterious effect on economic growth (Fischer 1993; Bleaney 1996; Barro 1997). One mechanism by which it may occur is via the efficiency of investment. A high inflation rate is often correlated with higher variance in relative prices. If this is the case, episodes of high inflation may lead to the mis-allocation of investment across different sectors in the economy, and consequently, negatively impact on the efficiency of investment.[12] As is conventional in the literature, we use the inflation rate (*INF*) as a measure of macroeconomic stability.

Public Investment in Infrastructure

Public investment in infrastructure has occupied an important role in past debates both in India and elsewhere on the determinants of growth (see Ahluwalia (1985, 1991) and Bardhan (1998) for the Indian case; and Aschauer (1989a, b), Easterley and Rebelo (1993), and Gramlich (1994) for discussions of other countries). Infrastructure is defined as large capital-intensive natural monopolies such as roads and other transportation facilities, electricity (and other utilities), and communication systems. Historically, in India, as in other countries, the government has played a key role in the provision of infrastructure.[13] We have seen in the previous chapter that public investment is an important determinant of private investment. Clearly, public infrastructure investment can not only affect the volume of investment but also its efficiency—poor roads, an erratic supply of electricity, or inadequate communication facilities can negatively affect the amount

[11] We also attempted growth rate of manufacturing exports (following Riedel (1988) and Lal and Myint (1996) among others) as an alternative to the export–output ratio and found that the results were almost identical.

[12] Using cross-country data, Bleaney (1996) finds that good macroeconomic management is associated with faster growth for the same rate of investment.

[13] Since the 1991 reforms, the dominant role that the Indian government has played in infrastructure provision may be becoming less important over time as private firms are allowed in the construction of roads and bridges, electricity generation, and telecommunications.

of output that is possible to obtain from a given amount of investment. As we have noted in Chapter 3, there has been a fall in public infrastructure investment as a ratio of GDP in India since the early 1980s. We use the ratio of public infrastructure investment to GDP (*PBIINF*) as an additional variable to explain changes in the efficiency of investment.[14]

Financial Deepening

As in the case of public infrastructure investment, financial deepening can increase both the volume and efficiency of investment. The debt accumulation hypothesis of Gurley and Shaw (1955), and formalized more recently by Bencivenga and Smith (1991), argues that the spread of organized finance can help overcome indivisibilities in investment through the mobilization of otherwise unproductive resources. As Levine (1997) argues, financial intermediaries and markets play an important role in selecting the most promising firms and households for lending purposes and thus, contributing to the more efficient use of capital. Furthermore, financial intermediaries may also enhance the quality of investment by identifying those entrepreneurs with the best chances of successfully initiating new goods and production processes (King and Levine 1993). We use the M3/GDP ratio as a measure of financial deepening (*FIN*).[15]

Equipment Investment

One important strand of the recent empirical growth literature has argued that among the three components of total investment, namely investment in equipment, investment in structures, and investment in inventories, the most important for growth is equipment investment (De Long and Summers 1991, 1992, 1993; Temple 1998). This view holds that the social return to equipment investment is far greater than that for other types of investment. The reasons are not very clear though, as De Long and Summers argue, 'historical accounts of economic growth invariably assign a central role to mechanization' (1991: p. 447). It could be that the role of external economies may be greater for equipment investment than that for structures investment, possibly due to the greater amount of research and development expenditures in the machinery sector. To examine the role of equipment investment in relation to the role of other types of investment, we estimate the Scott equation decomposing total investment into its three components.

[14] Public infrastructural investment is as defined in Chapter 3.

[15] We also used the Finance Ratio, which is the ratio of total financial claims issued during the year as a ratio of national income, with no change in the results.

THE EMPIRICAL MODELS

As discussed, the right-hand variable of the Scott model is the growth of non-residential business sector. However, in this study, we also estimate an alternative equation for aggregate investment in common with other studies in the recent growth literature, purely for comparative purposes.

The models we estimate are:

Model 1A: The basic Scott model for aggregate GDP

$$GY = aRI + bGL$$

where *a* and *b* are parameters assumed to take values greater than zero.

Model 2A: The basic Scott model, for GDP in the non-residential business sector

$$GYNRB = cRINRB + dGL$$

where *c* and *d* are parameters assumed to take values greater than zero.

In these two models *GY* and *GYNRB* are the growth rates of GDP of the entire economy and the non-residential business sector respectively, *RI* and *RINRB* are the rate of investment (gross domestic capital formation) of the entire economy and the non-residential business sector respectively, and *GL* is the growth rate of the quality-adjusted labour force. The efficiency of investment is assumed to be constant over time.

Model 1B: The augmented Scott model for aggregate GDP

$$GY = a_0{*}RI + a_1{*}OPEN{*}RI + a_2{*}INF{*}RI + a_3{*}PBIINF{*}RI + a_4{*}FIN{*}RI + bGL$$

where a_0, a_1, a_2, a_3, a_4, and b are parameters assumed to take values greater than zero.

Model 2B. The augmented Scott model for the non-residential business sector

$$GYNRB = c_0{*}RINRB + c_1{*}OPEN{*}RINRB + c_2{*}INF{*}RINRB + c_3{*}PBIINF{*}RINRB + c_4{*}FIN{*}RINRB + dGL$$

where c_0, c_1, c_2, c_3, c_4, and *d* are parameters assumed to take values greater than zero.

The augmented Scott models allows efficiency of investment to differ across time and, in light of our earlier discussion, to be influenced by openness, the inflation rate, public investment in infrastructure, and financial deepening. As a proxy for openness, we will also use *MSI* and *SMX* instead of *OPEN*.

Finally, we will estimate the Scott model with total investment decomposed into machinery (*RIM*), construction (*RIC*), and change in stocks (*RIS*) to assess the role of equipment investment versus other types of investment in explaining growth (Model 1C). We will also estimate a further model (Model 1D), which will interact the variables found to influence efficiency in Model 1B with the investment rate variables found significant above. As before, we will re-estimate the Scott model, replacing the growth rate of total output in Models 1C and 1D with the growth rate of output of the non-residential business sector. As with Models 1C and 1D, we decompose total investment of the non-residential business sector into its components—machinery (*RIMNRB*), construction (*RICNRB*), and changes in stocks (*RISNRB*). We call these models 2C and 2D.

Data and the Econometric Procedure

The data used in estimating the growth equations are discussed and the data series listed in Appendix 3. Plots of the key variables are presented in Fig. 7.1–7.4 to facilitate the interpretation of results.

The two growth rates (*GY* and *GYNRB*) are very similar, with very little difference in the year-to-year movements of the two series (see Fig. 7.1).

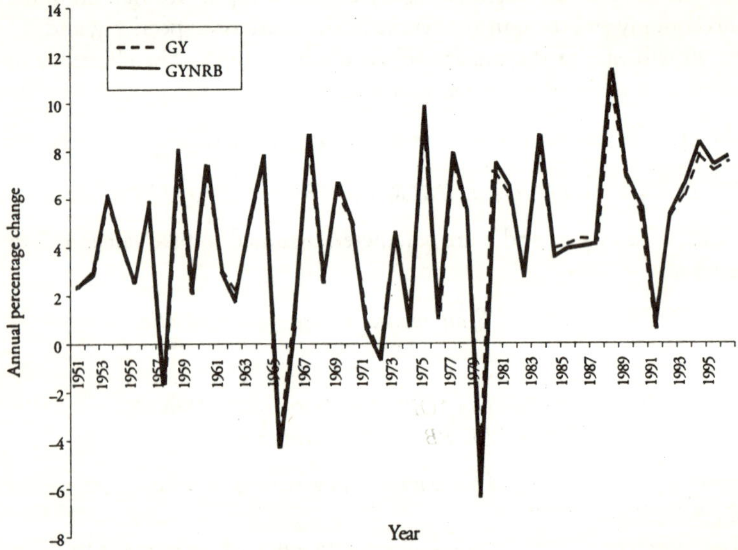

Figure 7.1: Growth Rate of GDP (GY) and GDP in Non-residential Business (GYNRB)

Source: Authors' calculations from CSO, *National Accounts Statistics*, various issues.

The plots of the investment rates for the whole economy and for the non-residential business sector indicate that while the behaviour of the two investment rates are broadly similar over time, the aggregate investment rate is more volatile (see Fig. 7.2). Plots of the three components of the aggregate investment indicate a significant increase in the rate of investment in machinery, particularly since 1991 (see Fig. 7.3). Construction investment as a ratio of GDP seems to be declining over time. Investment in inventories does not show any significant trend in either direction. A similar picture is obtained when we plot the rate of investment of the non-residential business sector in machinery and in construction in Fig. 7.4 (note that Indian national accounts data does not allow us to separate households' inventory holdings from that of the private corporate sector, so an estimate of inventory investment of the non-residential business sector is not possible).

Before estimation, we need to ascertain the time series properties of the variable. An issue that arises when testing for non-stationarity of *RI* and *RINRB* is the evidence from Fig. 7.2 of a structural break in 1958. This necessitates the use of Perron's test for non-stationarity for these two variables

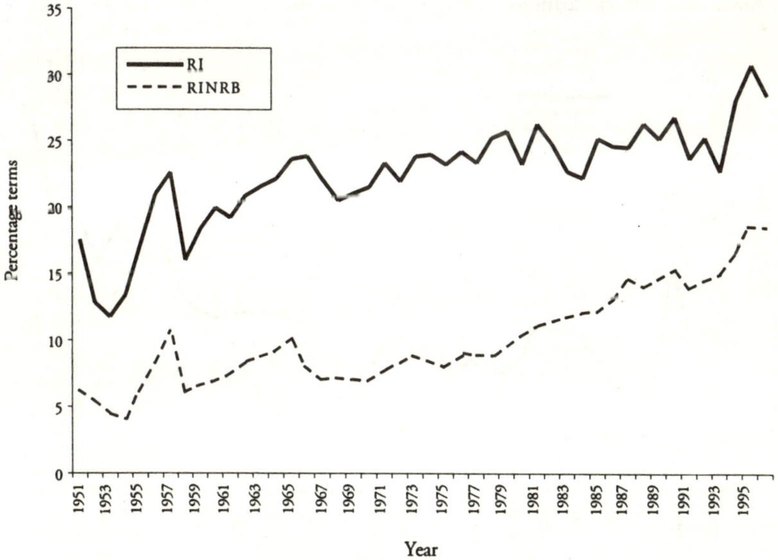

Figure 7.2: Rate of Aggregate Investment (RI) and Non-residential Business Investment (RINRB)

Source: Authors' calculations from CSO, *National Accounts Statistics*, various issues.

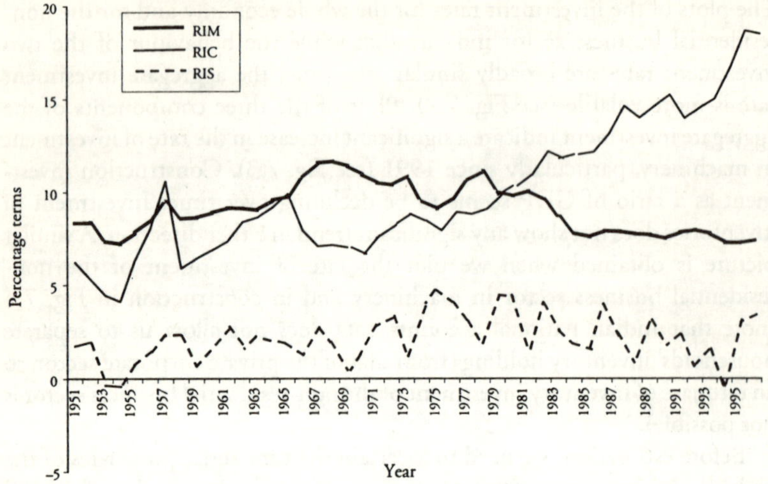

Figure 7.3: Rate of Investment in Machinery (RIM), Construction (RIC), and Change in Stocks (RIS)

Source: Authors' calculations from CSO, *National Accounts Statistics*, various issues.

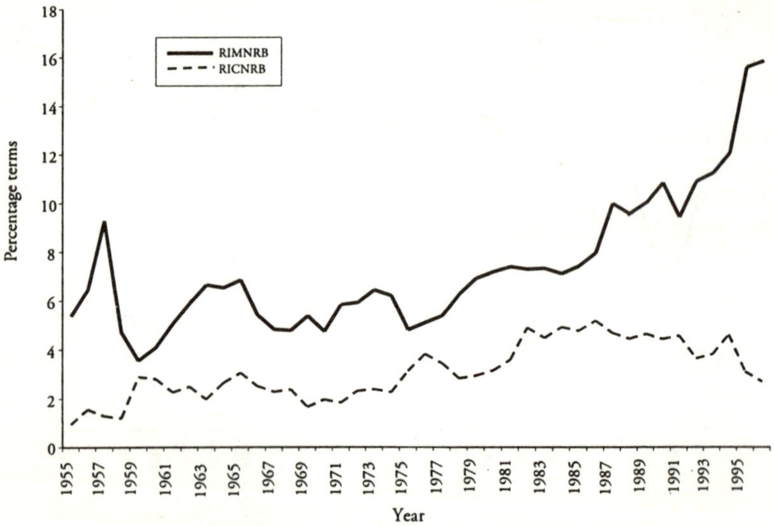

Figure 7.4: Rate of Investment in Machinery (RIMNRB) and Construction (RICNRB) in the Non-residential Business Sector

Source: Authors' calculations from CSO, *National Accounts Statistics*, various issues.

(for details, see Appendix 2). For the rest of the variables (*GY*, *GYNRB*, and *GL*) we apply the standard ADF test. The test statistics indicate that all five variables are integrated of order zero and thus, classical regression methods are appropriate.[16]

Two further econometric issues arise when estimating the Scott regressions. Firstly, even though the Scott's theory is designed to explain long-term growth, we are using annual data for the regressions, and hence, would also be capturing the influence of short-term factors on growth rates. The use of the general-to-specific econometric methodology allows us to control for cyclical influences on output by the appropriate inclusion of lags of the dependent and independent variables.[17] Also, as is clear from Fig. 7.1, there were particularly strong negative shocks to output growth in the years 1965 and 1979. We incorporate dummies for these two years.

The second econometric issue is the potential endogeneity of the investment rates (since higher output growth should lead to higher investment by increasing the returns to investment). To see whether our estimates are sensitive to simultaneity bias, we use both OLS and IV estimation techniques in our initial estimation of the Scott model.

RESULTS

Results from the estimation of Models 1A and 2A are reported in Table 7.1. The diagnostic statistics for these models indicate no problem of serial correlation, functional form mis-specification, and non-normality of the error term. The OLS estimates of the basic Scott model, with the growth rate of GDP as the dependent variable (column 1) indicate that *GL* is not statistically significant. In column 2, we present the model with *GL* omitted. We find that the rate of investment is significant, with a one per cent increase in the investment rate leading to a 0.24 per cent increase in GDP growth. Interestingly, the IV estimates are not very different from the OLS estimates (we use lags of *RI* as instruments of current *RI*). Examining the results of Model 2A, we find that *GL* has a higher significance in explaining growth of non-residential business output than total output (though *GL* is still not significant at conventional levels of significance). We also find the rate of investment variable having a far more important role in explaining growth in the case of the non-residential business sector than in the case of

[16] The ADF test statistics are as follows: *GY*: –7.4; *GYNRB*: –7.5; *RI*: –5.3; *RINRB*: –3.3; *GL*: –4.4.

[17] We also tried using an index of capacity utilization, constructed as the ratio of actual output to trend output obtained by fitting an exponential trend line. However, this led to significant serial correlation problems in the estimates.

TABLE 7.1

Investment and Growth: Models 1A and 2A

Explanatory Variables	*Model 1A OLS Dependent Variable: GY*		*Model 1A IV Dependent Variable: GY*	*Model 2A OLS Dependent Variable: GYNRB*	*Model 2A IV Dependent Variable: GYNRB*
	Col (1)	*Col (2)*	*Col (3)*	*Col (4)*	*Col (5)*
RI	0.253[c]	0.238[c]	0.241[c]	–	–
	(5.13)	(7.60)	(7.63)		
RINRB	–	–	–	0.456[c]	0.494[c]
				(4.79)	(5.08)
GL	–0.152	–	–	0.361	0.268
	(–0.40)			(1.03)	(0.75)
D65	–0.081[c]	–0.104[c]	–0.080[c]	–0.077[b]	–0.077[b]
	(–2.83)	(–2.83)	(–2.83)	(–2.40)	(–2.39)
D79	–0.104[c]	–0.161[c]	–0.105[c]	–0.107[c]	–0.106[c]
	(–3.63)	(–3.70)	(–3.71)	(–3.32)	(–3.30)
GY(–1)	–0.161	–0.161	–0.173	–	–
	(–1.18)	(–1.19)	(–1.27)		
GYNRB(-1)				–0.216	–0.246[a]
				(–1.53)	(–1.72)
R^{-2}	0.342	0.356	0.357	0.331	0.328
F statistic	6.05[c]	8.22[c]	8.21[c]	5.82[c]	5.75[c]
S.E. of Regression	0.0281	0.0277	0.0277	0.0314	0.0315
LM	1.74	1.56	1.36	1.79	1.14
RESET	0.001	0.005	0.47	0.87	0.62
JBN	1.41	1.42	1.45	0.74	0.80

Notes: t-ratios of regression coefficients are given in brackets. Approximate critical values for the *t*-ratios are as follows: 10 per cent = 1.69 ([a]), 5 per cent = 2.04 ([b]), and 1 percent = 2.75 ([c]). The test statistics are: *LM* = Lagrange multiplier test of residual serial correlation; *RESET* = Ramsey test for functional form mis-specification; and *JBN* = Jarque-Bera test for the normality of residuals.

the entire economy, with the IV estimate of the coefficient on *RINRB* almost double than the corresponding IV estimate on *RI*. The greater contribution of both *GL* and the rate of investment variable in explaining output growth in the case of the non-residential business sector provide support for Scott's suggestion that his model is more relevant to the non-residential business sector rather than the entire economy. Again, as in the case of Model 1A, the IV estimates of Model 2A are not very different from the OLS estimates. For this reason, we will use OLS for the estimation of the rest of the models.

In the next set of regressions, we allow the efficiency of investment to vary over time and to be influenced by policy variables. We first ran regressions as suggested by Models 1B and 2B with *RI* and *RINRB* respectively interacted with *OPEN*, *INF*, *PBIINF*, and *FIN*.[18] However, we found that in both the cases of *GY* and *GYNRB*, *PBIINF* and *FIN* were not statistically significant. We also experimented with interacting *RI* and *RINRB* with the other proxies of openness—*MSI* and *SMX*—and found that in none of these cases, the interactive terms were significant. The final results are presented in Table 7.2.

TABLE 7.2
Investment and Growth: Models 1B and 2B

Explanatory Variables	*Model 1B Dependent Variable: GY*	*Model 2B Dependent Variable: GYNRB*	
	Col (1)	*Col (2)*	*Col (3)*
RI	0.223^{c}	–	–
	(2.73)		
RINRB	–	0.805^{c}	0.856^{c}
		(4.55)	(5.65)
RI*INF	-0.011^{b}	–	–
	(–2.05)		
RI*OPEN	0.901	–	–
	(1.62)		
RINRB*INF	–	-0.035^{b}	-0.037^{b}
		(–2.29)	(–2.49)

(contd.)

[18] When estimating Models 2a and 2b with *PBIINF* interacted with the rate of investment variables, the sample period is restricted to 1960–95 for lack of data for the other years.

Table 7.2 (contd.)

Explanatory Variables	*Model 1B* *Dependent Variable: GY*	*Model 2B* *Dependent Variable: GYNRB*	
	Col (1)	*Col (2)*	*Col (3)*
GL	–	0.205 (0.61)	–
D65	–0.068[b] (–2.44)	–0.073[b] (–2.40)	–0.074[b] (–2.44)
D79	–0.085[c] (–2.97)	–0.079[b] (–2.44)	–0.076[c] (–2.39)
GY(–1)	–0.284[b] (–2.05)	–	–
GYNRB(–1)	–	–0.332[b] (–2.32)	–0.330[b] (–2.33)
R^{-2}	0.420	0.403	0.414
F statistic	6.65[c]	6.27[c]	7.89[c]
S.E. of Regression	0.0263	0.0297	0.0295
LM	1.83	2.12	1.90
RESET	0.08	0.77	1.36
JBN	1.40	0.80	0.96

Notes: t–ratios of regression coefficients are given in brackets. Approximate critical values for the *t*–ratios are as follows: 10 per cent = 1.69 ([a]), 5 per cent = 2.04 ([b]), and 1 per cent = 2.75 ([c]). The test statistics are: *LM* = Lagrange multiplier test of residual serial correlation; *RESET* = Ramsey test for functional form mis–specification; and *JBN* = Jarque–Bera test for the normality of residuals.

Perhaps the most noteworthy result is the importance of the inflation rate in influencing the efficiency of investment. For both total output growth and the rate of growth of output of the non-residential business sector, the inflation rate has a significant and negative impact on growth through an adverse impact on the efficiency of investment (column 3 of Table 7.2 omits *GL* in the final regression, as it is found not to be significant, when interactive terms for *RINRB* are added). We also find a clear role for openness (measured by the ratio of exports plus imports to GDP) in influencing growth through the efficiency of investment—an increase in openness has a significant positive impact on the efficiency of investment.

TABLE 7.3
Investment and Growth: Models 1C and 1D

Explanatory Variables	*Model 1C Dependent Variable: GY*		*Model 1D Dependent Variable: GY*
	Col (1)	*Col (2)*	*Col (3)*
RIM	0.346[c]	0.350[c]	–
	(3.18)	(3.27)	
RIC	0.171	0.210[a]	0.388[c]
	(1.20)	(1.82)	(4.26)
RIS	0.186	–	–
	(0.47)		
RIM*OPEN	–	–	2.429[c]
			(3.14)
RIM*INF	–	–	–0.016
			(–1.28)
D65	–0.077[b]	–0.080[c]	–0.072[b]
	(–2.60)	(–2.77)	(–2.51)
D79	–0.100[c]	–0.097[c]	–0.088[c]
	(–3.38)	(–3.42)	(–3.02)
GY(–1)	–0.196	–0.188	–0.211
	(–1.38)	(–1.35)	(–1.52)
R^{-2}	0.341	0.356	0.368
F statistic	5.04[c]	6.39[c]	5.53[c]
S.E. of Regression	0.0281	0.0277	0.0275
LM	2.09	2.51	2.16
RESET	0.23	0.57	2.93
JBN	1.10	0.92	0.71

Notes: t–ratios of regression coefficients are given in brackets. Approximate critical values for the *t*–ratios are as follows: 10 per cent = 1.69 ([a]), 5 per cent = 2.04 ([b]), and 1 per cent = 2.75 ([c]). The test statistics are: *LM* = Lagrange multiplier test of residual serial correlation; *RESET* = Ramsey test for functional form mis–specification; and *JBN* = Jarque–Bera test for the normality of residuals.

Finally, in Tables 7.3 and 7.4, we examine whether there are differences in the contributions of the three different components of the investment rate to economic growth. We first present estimates for the growth rate of total output (Models 1C and 1D). As has been found in the new growth literature, the estimates indicate that machinery investment has a much more important role in explaining growth than construction or inventory investment. In fact, the coefficient on inventory investment is insignificant, and we drop this variable in the final regression for Model 1C (column 2). We find that when both the machinery and construction investment rates are increased by one per cent, there is a 0.35 per cent increase in GDP growth in the former case as compared to a 0.21 per cent increase in the latter case. Interacting machinery investment with openness and the inflation rate variable, we find once again that the latter two variables are crucial in explaining the efficiency of investment (Model 1D).

TABLE 7.4
Investment and Growth: Models 2C and 2D

Explanatory Variables	*Model 2C Dependent Variable: GYNRB*	*Model 2D Dependent Variable: GYNRB*
	Col (1)	*Col (2)*
RIMNRB	0.363[b] (2.09)	–
RICNRB	0.664 (1.52)	0.897[b] (2.45)
RIMNRB*OPEN	–	1.645[b] (2.12)
RIS	0.431 (1.18)	0.555 (1.55)
D65	–0.076[b] (–2.38)	–0.070[b] (–2.17)
D79	–0.114[c] (–3.46)	–0.116[c] (–3.54)
GYNRB(–1)	–0.231 (–1.63)	–0.239 (–1.68)

(contd.)

Table 7.4 (contd.)

Explanatory Variables	*Model 2C* *Dependent Variable:* *GYNRB*	*Model 2D* *Dependent Variable:* *GYNRB*
	Col (1)	*Col (2)*
R^{-2}	0.324	0.326
F statistic	4.86[c]	4.88[c]
S.E. of Regression	0.0313	0.0312
LM	1.93	1.89
RESET	0.54	0.99
JBN	1.52	1.37

Notes: t–ratios of regression coefficients are given in brackets. Approximate critical values for the *t*–ratios are as follows: 10 per cent = 1.69 (a), 5 per cent = 2.04 (b), and 1 per cent = 2.75 (c). The test statistics are: *LM* = Lagrange multiplier test of residual serial correlation; *RESET* = Ramsey test for functional form mis–specification; and *JBN* = Jarque–Bera test for the normality of residuals.

The results for the non-residential business sector when investment is decomposed into its components are to some degree different than those for the entire economy (due to the lack of data for *RISNRB*, we use *RIS* in the regressions instead) (see Table 7.4). We find that in this case, the coefficient on construction investment (*RICNRB*) while greater than that on machinery investment (*RIMNRB*) is not statistically significant at the 10 per cent level. When *RIMNRB* is interacted with openness and the inflation rate, only the interactive term for openness (*RIMNRB*OPEN*) yielded a statistically significant coefficient. Thus, the robustness of the finding that openness has a positive effect on the growth rate of output via the efficiency of investment is striking.

CONCLUSIONS

This chapter has examined the role of investment in economic growth in India using an analytical framework developed using the new endogenous growth theory due to Scott (1989). The analytical framework provides a simple, yet persuasive approach to testing this relationship while allowing for key aspects of the policy regime to impact on growth through the quality of investment.

Our empirical analysis provides strong empirical support for the view that both the level of investment and its efficiency are the proximate causes of economic growth. The policy regime, as captured by the degree of openness and low inflation, seems to exert a significant positive influence on growth performance via investment efficiency. There is also empirical support for the view that investment in machinery and equipment has a larger growth effect compared to investment in construction or aggregate investment.

Throughout the post-independence era, the investment rate in India has remained well above that of many other developing countries—not only those belonging to the low-income category but also most middle-income countries in Latin America (see Chapter 3). However in terms of growth performance, India has continued to remain a typical low-income country. The empirical results reported in this chapter help understand this inconsistency between India's investment and growth performance. In the first three post-independence decades and also, to some extent, well into the 1980s, a dirigiste trade and industry policy regime constrained the potential growth effect of domestic investment. Thus, investment levels maintained through macroeconomic stability and financial sector reforms simply enabled India only to maintain growth of real GDP at a level just to offset population growth (Krueger 1992: p. 43). Higher growth rates during the post reform period can be explained in terms of both a more conducive setting for investment in machinery and equipment and greater efficiency of investment in a more liberal economic regime.

8

Conclusions

This book has examined the role of financial factors in economic growth in the light of the Indian experience during the post-independence era up to 1996. The determinants of saving and investment and the investment–growth nexus were subjected to careful scrutiny as the key themes which link the financial sector with the real economy. The book has drawn on both the recent theoretical and empirical literature in this subject area and recent advances in time-series econometrics. The findings were carefully analysed in relation to key policy shifts in India and in the wider developing country context to inform the ongoing policy debate. This final chapter summarizes the key findings and draws policy lessons.

Trends and Patterns of Saving and Investment

There was a consistent increase in domestic saving and investment rates in India throughout the period under study, though with considerable fluctuations from year to year and periodic cycles. The saving rate increased from about 10 per cent in the early 1950s to 17 per cent in the early 1970s, and then to over 25 per cent by the mid-1990s. The investment rate increased from 11 per cent in the early 1950s to around 19 per cent in the early 1970s, and then to 26 per cent by the mid-1990s.

Domestic investment was financed predominantly through domestic saving, with foreign capital inflows amounting to an average of 2 per cent of GDP during the period under consideration. Private saving accounted for the bulk of national saving, with the share of public saving declining persistently from the early 1980s onwards. By the mid-1970s, public saving accounted for a mere 5 per cent of total domestic saving, down from over 30 per cent in the mid-1950s. The annual increase in the private saving rate was much faster in the 1950s and 1960s, as compared to the period from the late 1960s to early 1980s. From then on, there was a significant increase in the rate well into the 1990s. Within private saving, household savings continued to remain the most important component. Its share in total private saving, however, declined from over 88 per cent in the early 1950s to 84 per cent in the mid-1990s, reflecting the increase in corporate saving.

On the investment side, the relative contribution of the public and private sectors to gross domestic capital formation has changed considerably in the period under consideration. From the mid-1960s to the early 1980s, the increase in the overall investment rate was driven mainly by increases in public investment. By contrast, the rise in the investment rate from the mid-1980s onwards emanated predominantly from the private sector. By the mid-1990s, the private sector accounted for over 80 per cent of total domestic investment compared to less than 60 per cent four decades ago. The dominance of household investment in total private investment has eroded sharply from the mid-1980s reflecting impressive growth in corporate investment. The share of corporate investment in total private investment, which varied in the range of 20 to 30 per cent during the first three decades of the post-independence period, increased to over 45 per cent in the 1990s.

India began the process of post-independence economic growth with a higher saving rate compared to many other developing country counterparts. Even in the early 1960s, India had high saving and investment rates compared to many other countries, including the present-day high-performing East Asian economies. From about the early 1970s, India has continuously lagged behind the latter set of countries. However, India's saving and investment performance has continued to remain impressive among countries in South Asia, Africa, and, to a lesser extent, those in Latin America. Among the Latin American countries (most of which belong to middle- or upper-middle income categories), only two countries—Chile and Costa Rica—consistently maintained superior saving rates compared to India. Countries like Brazil, Peru, Argentina, and Mexico, which had higher saving rates than India in the 1960s, ended up with lower or comparable rates in the mid-1990s.

On the investment side, India's relative performance among other countries and broader inter-country patterns are similar to those observed for the saving rates. Generally, countries with increasing saving rates also have increasing investment rates, while those with declining saving rates have slipped down in the investment ranking. These overall patterns are consistent with the Feldstein–Horioka proposition that, as against the popular perception about rapid globalization of capital, domestic investment is fundamentally determined by domestic saving. Among the countries covered in the comparison, India has one of the lowest degrees of reliance on net foreign capital inflows for financing domestic capital formation.

DETERMINANTS OF SAVING

The determinants of the domestic saving were examined using an analytical framework derived within the life-cycle model, the workhorse of modern saving analysis. The econometric evidence point to the real interest rate, growth and the level of per capita income, spread of banking facilities, and the rate of inflation as statistically significant positive influences on domestic saving. Terms of trade changes and inward remittances by expatriate Indians seems to have a significant negative impact on the saving rate. There is also a clear role for fiscal policy in increasing total saving in the economy, with the private sector considering public saving as an imperfect substitute for its own saving.

The results relating to the impact of real interest rate on domestic saving provides support for the McKinnon–Shaw proposition that, in an economy where the saving behaviour is highly intensive in money or near-money assets, high real interest rates promote private saving in the economy. Despite the fact that financial savings on average accounted for over 45 per cent of total private savings during the period under study, there is no evidence of substitution of other assets for financial assets in response to changes in the real deposit rate. A one per cent increase in the real interest rate seems to bring about a one percentage point increase in the national saving rate.

As postulated by the life-cycle model, income growth is an important determinant of the private saving rate; a one per cent increase in growth leads to a long-run increase in the saving rate by 0.14 per cent. However, we find that the Keynesian absolute income hypothesis also holds for saving performance in India—a one per cent increase in the level of per capita income leads to an increase in the private saving rate by 0.09 per cent. This provides support for the argument that for countries in the initial stages of development, the level of income is an important determinant of the capacity to save over and above the rate of income growth.

Bank density (population per bank branch) is a highly significant explicator of Indian saving performance. A one per cent decrease in bank density seems to bring about a 0.04 per cent increase in the private saving rate. This result provides strong support for the view that the expansion of banking facilities since the 1970s contributed significantly to improvement in saving propensities in the economy. There is no evidence to suggest that the expansion of bank branches generated greater financial savings in the form of bank deposits at the expense of the accumulation of other assets.

There is evidence that the private saving declines only by 0.53 percentage points for a given percentage point increase in the public saving . Thus, contrary to the prediction of the Ricardian equivalence hypothesis, an improvement in public saving will contribute to a net increase in total national saving in India.

While general economic performance (measured in terms of both income growth and the level of per capita income) has been a significant determinant of saving performance, the Indian economy has managed to maintain the saving rate at a level beyond what is permitted by economic performance alone. As noted, among the developing countries of similar income status, India has continued to maintain a relatively higher propensity to save. Our regression results suggest that a progressively important role of financial intermediation can help explain this relative performance. Two features of the financial intermediation process are important here. Firstly, while the nominal interest rate was an administered price changed at infrequent intervals, Indian policy makers ensured that there was no persistent adverse movement in real deposit rates. Secondly, the policy-induced push to spread banking facilities to rural and semi-urban areas played a useful supplementary role in increasing private (and hence total) saving through a persistent reduction in bank density in the country.

DETERMINANTS OF INVESTMENT

The determinants of private investment were examined using an analytical framework derived, with appropriate modification to suit the structural peculiarities of the Indian economy, from the neoclassical theory of business fixed investment. Given the nature of data availability, the prime focus of the analysis was on corporate investment. However, an investment function was also estimated for total non-residential business investment for the purpose of comparison.

The results support the hypothesis that corporate investment in a given year is negatively affected by the size of the initial capital stock; long-run investment elasticity with respect to the initial capital stock is estimated at –1.1. Moreover, the standard accelerator mechanism is important in explaining corporate investment behaviour. The cost of investment, which is measured so as to capture the cost of borrowing, the cost of capital goods, and depreciation, is found to have a significantly negative influence on corporate investment. This finding is of immense policy significance given that, of all the determinants of investment, the cost of capital is perhaps the one which is most influenced by economic policy.

In general, the determinants of private corporate investment were found to be different from those of non-residential business investment. While the rental cost of capital was an important determinant of private corporate investment, it is not the case for non-residential business investment. The responsiveness of investment to output was also weaker for the non-residential business sector. On the other hand, bank credit and public investment were important in explaining both corporate and non-residential business investment.

The estimated investment function for corporate investment sheds considerable light on the remarkable increase in corporate investment in India following the market-oriented structural adjustment reforms initiated in 1991. It is evident that the net impact of the reforms on corporate investment has been salutary. The decline in the rate of growth of real public sector investment brought about by the reform-related fiscal squeeze seems to have had a significant adverse impact on corporate investment. However, this adverse impact was outweighed by the salutary effects of the decline in real rental cost of capital brought about by the reform process, and favourable changes in investor perception in the aftermath of the reforms.

THE INVESTMENT–GROWTH NEXUS

The role of investment in economic growth was examined using an analytical framework derived from the *new view of economic growth* due to Scott (1989). Scott's model has a number of advantages over various other new (endogenous) growth models from both theoretical and empirical points of view. In particular, it provides a clear theoretical case for using the gross investment rate, rather than the stock of capital, as the appropriate indicator of investment in explaining long-term growth. It also provides an explicit role for policy to influence, interactively with gross investment, the relationship between investment and growth. By contrast, other formulations of endogenous growth theory redefine technology (which is exogenous in the orthodox Solow–Swan model) as another form of endogenously determined reproducible capital (termed knowledge), which combines with traditional capital to form a composite capital input. The shortcoming of this theory from an empirical point of view is that knowledge is unmeasurable. Moreover, the other endogenous growth theories do not provide for an explicit role for policy in influencing the efficiency of investment.

Our analysis provides strong empirical support for the view that *both* the level of investment and its efficiency are important in determining economic growth. Both the trade policy regime (as alternatively captured by the degree of openness and the availability of imported investment goods) and macroeconomic policy (as measured by the rate of inflation) seem to impact on growth performance via investment efficiency. As has been found in the new empirical growth literature, the estimates indicate that machinery investment has a much more important role in explaining growth than construction investment. There is no empirical evidence to suggest that financial deepening and public investment in infrastructure contribute directly to economic growth over and above their impact operating through raising saving and investment in the economy.

Throughout the post-war period, the investment rate in India remained well above that of many other developing countries—not only those belonging to the low-income category but also most middle-income countries in Latin America. However, in terms of growth performance, until recently India continued to remain a typical low-income country. The empirical results reported in this chapter help understand this inconsistency in India's investment and growth performance. In the first three decades of the post-independence period and well into the 1980s, a *dirigiste* trade and industry policy regime constrained the potential growth effect of domestic investment. Thus, investment levels maintained through macroeconomic stability and financial deepening simply enabled India to keep its head just above water. Higher growth rates since the mid-1980s can be explained both in terms of a more conducive setting for investment in machinery and equipment and the greater efficiency of investment in a more liberal economic regime.

POLICY IMPLICATIONS

The findings of this study provide useful guidance for development policy in India, particularly relating to macroeconomic, financial sector, and trade policies. In particular, they have a number of implications for identifying policy priorities for the speedy implementation of the unfinished agenda of the liberalization process initiated in 1991 in these areas.

Macroeconomic Policy

The study's findings suggest that the maintenance of a stable macroeconomic environment during most of the period under study was a key factor behind India's superior saving/investment performance compared to many other developing countries. While inflation does raise saving initially, it has a negative effect on the latter in the long run, via a decrease in the real interest rate. Inflation also has an unambiguously negative effect on the efficiency of investment.

There is also clear evidence that an increase in public sector saving has a net positive impact on total national saving. At the same time, public investment seems to play an important complementary role in promoting private investment. Thus, if fiscal policy has to promote *both* aggregate saving and investment in India, and if the reduction in the budget deficit is to be brought about by a cut in government expenditures, then the adjustment must necessarily be on public consumption and *not* on public investment. Of course, the long run solution to this painful compromise lies in initiatives to widen the domestic tax base and the efficacy of the revenue collection mechanism. Budgetary reforms in the overall economic reform process should be judged by their ability to achieve necessary fiscal prudence while maintaining growth of public investment levels in power, transport infrastructure, port, irrigation, and telecommunications and other infrastructure which underpin the expansion of private investment.

From about the mid-1980s, macroeconomic policy in India began to deviate significantly from the conventional prudential approach. Widening budget deficits and the resultant blow out in the balance of payments eventually set the stage for structural adjustment cum liberalization reforms in mid-1991. Regaining the lost macroeconomic prudence was a key emphasis of the reform package (Joshi and Little 1996). As part of the reforms, the government managed to cut the fiscal deficit from 9.9 per cent of GDP in 1990–1 to a little over 7 per cent in 1991–2. Commitment to sound budgetary policy was short lived, however. By 1993–4, the fiscal deficit was back to over 9 per cent of GDP and, despite policy rhetoric, the progress towards the reduction of the deficit has been barely perceptible in recent years (Joshi 1998). Despite economic recovery, government revenue has not increased significantly because rises in direct taxation have been largely offset by reform-related reduction in indirect taxation and also delays in the implementation of the proposed tax reforms. Moreover, given the little progress in the implementation of privatization proposals, deficits of the non-financial public sector enterprises (NFPS) have ballooned. In this context, the tendency for public consumption to crowd out public investment in total government expenditures, a disturbing development dating back to the early 1980s, has continued well into the post-reform period (Mundle and Rao 1997). Clearly, the inability of successive governments to control the revenue deficit (the difference between current revenues and expenditures), and the increasing reliance on capital expenditure cut-backs to adjust the fiscal account, may act as constraints on the possibility of any further increases in the national saving and private investment rates. Moreover, with the existing levels of the budget deficit, the use of monetary policy to keep inflation in check results in high interest rates too high for a desirable level of private investment to be sustainable. High interest rates also feed into NFPS deficits, aggravating budgetary imbalances in a feedback loop and thus limiting the degrees of freedom available for the authorities to use interest rate policy as an inflation control device. Thus unless concrete reforms measures (including privatization of loss-making NFPS) are taken, the inflation will get out of control, with adverse implications for domestic saving through reduced real interest rates (Joshi 1998; Srinivasan 2000, Chapter 4).

Financial Sector Policy

India's attempts in the post-independence period to promote the process of financial intermediation through the expansion of the geographical spread of the banking system are commendable by developing country standards. The increase in geographical spread has been the result of a strictly enforced branch licensing policy followed by the RBI. Under this policy, the RBI restricted banks from opening branches in urban and metropolitan areas. Instead, the thrust of branch expansion was mostly to the 'underbanked' districts in rural and semi-urban areas. Our results suggest that such a branch licensing policy that emphasized the spread of the banking system to rural and semi-urban areas has impacted positively on the saving rate. However, when we derive policy inferences from this finding we should not lose sight of the fact that the bank branch expansion policy also involved significant economic costs. In particular, the policy contributed to 'the poor profitability performance of public sector banks which had to shoulder most of the responsibility in providing banking access to the rural population' (Sen and Vaidya 1997: p. 43).

As part of economic liberalization reforms since 1991, banks have been given a certain degree of freedom in closing loss-making branches in rural and semi-urban areas or to convert them to satellite offices. Clearly, in the current deregulated environment, any further policy-induced emphasis on the branch expansion of commercial banks to 'underbanked' areas of the country cannot be considered as desirable. At the same time, our results suggest that a certain amount of caution should be exercised in allowing public sector banks to withdraw completely from rural areas as it may have an adverse effect on financial deepening, and consequently on the saving rate. As part of the banking sector reforms, it is important to set the stage for greater private sector participation and gradual opening to foreign banks. However, based on our results, we are of the view that the government has an important role to play in making banking accessible to the masses living in rural areas. To put it simply, the real challenge for reformers is to reform the inefficient banking system, while maintaining the favourable legacy of a countrywide banking system inherited from the controlled era.

Another important issue relating to financial sector liberalization, which is important from the perspective of this study, are the prevailing restrictions on private firms' access to bank credit. As a part of the financial sector reforms announced in 1991, the government proposed to scale down the mandatory requirements for banks to invest in government securities and cash reserves. Our findings suggest that further liberalization of flow of funds from the banking sector to private firms through the speedy implementation of this proposal will provide a significant impetus to private investment.

Trade Policy

This study has identified two significant ways in which recent changes in trade policy have positively impacted on growth performance of the Indian economy. Firstly, trade reforms brought about a fall in the relative price of capital goods, leading to a higher overall rate of investment in the economy. It should be noted that the most important change in trade policy in the immediate post-1991 period was the sharp reduction in the tariffs of capital goods, particularly in the higher rates (Joshi and Little 1997). The peak rate of tariff on capital goods was reduced from a high of 355 per cent in 1990 to 50 per cent in 1995. The fall in the relative price of capital goods due to the reduction in tariffs would have particularly led to an increase in equipment investment as the bulk of imported capital goods are machinery goods. As we have seen in Chapter 7, equipment investment has a larger growth effect than structures and inventory investment. Thus, the 1991 trade reforms pertaining to the capital goods sector can be expected to have a favourable effect on the growth performance of the Indian economy in the 1990s.

The second way in which recent trade policy changes may have had a positive effect on economic growth in India is the improvement in the efficiency of investment, both through the improved access to imported investment goods and an improvement in the general investment environment. While liberalization of capital goods imports is now more or less complete, further reductions in the relative price of capital goods may be possible with the privatization of public enterprises, most of which are in the intermediate and capital goods sectors.

Overall, our study makes a strong case for the speedy implementation of the unfinished liberalization agenda, particularly in the areas of macroeconomic stabilization, financial sector liberalization, and trade policy reforms.

Appendix 1

Indian Saving and Investment Data

The Central Statistical Organisation (CSO) is the agency responsible for the preparation of savings and investment data in India. This appendix discusses the methodology used by the CSO in the measurement of saving and investment in India and some key limitations of the data.

For the purpose of estimating saving and investment, the economy is divided into three broad institutional sectors, namely the public sector, the private corporate sector, and the household sector. The public sector covers government administration, departmental enterprises, and non-departmental enterprises.[1] The private corporate sector comprises all non-governmental financial/non-financial corporate enterprises and co-operative institutions. Non-government non-financial enterprises include public and private limited companies registered under the Indian Joint Stock Companies Act, 1956. Non-government financial institutions constitute all scheduled and non-scheduled commercial banks in the private sector and other financial and investment companies. Co-operative institutions comprise all co-operative banks and co-operative credit and non-credit societies. The household sector comprises, apart from individuals, all non-government non-corporate enterprises like sole proprietorships and partnerships owned and/ or controlled by individuals, and non-profit institutions.

Steps in the Estimation Procedure

A major constraint faced by the CSO in measuring saving and investment is the difficulty involved in direct estimation of household consumption and

[1] The non-departmental enterprises comprise government companies, statutory companies, and port trusts.

investment expenditures. Given this constraint, the household sector is treated as a 'residual' in the accounting procedure and household physical saving (that is, household saving in physical assets) is taken to be identical to household investment generated by investment estimation, as discussed below.

First, gross domestic capital formation (GDCF) or total investment is estimated as the sum of additions to fixed assets (that is, fixed capital formation) and inventories during the year. Here, fixed assets comprise construction and machinery and equipment (including breeding stock, draught animals, dairy cattle, and the like). Estimates are prepared separately for construction, machinery and equipment, and changes in stocks using the so-called commodity flow method. Under this method, GDCF is equal to the value of all commodities (for example, equipment, steel, cement, etc.) that can be used for investment. Adding imports to the domestic production of each such commodity in the relevant period, and subtracting exports and the amounts used for non-investment purposes provides an estimate of the quantities used for investment. The commodity vector so obtained is valued at producer's prices and to this value a trade and transportation margin and indirect taxes are added to arrive at an estimate of the value of investment at purchaser's prices (Srinivasan 1994). It should be noted that while the commodity flow method is used in estimating *pucca* construction as well as machinery and equipment, estimates of *kutcha* construction are prepared using the expenditure approach.[2]

The estimates of public and private corporate investment come directly from the financial statements of the public and private corporate sectors. Estimates of public and private corporate saving are obtained directly from the annual financial statements of the relevant enterprises/institutions.[3] Household investment, which is treated as identical to household physical saving, is then derived as a residual. Household financial saving in a given period is the increase in household financial assets over financial liabilities. Financial assets consists of currency, deposits, shares, debentures, bonds, life insurance funds, provident and pension funds, while financial liabilities are the household sector's borrowing from banks and non-bank finance companies.

As in the case of household physical saving, household financial saving is

[2] The term *pucca* construction refers to construction undertaken with the use of materials sold in the market such as cement, steel, bricks, timber, etc. Construction using freely available materials such as leaves, reeds, mud, etc. is known as *kutcha* construction.

[3] Estimates of private corporate saving are obtained from the RBI studies on the finances of public limited and private limited companies, and financial and investment companies, and from the RBI's database on banks and the co-operative movement.

estimated as a residual, that is, by deducting net financial assets of public and private corporate sectors from the total net financial assets of the economy. Gross domestic saving (GDS) is then estimated as the sum of household, private corporate, and public savings. Finally, foreign saving, coming from the balance of payments accounts, is added to GDS to obtain gross national saving (GNS).[4] Conceptually, GDS should be identical to GDCF, but in reality a sizeable discrepancy usually emerges. The CSO treats the savings estimate as more reliable and adjusts the total investment estimate (arrived at by the commodity flow method) for the discrepancy. As can be seen in Fig. A1.1, the unadjusted and adjusted GDCF series have differed substantially in some years.

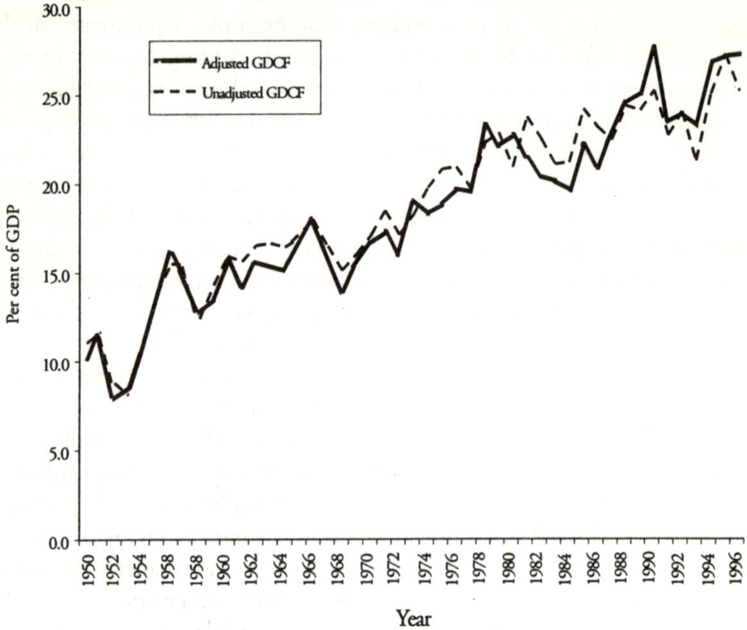

Figure A1.1: Adjusted and Unadjusted GDCF, 1950–96

Source: CSO, *National Accounts Statistics*, various issues.

[4] Estimates of foreign saving are also subject to errors and biases. In India, there are two quite different estimates of the trade deficit, which accounts for an important component of net external resource inflow. The first estimate is based on the flow of imports and exports through customs check-points. The other is based on foreign exchange receipts from exports and payments from imports that go through the banking system. As Srinivasan (1994: p. 12) points out, 'given the incentives the exchange control system in India and many other

LIMITATIONS

There are two important limitations with Indian saving/investment data. The first limitation stems from the estimation method for GDCF. While commenting on the measurement of GDCF, Srinivasan (1994: p. 11) notes that 'clearly at each step, there could be measurement errors: in estimating domestic availability, in the norms used to allocate investment and non-investment uses of a commodity, in valuing the commodity flow through a set of prices which are not necessarily the prices at which the goods were bought and sold, the trade and transport margin is often derived from some ancient benchmark survey etc.'. Furthermore, while data on domestic production of machinery and equipment in the organized manufacturing sector (provided in *The Annual Survey of Industries* (factory sector report)) and the imports of machinery and equipment can be considered to be reasonably reliable, the same cannot be said about the estimates of domestic production of machinery and equipment in the unorganized (or unregistered) manufacturing sector. Similarly, while estimates of *pucca* construction can be considered to be reliable, the estimates of *kutcha* construction would be less so as most of it occurs in the unorganized manufacturing sector and in the agricultural sector, where precise data are difficult to obtain. It would then be reasonable to conclude that there may be significant errors in the computation of total investment in India. Such errors directly flow on to estimates of household investment (which is residually obtained by deducting public and private corporate investment from total investment) and on to gross domestic savings (since household physical saving component therein is taken to be identical to household investment).

A second limitation of saving/investment data has to do with the treatment of the household sector. As the K. N. Raj Working Group on Saving[5] aptly noted, 'the household sector is highly heterogeneous in its composition, consisting of farm households, unincorporated enterprises in other sectors (such as manufacturing, transport and trade) and households proper' (RBI 1982: p. 45). The Working Group recommended in its report to estimate savings and investment separately for farm households, unincorporated enterprises in industry; trade, and transport, and households proper.

countries create for smuggling, capital flight and evasion of high tariffs, it is likely that both estimates based on officially recorded data are wide off the mark'. The second of the two estimates of the trade deficit is used in estimating foreign saving and, consequently, GNS (CSO 1989: p. 329).

[5] This working group was set up by the RBI in May 1981 to undertake a critical review of the available estimates of saving and investment in the Indian economy and to make recommendations for their improvement.

However, for want of requisite data, the CSO has not yet been able to implement its recommendation.

Failure to take into account the highly heterogeneous nature of the household sector impacts on the quality of saving/investment estimates in two ways. Firstly, while most financial assets held by households would constitute pure financial savings by the households proper, most financial liabilities would be in the form of borrowing by farm-households and unincorporated enterprises (consumer credit has been relatively insignificant in India in the past). Therefore, the actual estimate of financial saving would be an underestimate of true financial savings in the economy. Secondly, household investment in construction consists of both non-residential investment in structures by farm-households and unincorporated enterprises, and residential construction by the households proper. As we have noted in Chapter 6, the determinants of the former may be quite different from that of the latter. In fact, it would be more meaningful to add non-residential investment in structures by farm-households and unincorporated enterprises to investment in structures by the private corporate sector. By doing so, one can obtain an estimate of total investment in structures by the private sector, and consequently, an estimate of *total private investment.*[6] Data are not available for constructing such an series for India.[7]

While the Indian saving/investment data suffer from considerable measurement errors as discussed above, the CSO, by and large, has followed a uniform methodology in preparing these estimates throughout the period under study. The data can, therefore, be used in econometric analysis on the assumption that the degree of errors and biases in the estimates are constant over time. Indeed, in the developing world, India is one of the few countries for which reasonably consistent saving and investment estimates are available for a period of sufficient length required for econometric analysis.

[6] Here, one makes the reasonable assumption that household investment in machinery and equipment is undertaken only by farm households and unincorporated enterprises and *not* by households proper.

[7] The quality of Indian saving/investment data have also been questioned on grounds of using potentially biased sample studies and outdated benchmark ratios to obtain estimates of aggregate and sectoral saving and investment estimates. See EPWRF (1996: pp. 15-16).

Appendix 2

The Econometric Methodology

Suppose the theory suggests that there is a linear relationship between a pair of random variables X and Y for which time-series data are available for a period of sufficient length. Then the obvious way to test the theory is to estimate a linear equation of the form

$$Y = \alpha + \beta X + e \qquad \text{(A2.1)}$$

where e is a stochastic error term. The estimation is conventionally done by the Ordinary Least Squares (OLS) method, the overall fit is tested by R^2, and the statistical significance of β is tested using the standard t-test.

This classical approach to statistical inference is based on the assumption that the data series are stationary. That is, data series grow over time in a fairly steady, constant manner, reflecting smoothly evolving economic forces. In this sense, fluctuations in the series are taken to imply the influence of cyclical or temporary factors, and eventually the series return to their trend growth values. The mean, variance, and co-variances of the series, therefore, tend to remain constant over time.

Most economic time series are, however, not stationary around a deterministic trend. Rather they have stochastic trends; that is, at least some shocks that affect a series will have a permanent effect on the level of the series, making the series 'wander' without a tendency to revert to mean value. Thus, the mean, variance, and co-variances of the series tend to vary over time.

If variables are non-stationary, the OLS estimates tend to have sample distributions with properties very different from those assumed under the conventional procedure, and regression coefficients tends to appear spuriously significant. In other words, when we work with non-stationary variables, there is always the possibility of a 'Type 1' error; that is, accepting the relationship as significant when, in fact, X and Y are uncorrelated. Also, measures of the overall fit of the regression, such the coefficient of determination R^2, tend to provide an artificially high explanatory power of the regression. This is the problem of 'nonsense correlation' or 'spurious regression' alluded to by Yule in a classic article in 1927. However, until the publication of Granger and Newbold (1974), applied econometricians paid far too little attention to this problem.

Granger and Newbold (1974) showed by simulation how misleading standard regression procedure can be when applied to non-stationary variables. According to their experiments, high R^2 values can occur together with apparently significant t-values in regressions involving two completely unrelated series if both are integrated at order 1 (a series is said to be integrated of order 1 if the differenced series is stationary with positive spectrum at zero frequency).[1] They further demonstrated that, if more than two independent I(1) series are used in a regression, the possibility of a spurious relationship increases further. In sum, Granger–Newbold results exposed the need to rework the basic statistical techniques used in econometrics.

A simple cure to the problem of spurious correlation when modelling with non-stationary variables is to estimate relationships using differenced series rather than using their absolute levels (Nelson and Plosser 1982; Mills 1990). The effect of taking the rate of change in a variable is typically to remove any trend element. That is, many non-stationary economic time series become stationary when they are first differenced. Unfortunately, there is a real danger that, when differenced, important parts of the potential relationship between the variables can be lost (Granger 1987). In particular, estimates based on differences are therefore likely to provide poor forecasts for even a few periods ahead if a long-run relationship exists but is ignored. Differencing is thus an unsatisfactory method of dealing with a spurious correlation problem.

Recent advances in time-series econometrics have come up with two alternative approaches to address the spurious regression problem, without sacrificing important 'level' information. These are the general to specific modelling procedure developed by David Hendry and his co-researchers (for example, Davidson et al. 1978; Hendry 1996) and the second is the cointegration approach pioneered by Engle and Granger (1987).

GENERAL TO SPECIFIC METHODOLOGY

The general to specific methodology (GSM) (also known as the Hendry methodology or the London School of Economics method) has its origins

[1] Another way of stating this is 'that the variable has a unit root'.

in Sargan's seminal (1964) paper on error correction approach to time-series modelling, but it also reflects an oral tradition developed largely at the London School of Economics from the early 1960s.[2]

The essence of GSM is to embed the relationship being investigated within a sufficiently complex dynamic specification, including lagged dependent and independent variables so that a parsimonious specification of the model can be uncovered (Hendry, Pagan and Sargan 1985). A major advantage of this method is that it results in equations with first-differenced and stationary dependent variables, but unlike simple first-differenced equations, appropriately makes use of long-run information in the data (Wickens and Breucsh 1988).

Under this procedure, estimation starts with an over-parameterized autoregressive distributed lag (ADL) specification of an appropriate lag order:

$$Y_t = \alpha + \sum_{i=1}^{m} A_i\, Y_{t-i} + \sum_{i=0}^{m} B_i X_{t-i} + \mu_t, \tag{A2.2}$$

where a is a vector of constants, Y_t is a $(n \times 1)$ vector of endogenous variables, X_t is a $(k \times 1)$ vector of explanatory variables, and A_i and B_i are $(n \times n)$ and $(n \times k)$ matrices of parameters.

Equation (A2.2) can be re-parameterised in terms of differences and lagged levels so as to separate the short-run and long-run multipliers of the system as follows:

$$\Delta Y_t = \alpha + \sum_{i=1}^{m-1} A_i^{*} \Delta Y_{t-i} + \sum_{i=0}^{m-1} B_i^{*} \Delta X_{t-i} + C_0 Y_{t-m} + C_1 X_{t-m} + \mu_t,$$

where (A2.3)

$$C_0 = -I - \left[\sum_{i=1}^{m} A_i\right] \qquad C_1 = \left[\sum_{i=1}^{m} B_i\right]$$

and where the long-run multipliers of the system are given by $C_0^{-1}C_1$ and I is the identity matrix. Equation (A2.3) is known as the error correction mechanism(ECM) representation of the model. This is the particular formulation generally used as the 'maintained hypothesis' of the specification search.

The dynamics of the general model could be written in many different ways, all of which would yield the same estimates of the unknown parameters, but each of which package the information differently and consequently may be easier to interpret and understand (Pagan 1987). But the ECM is generally preferred over the other formulations because of a number

[2] For highly accessible discussions of the methodology, see Pagan (1987, 1995). Gilbert (1989) provides an interesting historical account of its evolution.

of reasons. The ECM has a first-differenced dependent variable, not a typical trending variable. Moreover, provided the model is correctly specified, the disequilibrium error of the specification will also be stationary. It can therefore be estimated by standard estimation methods such as OLS. An ECM also involves a parameterization that clearly distinguishes between long- and short-run effects. This separation between long- and short-run parameters in an ECM makes it an excellent vehicle for either assessing the validity of the long-run implications of theory or of incorporating them into the estimation process.

The estimation procedure involves first estimating the unrestricted equation (A2.3), and then progressively simplifying it by restricting statistically insignificant coefficients to zero and reformulating the lag patterns where appropriate in terms of levels and differences to achieve orthogonality. As part of the specification search, it is necessary to check rigorously at every stage even the more general of models for possible misspecification. Such checks will involve both a visual examination of the residual from the fitted version of the model and the use of tests for serial correlation, heteroskedasticity and normality in the residual, and the appropriateness of the particular functional form used. In particular, any suggestion of autocorrelation in the residual should lead to a rethink about the form of the general model. Above all, theoretical consistency must be born in mind throughout the testing down procedure.[3]

COINTEGRATION TECHNIQUES

Engle and Granger (1987) developed the concept of cointegration as an extension to the earlier work by Granger and Newbold (1974) on the spurious regression problem. They observed that while the individual economic series may be non-stationary, a vector of variables, taken together, may be cointegrated (generating a stationary residual), provided these variables are individually integrated of the same order. If the particular vector of the variables is put together on the basis of sound economic theory, then a cointegration relationship among them can be interpreted as the equilibrium (long-run) relationship described by that theory.

Based on the equivalence of cointegration and the economic concept of equilibrium, Engle and Granger propose a constructive two-stage approach to modelling economic relationships involving non-stationary variables, provided the variables are integrated of the same order. The first stage involves modelling the long run or cointegrating the relationship. The

[3] Further details of these tests can be found in Hendry (1996) and Greene (1999).

short-run dynamic relationship among the variables is estimated at the second stage. The second stage relationship can best be modelled with an error correction model. Engle and Granger (1987) prove that if the variables are cointegrated (that is, if an equilibrium relationship exists), then the short-run disequilibrium relationship between them can be represented by an ECM. This result is referred to as the Granger representation theorem.

A data series is said to be *integrated* of order d, or $I(d)$, if it requires to be differenced d times to yield a stationary series. Suppose that we have a vector (a set of variables) X_t containing n variables, all of which are I(1).[4] This set of variables are said to be cointegrated if they form a linear combination $Z_t = a\ X_t$ such that Z_t is I(0), where a is known as the cointegrating vector.

An essential first step in the implementation of this two-stage modelling procedure is testing the integration properties of the variables involved. The standard tests are the Dickey–Fuller (DF) and Augmented Dickey-Fuller (ADF) tests.[5]

The DF test involves running a regression of the following type:

$$\Delta Y_t = a_0 + a_1 t + a_2 Y_{t-1} + e_t \tag{A2.4}$$

where Y is the variable under investigation, t is the time trend, and e is the error term.

The terms a_0 and a_1 are excluded from the regression if they are statistically insignificant (for more details see chapter 4 of Enders). If the error term is found to be serially correlated, lags of ΔY_t are added to the above regression until one achieves independence of the error term:

$$\Delta Y_t = a_0 + a_1 t + a_2 Y_{t-1} + a_3 \Delta Y_{t-2} + a_4 \Delta Y_{t-3} + \ldots + a_k \Delta Y_{t-k-1} + e_t \tag{A2.5}$$

The above is the regression for the ADF test. The null hypothesis of stationarity (no unit root) is rejected if a_2 is negative and its t-statistic is greater than the Dickey–Fuller critical value.

In the presence of structural change (defined to be either a one-period shock to the series or a change in the level of the series), the DF and ADF

[4] Normally non-stationary economic variables are integrated of order I(1), that is stationarity is achieved by first-differencing.

[5] While several alternate procedures exist to test for unit roots, the Dickey–Fuller test (appropriately augmented to allow for autocorrelation) is the most widely used one. It has been found that the asymptotic properties for other procedures are the same as those of Dickey–Fuller, though they may differ in their small sample properties (for a discussion, see Enders 1995).

tests have a bias towards accepting the null hypothesis of a unit root. Perron (1989) provides an extension of the DF and ADF tests in the presence of structural change. Essentially, Perron's test involves adding a dummy variable to the DF and ADF regressions to incorporate the episode of structural change. Critical values in this case would be different from those provided by Dickey–Fuller and are given in Perron's paper.

If all variables are found to be integrated of the same order,[6] the long-run relationship (the first-stage regression) is then estimated using OLS. If the residual of this estimated regression is found to be stationary (in terms of the Dickey–Fuller test, conducted without a constant term in the auxiliary regression), then the coefficients of the regression can be interpreted as representing a long-term (steady state) relationship. Engle and Granger (1987) have demonstrated that for non-stationary variables, the OLS estimator is super consistent ; that is, it converges to the true value at a rate faster than in normal asymptotics.

Finally, the short-run relationship is modelled in terms of first differences of all variables, and the lagged residual of the first stage (cointegrating) regression is included to represent the disequilibrium error. As all variables are stationary, the standard tests are applicable.

Suppose our model aims to explain variable Y_t in terms a vector of explanatory variable X_t. First we perform a static OLS regression of the following form in order to obtain the cointegrating vector:

$$Y_t = \alpha + \beta X_t + \mu_t, \tag{A2.6}$$

After obtaining an estimate of the the long-run relationship of the model, b_t, and having satisfied that μ_t is I(0), we construct the ECM term,

$$Z_t = Y_t - \beta X_t \tag{A2.7}$$

which is then inserted in a dynamic second-stage model in the form of,

$$\Delta Y_t = \alpha + \sum_{i=1}^{m-1} A_i \Delta Y_{t-i} + \sum_{i=0}^{m} B_i \Delta X_{t-i} + C_0 Z_{t-1} + \mu_t. \tag{A2.8}$$

This equation is then 'tested down' (using OLS),[7] by dropping statistically insignificant lag terms and imposing, if need be, data-acceptable restrictions on the regression parameters.[8]

[6] In most cases this means that all variables are I (1). See fn. 5.

[7] Note that all variables in A2.8 are stationary (I(0)). So the error term (u_t) satisfies the standard assumption of the OLS estimator.

[8] For further details, see various contributions in Granger (1990) and the excellent survey article by Muscatelli and Hurns (1995).

Subsequent research has revealed a number of problems with the Engle–Granger two-stage procedure. Although the OLS estimator from the cointegrating regression possesses the large sample property of consistency and are highly efficient, they are still biased in small samples. In the case of small samples, the OLS estimator in the first step has an asymptotic distribution, which is non-normal and is affected by nuisance parameters. This makes statistical inference difficult since the standard *t*-statistics will not be valid asymptotically. This bias is carried over to the second stage estimation through the disequilibrium errors. Another problem is that when there are more than two variables, all integrated to order 1, in the model, it is possible that there will be more than one linear combination of these variables that is integrated to order zero. That is, there may be more than one cointegrating vector. These considerations have led to the development of a number of alternative procedures for the estimation of the first-stage regression in the Engle–Granger two-step procedure. Two most widely used alternatives are the fully-modified OLS estimator proposed by Phillips and Hansen (1989) and the maximum-likelihood procedure developed by Johansen (1988) and Johansen and Juselius (1990).[9]

The Phillips–Hansen method is an optimal single-equation technique which is asymptotically equivalent to maximum-likelihood. It applies a semi-parametric correction to the OLS estimator to eliminate dependency on the nuisance parameters, and to give median-unbiased *t*-statistics which follow a standard normal distribution asymptotically (and thus the label 'fully-modified').

In theory, the maximum-likelihood method for the estimation of cointegration vectors developed by Johansen (1988) is superior to the Phillips–Hansen method. Under this method, unit roots are explicitly incorporated in the specification. It too takes into account short-run dynamics in estimating the cointegrating vector, and additionally provides for testing for the existence of more than one cointegrating vector. However, the small-sample properties of this method are still unknown. Moreover, recent applications of this technique have encountered at least three practical difficulties (Hall 1991). The first problem is that both the trace and determinant test statistics used to determine the degree of cointegration, and the estimates of the long-run cointegrating vector, are very sensitive to the choice of lag length for the VAR. Second, severe collinearity may emerge between some of the regressors, particularly when dealing with VARs of a reasonable size. This in turn renders the point estimates of the long-run

[9] For a succinct text-book treatment of the Phillips–Hansen procedure, see Banerjee et al. (1993: pp. 239–52).

elasticities even more sensitive to the choice of lag specification. Finally, when there are more than one cointegrating relationships between the variables in the model, it is sometimes difficult to provide an economic interpretation of the cointegrating vectors (Wickens 1996).

To summarize the discussion so far, if all the variables under consideration are found to be non-stationary, then the Engle–Granger two-step procedure, with the Johansen or Phillip–Hansen procedures (or any other technique) appropriately chosen for the first stage estimator, provides a neat way of modelling time-series data. This has the advantage of separately identifying long-term and short-term relationships, while cushioning against the possibility of uncovering spurious relationships.

What if the set of variables under consideration is a mixture of stationary and non-stationary series?[10] Research in time-series econometrics over the past two decades have ended in a virtual agreement in this regard to work with the general to specific methodology (GSM). Interestingly, recent comparative Monte Carlo studies of cointegrating techniques (for example, Phillips and Loretan 1991; Inder 1993) have found the general to specific procedure to be equally good as, if not more appropriate than, the Phillips–Hansen procedures as an alternative estimation procedure in dealing with small data samples even when all data series under consideration are non-stationary. These findings in fact provide support for the view of the principal creators of GSM that it is perfectly legitimate for one to proceed directly with an estimation process based on a general unrestricted ADL specification (as given by eqn A2.2), without testing the time-series properties of the data series. However, it has now become the standard practice in applied time-series analyses to begin with testing time-series properties of the data series. This is because if the variables are found to be integrated of the same order and they form a cointegrating vector, then the two-stage procedure provides a neat way of separating the long-run equilibrium relationship from short-run dynamics (Pagan 1995).

[10] As Engle and Granger (1987) has pointed out, in reality, researchers more often encounter these types of data situations than having to estimate models with variables that are all non-stationary.

Appendix 3

Data used in the Econometric Analysis

Most of the data series used in this study have been directly obtained or compiled from the following publications: (i) Central Statistical Organisation (CSO), *National Accounts Statistics (NAS)*, Delhi (various issues); and (ii) Reserve Bank of India, *Report on Currency and Banking*, Delhi (various issues). However, the choice of data series for the compilation and the construction of some of the variables used in the empirical analyses of Chapters 5, 6, and 7 need some explanation.

CHAPTER 5

Private saving (*SPRV*), national saving (*SNAT*), wealth (*W*), borrowing (*BOR*), public saving (*SPB*) and current private transfers (*TRN*) are all used in the regressions as ratios of gross national disposable income (GNDI). The data series on GNDI is constructed by adding net current private transfers (obtained from the RBI's *Reports on Currency and Finance*) to gross national product (GNP) in market prices. The real interest rate on bank deposits (*RID*) is the difference between the average one-to-three year bank deposit rate and the inflation rate (measured by the GDP deflator).

CHAPTER 6

Investment by the non-residential business sector (*INRB*) is the real investment in fixed capital (both machinery and structures) by the private corporate sector plus real investment in machinery by the household sector. Real bank credit to the private sector (*BC*) is the ratio of nominal bank credit to the price deflator for gross domestic fixed capital formation. Nominal bank credit is taken to be domestic credit – claims on the private sector (obtained from IMF, *International Financial Statistics*).

Cost of capital for private corporate (*CCP*) and non-residential business sectors (*CNRB*) is measured using the formula:[1]

$$C_t = [PK_t[r_t - \pi_t^e + \delta_t]/P_t], \tag{A3.1}$$

where r = bank lending rate, PK = price of capital good, π^e = expected rate of change in capital goods price, δ = rate of depreciation, and P = the general price level.

The bank lending rate (r) is the one year lending rate of the State Bank of India (the premier commercial bank in India). The measure of the general price level is the GDP deflator (1980 = 1.00). Capital good price (*PK*) is measured in terms of the implicit deflators for private corporate and non-residential business fixed capital formation (1980 = 1.00). The expected rate of change in capital goods price (p^e) is measured as the three year moving average of the rate of change of capital goods price (measured by the implicit deflators for private corporate and non-residential business fixed capital formation) with a one-year lag. The adaptive expectation hypothesis that undergirds this variable choice is considered appropriate for a low-inflation country like India, especially when working with annual data. The depreciation rate (δ) is calculated from the CSO's *National Account Statistics* [for the non-residential business sector, we used the depreciation rate for the total private sector; see below]. And finally, the general price level (P) is measured in terms of the GDP deflator. The base year for *PK* and *P* is 1980

Data on the real capital stock of the private corporate sector (*KCP*) is readily available from the CSO's *NAS* for the years since 1980. This series was extended back to 1951 applying the following formula,

$$K_{t-1} = K_t + DEP_t - I_t \tag{A3.2}$$

where K is real capital stock at the end of year 1981, and *DEP* and I denote real depreciation and real private corporate fixed investment during each year.

The *NAS* does not, however, provide disaggregated data on capital stock by type of asset. As a proxy for other capital stock series for the non-residential business sector (*KNRB*), we, therefore, used the capital stock of the total private sector. As in the case of the private corporate sector, capital stock data for the total private sector was not directly available prior to 1980. We backdated the series to 1951 using formula (A3.2).

[1] See Chapter 6.

CHAPTER 7

The real GDP of the non-residential business sector (*GDPNRB*) is obtained by deducting from real GDP, the contribution of the real estate and public administration sectors. The real investment of the non-residential business sector (*RINRB*) is the ratio of INRB to GDPNRB.

GQL is the growth in the quality adjusted labour force, *QLF*, where *QLF* is obtained as follows:

$$QLF = (1 + LF^{*}SS)LF, \tag{A3.3}$$

and where *LF* is the total labour force and *SS* is the ratio of the population who have attained secondary school. Both *LF* and *SS* are obtained from the World Bank, *World Tables*.

The share of machinery imports in total investment (*MSI*) is total machinery imports (obtained from the *Reports on Currency and Finance*) as a ratio of GDCF. The share of manufacturing in total exports (*SMX*) is India's manufacturing exports as a ratio of its total exports. The data for computing *SMX* was obtained from the UN Trade Database.

Public Investment in Infrastructure (*PBIINF*) is total Public GDCF in electricity, gas and water supply, and transport, storage and communications, as a ratio of GDP.

Table A3.1

Data Used in the Regression Analysis for Saving

Year	*SPRV*	*SNAT*	*GPOP*	*GY*	*RID*	*W*	*LY*	*BOR*	*INF*	*TOT*	*SPB*	*TRN*	*AGS*	*BDN*
1955	0.120	0.136	0.018	0.036	0.038	0.283	1419	0.012	–0.015	0.851	0.016	0.005	0.480	937
1956	0.110	0.128	0.020	0.055	–0.106	0.253	1467	0.008	0.128	0.793	0.019	0.005	0.463	917
1957	0.088	0.107	0.020	–0.003	–0.008	0.272	1435	0.004	0.033	0.768	0.019	0.005	0.470	888
1958	0.083	0.099	0.022	0.072	–0.010	0.265	1505	0.007	0.038	0.829	0.016	0.003	0.453	862
1959	0.102	0.118	0.019	0.025	0.007	0.282	1515	0.009	0.026	0.872	0.016	0.003	0.430	847
1960	0.101	0.127	0.019	0.050	–0.009	0.261	1561	0.008	0.042	0.872	0.026	0.002	0.414	849
1961	0.093	0.122	0.023	0.037	0.020	0.264	1582	0.008	0.020	0.878	0.029	0.002	0.421	844
1962	0.103	0.134	0.023	0.031	–0.003	0.265	1595	0.009	0.043	0.878	0.031	0.002	0.384	827
1963	0.099	0.133	0.022	0.063	–0.042	0.257	1659	0.012	0.082	0.878	0.033	0.002	0.380	796
1964	0.094	0.127	0.022	0.073	–0.046	0.259	1742	0.008	0.086	0.870	0.033	0.002	0.405	773
1965	0.114	0.145	0.023	–0.024	–0.021	0.255	1661	0.010	0.081	0.888	0.031	0.002	0.390	735
1966	0.130	0.152	0.021	–0.002	–0.075	0.250	1624	0.012	0.135	0.870	0.023	0.004	0.390	709
1967	0.111	0.130	0.022	0.076	–0.026	0.232	1709	0.009	0.086	0.875	0.019	0.003	0.397	662
1968	0.105	0.128	0.024	0.037	0.037	0.245	1731	0.014	0.023	0.870	0.023	0.003	0.382	627
1969	0.124	0.150	0.021	0.065	0.026	0.258	1805	0.017	0.034	0.913	0.026	0.002	0.365	522
1970	0.128	0.158	0.023	0.052	0.044	0.275	1857	0.014	0.016	0.893	0.029	0.002	0.380	450
1971	0.135	0.163	0.024	0.018	0.007	0.300	1845	0.015	0.053	1.067	0.028	0.002	0.370	407

(contd.)

Table A3.1 (contd.)

Year	SPRV	SNAT	GPOP	GY	RID	W	LY	POR	INF	TOT	SPB	TRN	AGS	BDN
1972	0.128	0.154	0.023	–0.006	–0.049	0.323	1792	0.012	0.109	0.904	0.026	0.002	0.383	369
1973	0.156	0.185	0.023	0.033	–0.121	0.308	1809	0.013	0.181	0.983	0.029	0.002	0.354	342
1974	0.137	0.174	0.022	0.016	–0.087	0.290	1798	0.011	0.167	0.821	0.037	0.002	0.364	317
1975	0.147	0.189	0.024	0.095	0.095	0.314	1923	0.014	–0.015	0.729	0.042	0.004	0.352	286
1976	0.162	0.211	0.021	0.020	0.021	0.359	1920	0.017	0.059	0.616	0.049	0.007	0.324	250
1977	0.166	0.209	0.023	0.074	0.004	0.380	2016	0.018	0.056	0.841	0.043	0.008	0.343	226
1978	0.184	0.229	0.022	0.059	0.035	0.429	2089	0.026	0.025	0.784	0.045	0.009	0.341	215
1979	0.170	0.213	0.025	–0.048	–0.088	0.463	1941	0.031	0.158	0.860	0.043	0.010	0.325	205
1980	0.174	0.208	0.023	0.075	–0.041	0.460	2040	0.025	0.116	1.000	0.034	0.015	0.335	190
1981	0.151	0.195	0.019	0.062	–0.023	0.441	2125	0.025	0.103	1.072	0.045	0.013	0.323	177
1982	0.145	0.188	0.023	0.035	0.006	0.461	2150	0.020	0.074	1.038	0.044	0.014	0.307	168
1983	0.156	0.188	0.021	0.072	–0.005	0.462	2257	0.026	0.085	1.286	0.032	0.013	0.288	160
1984	0.154	0.182	0.022	0.037	0.005	0.490	2291	0.025	0.075	1.013	0.028	0.013	0.276	144
1985	0.165	0.198	0.022	0.053	0.010	0.507	2361	0.027	0.075	1.284	0.032	0.011	0.292	143
1986	0.160	0.187	0.021	0.046	0.020	0.541	2419	0.029	0.065	1.371	0.027	0.010	0.278	143
1987	0.188	0.209	0.022	0.048	0.004	0.551	2480	0.028	0.086	1.147	0.022	0.011	0.273	142
1988	0.195	0.215	0.022	0.095	0.009	0.539	2658	0.032	0.081	1.155	0.021	0.010	0.266	142
1989	0.210	0.226	0.021	0.054	0.007	0.561	2771	0.023	0.083	1.020	0.016	0.008	0.267	139
1990	0.235	0.245	0.021	0.054	–0.019	0.555	2863	0.017	0.109	0.960	0.010	0.007	0.264	141

(contd.)

Table A3.1 (contd.)

Year	*SPRV*	*SNAT*	*GPOP*	*GY*	*RID*	*W*	*LY*	*BOR*	*INF*	*TOT*	*SPB*	*TRN*	*AGS*	*BDN*
1991	0.212	0.231	0.020	0.025	–0.027	0.649	2877	0.010	0.147	0.857	0.019	0.015	0.257	143
1992	0.207	0.223	0.019	0.046	0.024	0.574	2955	0.022	0.086	0.991	0.015	0.012	0.232	145
1993	0.223	0.229	0.018	0.060	0.016	0.585	3076	0.019	0.094	1.002	0.006	0.014	0.233	146
1994	0.240	0.259	0.018	0.095	0.001	0.607	3308	0.033	0.099	1.093	0.018	0.017	0.257	148
1995	0.232	0.254	0.018	0.104	0.038	0.595	3589	0.024	0.082	1.050	0.023	0.023	0.232	143
1996	0.243	0.263	0.017	0.079	0.037	0.609	3808	0.015	0.063	0.958	0.019	0.023	0.233	144

Notations:

SPRV	Private saving as a ratio of GNDI
SNAT	Gross domestic saving as a ratio of GNDI
GPOP	Annual growth rate of population
GY	Annual growth rate of GNDI
RID	Real interest rate on bank deposit
W	Money stock as a ratio of GNDI
LY	Per capita GNDI
BOR	Household financial liabilities as a ratio of GNDI
INF	Change in the GDP deflator
TOT	Price of exports as a ratio of price of imports
SPB	Public saving as a ratio of GNDI
TRN	Current private transfers as a ratio of GNDI
AGS	Agricultural output (GDP) as a ratio of total GDP (in constant prices)
BDN	Total population as a ratio of total branches of scheduled commercial banks (in '000)

TABLE A3.2

Data Used in the Regression Analysis for Investment (all variables except CCP and CNRB in rupees billion)

Year	ICP	INRB	KCP	KNRB	CCP	CNRB	Y	BC	PB
1954	7	16	42	539	0.089	–0.044	539	4	24
1955	7	26	44	561	0.088	–0.068	558	5	32
1956	13	33	53	597	0.096	0.015	589	11	36
1957	21	48	69	640	0.085	0.017	587	8	37
1958	12	27	77	661	0.114	0.108	631	1	36
1959	12	21	83	680	0.046	–0.024	648	6	45
1960	17	28	93	700	0.050	–0.037	681	11	52
1961	25	34	110	726	0.035	–0.068	707	10	51
1962	19	40	121	751	0.078	0.031	730	10	59
1963	28	48	139	779	0.091	0.041	775	13	66
1964	25	50	152	813	0.086	0.026	833	8	74
1965	16	49	156	851	0.085	0.035	813	13	78
1966	14	37	159	887	0.077	0.027	810	14	68
1967	16	38	163	933	0.048	–0.020	873	11	62
1968	15	39	166	980	0.041	–0.032	904	14	63
1969	13	45	167	1033	0.044	–0.021	964	18	62
1970	16	41	171	1084	0.093	0.068	1014	19	63
1971	20	53	178	1138	0.093	0.073	1032	25	70
1972	19	52	183	1186	0.085	0.064	1026	20	83
1973	22	58	192	1234	0.076	0.045	1056	34	81
1974	18	56	196	1286	0.097	0.072	1069	24	70
1975	25	49	205	1339	0.065	0.009	1167	36	82
1976	16	51	205	1397	0.054	0.004	1187	53	101
1977	21	59	211	1468	0.084	0.034	1273	33	108
1978	15	70	210	1538	0.163	0.135	1346	44	108
1979	20	73	214	1594	0.180	0.160	1276	41	111
1980	35	83	232	1668	0.153	0.119	1360	43	117
1981	54	93	267	1725	0.123	0.089	1449	58	132
1982	66	94	315	1783	0.117	0.093	1504	59	152

(contd.)

Table A3.2 (contd.)

Year	*ICP*	*INRB*	*KCP*	*KNRB*	*CCP*	*CNRB*	*Y*	*BC*	*PB*
1983	54	102	343	1829	0.154	0.162	1615	56	156
1984	62	102	381	1883	0.150	0.138	1675	65	164
1985	64	106	422	1939	0.174	0.140	1766	53	171
1986	78	124	470	1994	0.116	0.073	1853	71	192
1987	66	157	503	2066	0.142	0.118	1941	54	187
1988	70	169	537	2144	0.166	0.147	2133	83	195
1989	81	187	580	2235	0.189	0.164	2274	80	197
1990	100	216	636	2352	0.155	0.130	2402	71	206
1991	148	194	735	2465	0.139	0.115	2413	51	210
1992	162	236	841	2609	0.150	0.122	2543	100	195
1993	188	259	965	2774	0.141	0.118	2669	66	209
1994	197	296	1089	2988	0.119	0.099	2886	101	252
1995	283	412	1288	3233	0.148	0.132	3099	78	233
1996	313	450	1502	3509	0.133	0.118	3327	143	223

Notations:

ICP	Real private corporate fixed investment
INRB	Real fixed investment, non-residential business sector
KCP	Real fixed capital stock, private corporate sector
KNRB	Real fixed capital stock, non-residential business sector
CCP	Rental cost of capital, private corporate sector
CNRB	Rental cost of capital, non-residential business sector
Y	Real GDP (in market prices)
BC	Real bank credit to the private sector
IPB	Real public fixed investment

TABLE A3.3

Data Used in the Construction of the Capital Stock and the Cost of Capital Series

Year	R	P	PKCP	PKNRB	DEPCP	DEPNRB	π^e_{CP}	π^e_{NRB}	δ_{CP}	δ_{NRB}
1954	0.04	0.187	0.165	0.159	4	25	0.006	0.106	0.102	0.015
1955	0.04	0.184	0.171	0.147	4	26	–0.012	0.140	0.101	0.015
1956	0.05	0.208	0.184	0.139	4	26	–0.002	0.043	0.099	0.016
1957	0.05	0.214	0.194	0.131	5	27	0.030	0.037	0.087	0.016
1958	0.05	0.223	0.200	0.184	5	31	0.056	–0.063	0.072	0.018
1959	0.05	0.228	0.206	0.184	6	32	0.054	0.098	0.072	0.019
1960	0.05	0.238	0.215	0.193	6	34	0.038	0.115	0.076	0.020
1961	0.05	0.243	0.226	0.203	8	35	0.035	0.153	0.082	0.021
1962	0.05	0.253	0.235	0.204	8	37	0.042	0.033	0.076	0.022
1963	0.06	0.274	0.239	0.230	10	40	0.045	0.035	0.084	0.024
1964	0.07	0.297	0.251	0.238	11	42	0.036	0.062	0.082	0.025
1965	0.075	0.322	0.270	0.250	11	43	0.036	0.055	0.074	0.025
1966	0.075	0.365	0.290	0.324	12	47	0.048	0.072	0.076	0.027
1967	0.075	0.397	0.306	0.349	12	50	0.067	0.127	0.075	0.029
1968	0.075	0.406	0.324	0.350	12	50	0.068	0.141	0.074	0.030
1969	0.07	0.419	0.349	0.365	12	52	0.063	0.125	0.071	0.031

(contd.)

Table A3.3 (contd.)

Year	R	P	PKCP	PKNRB	DEPCP	DEPNRB	π^e_{CP}	π^e_{NRB}	δ_{CP}	δ_{NRB}
1970	0.085	0.426	0.373	0.387	12	52	0.064	0.041	0.073	0.031
1971	0.085	0.448	0.400	0.401	12	53	0.068	0.035	0.073	0.032
1972	0.085	0.497	0.430	0.446	13	55	0.072	0.047	0.073	0.033
1973	0.09	0.587	0.495	0.488	13	54	0.072	0.069	0.071	0.033
1974	0.125	0.685	0.600	0.633	14	57	0.100	0.082	0.075	0.034
1975	0.14	0.675	0.651	0.715	16	61	0.146	0.168	0.081	0.036
1976	0.14	0.715	0.675	0.716	16	62	0.150	0.174	0.076	0.037
1977	0.14	0.755	0.705	0.721	15	62	0.111	0.142	0.074	0.038
1978	0.14	0.774	0.766	0.782	16	66	0.056	0.046	0.074	0.040
1979	0.145	0.896	0.879	0.920	16	69	0.056	0.031	0.078	0.042
1980	0.165	1.000	1.000	1.000	17	72	0.093	0.090	0.079	0.043
1981	0.165	1.103	1.086	1.046	19	75	0.124	0.116	0.080	0.045
1982	0.165	1.185	1.126	1.028	21	79	0.123	0.103	0.078	0.046
1983	0.165	1.285	1.256	1.200	22	83	0.087	0.038	0.071	0.047
1984	0.165	1.381	1.325	1.293	24	87	0.079	0.066	0.071	0.048
1985	0.165	1.485	1.573	1.510	26	92	0.069	0.076	0.068	0.049
1986	0.165	1.581	1.560	1.505	30	95	0.119	0.138	0.071	0.049

(contd.)

Table A3.3 (contd.)

Year	*R*	*P*	*PKCP*	*PKNRB*	*DEPCP*	*DEPNRB*	π^e_{CP}	π^e_{NRB}	δ_{CP}	δ_{NRB}
1987	0.165	1.717	1.560	1.508	33	100	0.078	0.081	0.069	0.050
1988	0.165	1.855	1.755	1.697	35	106	0.060	0.056	0.070	0.051
1989	0.165	2.009	1.917	1.869	39	113	0.039	0.041	0.072	0.053
1990	0.165	2.229	2.084	2.032	43	121	0.072	0.076	0.074	0.054
1991	0.175	2.557	2.367	2.344	49	129	0.101	0.105	0.077	0.055
1992	0.19	2.776	2.595	2.564	56	138	0.105	0.114	0.076	0.056
1993	0.19	3.037	2.682	2.650	65	149	0.106	0.112	0.076	0.057
1994	0.15	3.338	2.923	2.886	74	161	0.089	0.094	0.075	0.059
1995	0.165	3.611	3.152	3.113	84	179	0.073	0.072	0.078	0.060
1996	0.145	3.838	3.298	3.257	99	198	0.067	0.067	0.077	0.061

Notations:

R	nominal interest rate
P	GDP price deflator
PKCP	Price deflator for private corporate fixed investment
PKNRB	Price deflator for non-residential business fixed investment
DEPCP	Real depreciation, private corporate sector (rupees billion)
DEPNRB	Real depreciation, non-residential business sector (rupees billion)
π^e_{CP}	3 year moving average of the rate of change in PKCP
π^e_{NRB}	3 year moving average of the rate of change in PKNRB
δ_{CP}	Rate of depreciation, private corporate sector
δ_{NRB}	Rate of depreciation, non-residential business sector

Table A3.4

Data Used in the Regression Analysis of Economic Growth

Year	*GY*	*GYNRB*	*RI*	*RINRB*	*RIM*	*RIC*	*RIS*	*GQLF*	*MSI*	*SMX*	*OPEN*	*FINT*	*PBINF*
1955	0.026	0.026	0.172	0.063	0.063	0.085	0.015	0.015	0.192	0.006	0.132	0.276	–
1956	0.057	0.059	0.210	0.080	0.080	0.095	0.024	0.021	0.142	0.006	0.144	0.247	–
1957	–0.012	–0.017	0.226	0.106	0.106	0.086	0.023	0.020	0.195	0.006	0.153	0.267	–
1958	0.076	0.081	0.160	0.059	0.059	0.086	0.006	0.020	0.155	0.004	0.120	0.262	–
1959	0.022	0.021	0.183	0.064	0.064	0.089	0.019	0.020	0.153	0.005	0.115	0.279	–
1960	0.071	0.075	0.199	0.069	0.069	0.091	0.029	0.009	0.165	0.005	0.127	0.260	0.023
1961	0.031	0.031	0.192	0.073	0.073	0.091	0.018	0.016	0.163	0.005	0.112	0.264	0.031
1962	0.021	0.018	0.208	0.084	0.084	0.090	0.023	0.016	0.155	0.005	0.112	0.265	0.037
1963	0.051	0.050	0.216	0.086	0.086	0.096	0.020	0.016	0.148	0.006	0.113	0.256	0.039
1964	0.076	0.078	0.221	0.092	0.092	0.097	0.019	0.016	0.140	0.005	0.105	0.259	0.035
1965	–0.037	–0.043	0.236	0.099	0.099	0.108	0.014	0.016	0.127	0.006	0.092	0.255	0.036
1966	0.010	0.007	0.238	0.079	0.079	0.116	0.027	0.016	0.134	0.009	0.114	0.249	0.030
1967	0.081	0.087	0.220	0.071	0.071	0.116	0.019	0.016	0.112	0.008	0.104	0.232	0.025

(contd.)

Table A3.4 (contd.)

Year	*GY*	*GYNRB*	*RI*	*RINRB*	*RIM*	*RIC*	*RIS*	*GQLF*	*MSI*	*SMX*	*OPEN*	*FINT*	*PBINF*
1968	0.026	0.025	0.205	0.072	0.072	0.114	0.005	0.024	0.105	0.009	0.096	0.245	0.024
1969	0.065	0.067	0.210	0.070	0.070	0.109	0.016	0.016	0.068	0.010	0.083	0.258	0.023
1970	0.050	0.050	0.215	0.067	0.067	0.105	0.028	0.016	0.064	0.010	0.082	0.276	0.029
1971	0.010	0.006	0.233	0.077	0.077	0.104	0.035	0.030	0.068	0.010	0.074	0.300	0.029
1972	–0.003	–0.007	0.219	0.082	0.082	0.108	0.013	0.030	0.068	0.013	0.075	0.323	0.032
1973	0.046	0.046	0.238	0.088	0.088	0.095	0.040	0.036	0.074	0.014	0.088	0.309	0.025
1974	0.012	0.007	0.240	0.085	0.085	0.091	0.049	0.030	0.066	0.019	0.107	0.290	0.032
1975	0.090	0.099	0.232	0.079	0.079	0.097	0.041	0.030	0.073	0.018	0.118	0.313	0.036
1976	0.012	0.010	0.242	0.089	0.089	0.106	0.031	0.030	0.071	0.026	0.120	0.356	0.034
1977	0.075	0.079	0.233	0.088	0.088	0.111	0.020	0.030	0.067	0.028	0.119	0.377	0.034
1978	0.055	0.056	0.252	0.091	0.091	0.100	0.045	0.088	0.069	0.028	0.120	0.425	0.036
1979	–0.052	–0.063	0.257	0.098	0.098	0.098	0.045	0.030	0.068	0.032	0.136	0.457	0.040
1980	0.072	0.075	0.232	0.103	0.103	0.100	0.016	0.030	0.073	0.032	0.142	0.452	0.039
1981	0.061	0.065	0.263	0.109	0.109	0.096	0.042	0.019	0.067	0.035	0.134	0.436	0.041
1982	0.031	0.027	0.248	0.122	0.122	0.087	0.026	0.019	0.076	0.034	0.130	0.457	0.044

(contd.)

Table A3.4 (contd.)

Year	*GY*	*GYNRB*	*RI*	*RINRB*	*RIM*	*RIC*	*RIS*	*GQLF*	*MSI*	*SMX*	*OPEN*	*FINT*	*PBINF*
1983	0.082	0.087	0.227	0.118	0.118	0.078	0.020	0.019	0.083	0.039	0.123	0.460	0.039
1984	0.038	0.035	0.222	0.120	0.120	0.076	0.016	0.019	0.070	0.048	0.125	0.489	0.041
1985	0.041	0.039	0.252	0.121	0.121	0.079	0.039	0.019	0.079	0.045	0.117	0.506	0.045
1986	0.043	0.040	0.246	0.131	0.131	0.079	0.023	0.019	0.088	0.055	0.111	0.541	0.055
1987	0.043	0.041	0.245	0.146	0.146	0.078	0.009	0.019	0.091	0.070	0.114	0.552	0.049
1988	0.106	0.113	0.263	0.140	0.140	0.077	0.032	0.026	0.081	0.090	0.122	0.542	0.047
1989	0.069	0.070	0.252	0.146	0.146	0.075	0.018	0.019	0.086	0.118	0.138	0.566	0.047
1990	0.054	0.057	0.268	0.152	0.152	0.078	0.024	0.019	0.084	0.123	0.141	0.561	0.045
1991	0.008	0.006	0.237	0.140	0.140	0.080	0.007	0.020	0.065	0.177	0.149	0.656	0.048
1992	0.053	0.054	0.253	0.145	0.145	0.078	0.017	0.020	0.068	0.202	0.166	0.582	0.045
1993	0.062	0.065	0.227	0.150	0.150	0.073	–0.004	0.020	0.095	0.244	0.176	0.592	0.046
1994	0.078	0.083	0.281	0.166	0.166	0.073	0.030	0.020	0.092	0.276	0.181	0.612	0.041
1995	0.072	0.074	0.308	0.187	0.187	0.074	0.034	0.020	0.104	0.334	0.208	0.598	0.038
1996	0.075	0.077	0.284	0.185	0.185	0.073	0.015	0.020	0.098	0.332	0.201	0.612	–

(contd.)

Table A3.4 (contd.)

Notations:

GY	Growth rate of real GDP
GYNRB	Growth rate of real GDP of the non-residential business sector
RI	Gross domestic capital formation as a ratio of GDP
RINRB	Investment of non-residential business sector as a ratio of its GDP
RIM	Total fixed capital formation in machinery as a ratio of GDP
RIC	Total fixed capital formation in construction as a ratio of GDP
RIS	Change in stocks as a ratio of GDP
GQL	Growth rate of quality-adjusted labour force
MSI	Share of machinery imports in total investment
SMX	Share of manufacturing in total exports
OPEN	Exports plus imports as a ratio of GDP
FINT	M3/GDP
PBIINF	Public investment in infrastructure as a ratio of GDP

Appendix 4

Growth Models

Growth models are broadly of two types, the neoclassical models that originated from the work of Solow (1956) and Swan (1956), and endogenous growth models pioneered by Romer (1986) and Lucas (1988). This appendix provides a brief exposition of these two types of models with particular emphasis on the role that the saving/investment rate plays in these models.[1]

The Neoclassical Growth Models

Two crucial assumptions underpin the neoclassical growth model: firstly, the rates of saving, population growth, and technological progress are exogenous; and secondly, labour and capital, the two inputs in the production process, are paid their marginal products.

Consider an economy that produce and consume only one good (Y) using capital (K) and labour (L). Assume that the production function is Cobb–Douglas, so that production at time t is given by:

$$Y(t) = F(K(t), A(t)L(t)) = K(t)^{a}(A(t)L(t))_{,}^{1-a} \quad 0 < a < 1. \qquad (A4.1)$$

Here, A is the level of technology and is labour-augmenting (or 'Harrod-neutral').

L and A are assumed to grow exogenously at rates n and g:

$$\begin{aligned} L(t) &= L(0)e_{g}^{nt} \\ A(t) &= A(0)e^{nt} \end{aligned} \qquad (A4.2)$$

AL is the effective amount of labour used in production and its rate of growth is n+g.

[1] For more elaborate expositions of the neoclassical growth model, see Solow (1970), Barro and Sala-i-Martin (1995: Chapter 1), and Jones (1998: Chapter 2).

The model assumes that a constant fraction of output, *s*, is invested. Defining k as the stock of capital per effective unit of labour, $k = K/AL$, and y as the level of output per effective unit of labour, $y = Y/AL$, the production function can be re-written as:

$$y(t) = f(k(t)),\ f' > 0,\ f'' < 0. \tag{A4.3}$$

Thus, the production function exhibits diminishing returns to capital per effective unit of labour.

Furthermore, the evolution of k is governed by:

$$\begin{aligned} \dot{k}(t) &= sy(t) - (n + g + \delta)k(t) \\ &= sk(t)^{\alpha} - (n + g + \delta)k(t), \end{aligned} \tag{A4.4}$$

where δ is the rate of depreciation.

Equation (A4.3) is best analysed in terms of the Solow diagram (Fig. A4.1). It consists of two curves, plotted as functions of the capital-effective labour ratio, K/AL. The first curve is the amount of investment per person, $sy = sk^{\alpha}$. This curve has the same shape as the production function (since s is just a parameter) and thus, concave to the origin. The second curve is the line $(n+g+\delta)k$, which represents the amount of new investment per effective

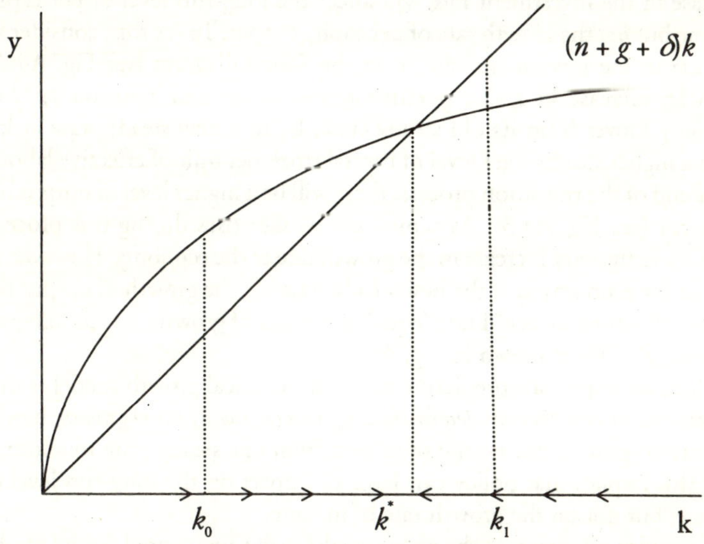

Figure A4.1: The Solow Diagram

unit of labour required to keep the amount of capital per effective unit of labour constant. The difference between the two curves is the change in the amount of capital per effective unit of labour. In the diagram, k^* is the steady state capital per effective unit of labour. If k is at k^*, there will be no change in the level of capital per effective unit of labour. However, if k is at k_0, the amount of investment per effective unit of labour exceeds the amount needed to keep capital per effective unit of labour constant, and hence, k will increase. Using the same logic, it can be shown that k will fall if k is at k_1.

The steady state level of k is given by:[2]

$$k^* = [s/(n + g + \delta)]^{1/(1-\alpha)} \tag{A4.5}$$

Substituting eqn (A4.5) into the production function and taking logs, we find that the steady-state income per capita is:

$$\ln\left[\frac{Y(t)}{L(t)}\right] = \ln A(0) + gt + \frac{\alpha}{1-\alpha}\ln(s) - \frac{\alpha}{1-\alpha}\ln(n + g + \delta) \tag{A4.6}$$

Thus, the lower the population growth, the higher the level of initial efficiency A(0), and the saving/investment rate, the higher is the level of per capita income.

It is important to realize that in the neoclassical growth model, an increase in the investment rate will affect the long-run level of per capita income but *not* the growth rate of per capita output. To see this, consider an increase in the investment rate, *s*, in the Solow diagram (see Fig. A4.2). With an increase in *s*, the *sy* curve moves to its new position *s'y*. The economy moves from its old steady state, k^*, to a new steady state at k^{**}. With a higher steady-state level of capital stock per unit of effective labour, at the end of the transition process, there will be a higher level of output per worker, *y* (see Fig. A4.3). As capital per worker rises during this process, there is a temporary increase in the growth rate of the economy. However, as soon as the economy is at the new steady state k^{**}, the growth of output per capita will return to its old rate (equal to the rate of growth in technological progress, *g*). This is shown in Fig. A4.3.

Thus, an important prediction of the neoclassical growth model is that *the investment rate does not determine long-run (or steady state) growth;* it only impacts on growth during the transition from one steady state to another. This also implies that policy can have an impact on the long-run level of income, but not on the growth rate of income.

A popular extension of the above model is the augmented Solow model

[2] Set equation (A4.4) to zero and solve for k.

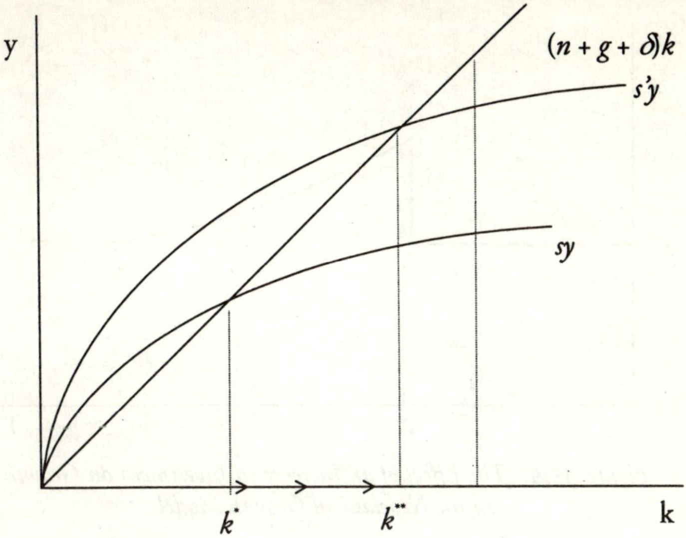

Figure A4.2: The Effect of an Increase in the Investment Rate in the Solow Diagram

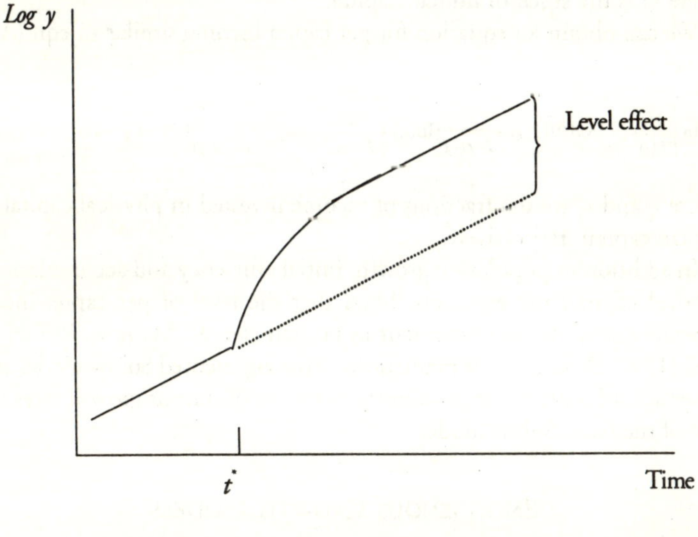

Figure A4.3: The Effect of an Increase in Investment on Per Capita Income in the Neoclassical Growth Model

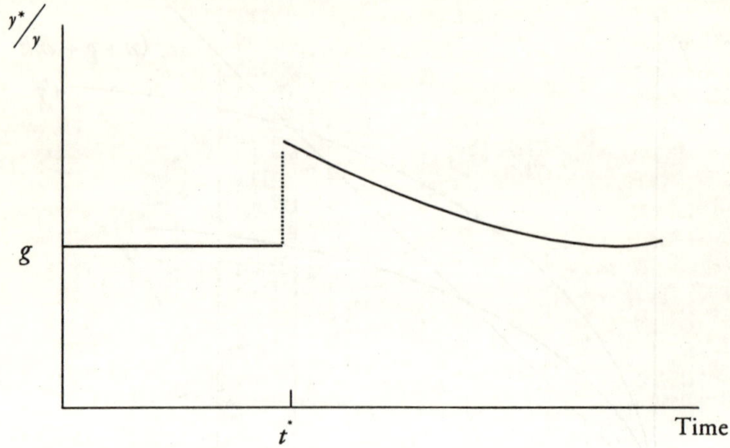

Figure A4.4: The Effect of an Increase in Investment on Growth in the Neoclassical Growth Model

of Mankiw, Romer and Weil (1992). This model incorporates human capital as an additional input in the production process as follows:

$$Y(t) = K(t)^{\alpha} H(t)^{\beta} (A(t)L(t))^{1-\alpha-\beta} \quad \text{(A4.7)}$$

where H is the stock of human capital.

We can obtain an equation for per capita income similar to eqn (A4.6) above:

$$\text{In}\left[\frac{Y(t)}{L(t)}\right] = \text{In}\, A(0) + gt + \frac{\alpha}{1-\alpha-\beta}\text{In}(s_k) + \frac{\beta}{1-\alpha-\beta}\text{In}(s_k) - \frac{\alpha+\beta}{1-\alpha-\beta}\text{In}\,(n+g+\delta) \quad \text{(A4.8)}$$

where s_k and s_h are the fractions of income invested in physical capital and human capital, respectively.

In addition to population growth, initial efficiency and accumulation of physical capital, the equation shows that the level of per capita income depends positively on investment in human capital. Mankiw, Romer and Weil (1992) show that the predictions of the augmented Solow model are in closer accord with the cross-country variation of output growth rates than that of the basic Solow model.

ENDOGENOUS GROWTH MODELS

There are a number of alternative formulations of the endogenous growth model. Here we provide an exposition of the simplest of these models, known as the AK model. However, the AK model, while simple, allows us to understand the key insights of the endogenous growth models.

Consider the production function

$$Y = AK, \tag{A4.9}$$

where A is a positive constant.[3]

Assuming no population growth, the accumulation of capital is governed by the following equation:

$$\dot{K} = sY - \delta K, \tag{A4.10}$$

where, as before, s is the investment rate and δ is the depreciation rate. Dividing both sides of eqn (A4.10) by K and noting that the output–capital ratio, $Y/K = A$, we obtain:

$$\frac{\dot{K}}{K} = sA - \delta. \tag{A4.11}$$

Finally, taking logs and derivatives of the production function, we note that the growth rate of output is equal to the rate of growth of capital, and therefore,

$$g_Y \equiv \frac{\dot{Y}}{Y} = \frac{\dot{K}}{K} = sA - \delta. \tag{A4.12}$$

The main implication of this equation is that the higher is the investment rate, the higher is the growth rate of the economy. Thus, unlike in the neoclassical growth model, changes in the investment rate can have a *permanent* effect on the growth rate of the economy.[4] Furthermore, in contrast to the neoclassical growth models, this model allows for policy to have permanent effects on long-run growth, and not just the long-run level of income.

[3] It is this production function that gives the AK model its name.

[4] The reason why the AK model gets this result is that the latter assumes that there are constant returns to capital accumulation, in contrast to neoclassical models that assume diminishing returns to capital. Moreover, in more complicated endogenous growth models (such as Lucas 1988), a similar result may be obtained as long as there are constant returns to the *reproducible* factors of production, such as physical or human capital.

References

Abel, A. (1990), 'Asset Prices under Habit Formation and Catching Up with the Joneses', *American Economic Review*, Vol. 80, No. 2, pp. 38–42.

Ady, P. (1976), 'Growth Models for Developing Countries', in A. Cairncross and M. Puri (eds), *Employment, Income Distribution and Development Strategy: Problems of the Developing Countries*, Macmillan, London, pp. 106–19.

Agenor, P. and P. J. Monteil (1996), *Development Macroeconomics*, Princeton University Press, Princeton, NJ.

Agrawal, P., S. V. Gokarn, V. Mishra, K. S. Parikh and K. Sen (1995), *Economic Restructuring in East Asia and India: Perspectives on Policy Reform*, Macmillan, London.

Agrawal, R. N. (1987), *Corporate Investment and Financing Behaviour*, Commonwealth Publishers, Delhi.

Ahluwalia, I. J. (1985), *Productivity and Growth in Indian Manufacturing*, Oxford University Press, Delhi.

—— (1991), *Industrial Growth in India*, Oxford University Press, Delhi.

Aivazian, V. (1998), 'Microeconomic Elements and Perspectives From Finance Theory', in J. M. Fanelli and R. Medhora (eds), *Financial Reform in Developing Countries*, Macmillan, Basingstoke, U.K., pp. 328–51.

Aksoy, M. A. (1992), *The Indian Trade Regime*, WPS 989, The World Bank, Washington, D.C.

Arrow, K. (1962), 'The Economic Implications of Learning by Doing', *Review of Economic Studies*, Vol. 29, No. 1, pp. 153–73.

Aschauer, D. (1989a), 'Is Public Expenditure Productive?', *Journal of Monetary Economics*, Vol. 23, No. 2, pp. 177–200.

—— (1989b), 'Does Public Capital Crowd Out Private Capital?', *Journal of Monetary Economics*, Vol. 24, No. 2, pp. 171–88.

Athey, M. J. and P. S. Laumas (1994), 'Internal Funds and Corporate Investment in India', *Journal of Development Economics*, Vol. 45, No. 2, pp. 287–303.

Athukorala, P. (1998), 'Interest Rates, Saving and Investment: Evidence from India', *Oxford Development Studies*, Vol. 26, No. 2, pp. 153–69.

Athukorala, P. and S. Rajapatirana (1993), 'Domestic Financial Market and Trade Liberalization Outcome', *World Development*, Vol. 21, No. 7, pp. 1191–203.

—— (2000), *Liberalization and Industrial Transformation: Sri Lanka in International Perspective*, Oxford University Press, Delhi.

Athukorala, P. and K. Sen (1995), 'Economic Reforms and the Rate of Saving in India: Some Observations', *Economic and Political Weekly*, Vol. 30, No. 35, pp. 2184–90.

Balassa, B. (1982), *Development Strategies in Semi-Industrial Economies*, Johns Hopkins University Press, Baltimore.

Bandiera, O., G. Caprio, P. Honohan and F. Schiantarelli (2000), 'Does Financial Reform Raise or Reduce Saving?', *The Review of Economics and Statistics*, Vol. 82, No. 2, pp. 239–63.

Banerjee, A., J. J. Dolado, J. W. Galbraith, and D. F. Hendry (1993), *Cointegration, Error Correction, and the Econometric Analysis of Non-Stationary Data*, Oxford University Press, Oxford.

Bardhan, P. (1998), *The Political Economy of Development in India*, Oxford University Press, Oxford.

Barro, R. J. (1974), 'Are Government Bonds Net Worth?', *Journal of Political Economy*, Vol. 82, No. 6, pp. 1095–117.

Barro, R. J. (1991), 'Economic Growth in a Cross-section of Countries', *Quarterly Journal of Economics*, Vol. 106, No. 2, pp. 407–33.

Barro, R. (1997), *Determinants of Economic Growth*, The MIT Press, Cambridge, Mass.

Barro, R. J. and X. Sala-i-Martin (1995), *Growth Economics*, McGraw-Hill, New York.

Bayoumi, T. A. (1993), 'Financial Deregulation and Household Saving', *Economic Journal*, Vol. 103, pp. 1432–43.

Bencivenga, V. and B. Smith (1991), 'Financial Intermediation and Endogenous Growth', *Review of Economic Studies*, Vol. 58, No. 2, pp. 195–209.

Bernheim, B. D. (1987), 'Ricardian Equivalence: An Evaluation of Theory and Evidence', *NBER Macroeconomics Annual*, NBER, Cambridge.

Bhagwati, J. N. (1978), *Anatomy and Consequences of Exchange Control Regimes*, Ballinger, Cambridge, Mass.

—— (1993), *India in Transition: Freeing the Economy*, Clarendon Press, Oxford.

—— and P. Desai (1970), *India: Planning for Industrialization*, Oxford University Press, Oxford.

Bhagwati, J. N. and T. N. Srinivasan (1975), *Foreign Trade Regimes and Economic Development: India*, Columbia University Press, New York.

—— (1979), 'Trade Policy and Development', in R. Dornbusch and J. A. Frankel (eds), *International Economic Policy: Theory and Evidence*, Johns Hopkins University Press, Baltimore, pp. 1–35.

Bleaney, M. (1996), 'Macroeconomic Instability, Investment and Growth in Developing Countries', *Journal of Development Economics*, Vol. 48, No. 2, pp. 461–77.

Blejer, M. and M. S. Khan (1984), 'Government Policy and Private Investment in Developing Countries', *IMF Staff Papers*, Vol. 31, No. 2, pp. 379–403.

Booth, A. (1999), 'Initial Conditions and Miraculous Growth: Why is Southeast Asia Different from Taiwan and South Korea', *World Development*, Vol. 2, No. 2, pp. 301–21.

Campbell, J. and N. G. Mankiw (1987), 'Permanent Income, Current Income and Consumption', *NBER Working Paper No. 2436*, NBER, Cambridge.

Carroll, C. and D. Weil (1994), 'Saving and Growth: A Reinterpretation', *Carnegie–Rochester Conference Series on Public Policy*, Vol. 40, pp. 133–92.

Central Statistical Organisation (CSO) (1988), *National Accounts Statistics: Sources and Methods*, Delhi.

Chibber, A., M. Dailami and N. Shafik (1992), *Reviving Private Investment in Developing Countries: Empirical Studies and Policy Lessons*, North-Holland, Amsterdam.

Chirinko, R. (1993), 'Business Fixed Investment Spending: Modeling Strategies, Empirical Results and Policy Implications', *Journal of Economic Literature*, Vol. 31, No. 4, pp. 1875–1911.

Choudhuri, Uma Datta Roy (1988), 'New Series on National Accounts Statistics', *Economic and Political Weekly*, Vol. 23, No. 30, pp. 1527–1540.

Choudhuri, Uma Datta Roy and A. Bagchi (eds) (1990), *Domestic Savings in India: Trends and Issues*, Vikas Publishing House, Delhi.

Collins, S. (1994), 'Saving, Investment and External Balance in South Korea', in S. Haggard, R. N. Cooper, S. M. Collins, C. Kim, and S. Ro (eds), *Macroeconomic Policies and Adjustment in Korea, 1970–1990*, The MIT Press, Cambridge, Mass.

Collins, S. and B. Bosworth (1996), 'Economic Growth in East Asia: Accumulation Versus Accumulation', *Brookings Papers on Economic Activity*, No. 2, pp. 135–91.

Corbo, V. and K. Schmidt–Hebbel (1991), 'Public Policies and Saving in Developing Countries', *Journal of Development Economics*, Vol. 36, No. 1, pp. 89–115.

CSO (1989), *National Accounts Statistics: Sources and Methods*, Central Statistical Organization, Department of Statistics, Government of India, New Delhi.

Davidson, J.E.H, D.F. Hendry, F. Saba and S. Yeo (1978), 'Econometric Modelling of the Aggregate Time–Series Relationship between Consumers' Expenditure and Income in the United Kingdom', *Economic Journal*, Vol. 88, No. 352, pp. 661-92.

Davidson, P. (1986), 'Finance, Funding, Saving and Investment', *Journal of Post Keynesian Economics*, Vol. 9, No. 1, pp. 101–10.

Dayal–Ghulati, A. and C. Thimann (1997), 'Saving in Southeast Asia and Latin

America Compared: Searching for Policy Lessons', IMF Working Paper WP/97/110.

De Long, J. B. and L. H. Summers (1991), 'Equipment Investment and Economic Growth', *Quarterly Journal of Economics*, Vol. 106, No. 2, pp. 455–502.

—— (1992), 'Equipment Investment and Economic Growth: How Strong is the Nexus?', *Brookings Papers on Economic Activity*, pp. 157–99.

—— (1993), 'How Strongly do Developing Countries Benefit from Equipment Investment?', *Journal of Monetary Economics*, Vol. 32, No. 3, pp. 395–415.

De Melo, J. and J. Tybout (1986), 'The Effect of Financial Liberalisation on Savings and Investment in Uruguay', *Economic Development and Cultural Change*, Vol. 34, No. 3, pp. 561–87.

Deaton, A. (1977), 'Involuntary Saving through Unanticipated Inflation', *American Economic Review*, Vol. 67, No. 5, pp. 899–910.

—— (1989), 'Saving in Developing Countries: Theory and Review', *Proceedings of the World Bank Annual Conference on Development Economics – 1989*, The World Bank, pp. 61–108.

—— (1991), 'Saving and Liquidity Constraints', *Econometrica*, Vol. 59, No. 5, pp. 1221–448.

—— (1992), *Understanding Consumption*, Clarendon Press, Oxford.

Deaton, A. and C. Paxson (1994), 'Saving, Growth and Aging in Taiwan', in D. Wise, *Studies in the Economics of Saving*, University of Chicago Press, Chicago, pp. 331–64.

—— (2000), 'Growth and Saving Among Individuals and Households', *The Review of Economics and Statistics*, Vol. 82, No. 2, pp. 212–25.

Denison, E. F. (1962), *The Sources of Economic Growth in the U.S. and the Alternatives Before Us*, Committee for Economic Development, Library of Congress, New York.

—— (1991), 'Scott's New View of Economic Growth: A Review Article', *Oxford Economic Papers*, Vol. 43, pp. 224–36.

Devereux, M. and F. Schianterelli (1990), 'Investment, Financial Factors and Cash Flow: Evidence from U. K. Panel Data', in R. G. Hubbard (ed.), *Asymmetric Information, Corporate Finance and Investment*, University of Chicago Press, Chicago.

Diaz–Alejandro, C. F. (1975), 'Trade Policy and Economic Development', in P. B. Kenen (ed.), *International Trade and Finance: Frontiers for Research*, Cambridge University Press, Cambridge, pp. 93–150.

Dixit, A. and R. Pindyck (1994), *Investment under Uncertainty*, Princeton University Press, Princeton.

Domar, E. (1947), 'Expansion and Employment', *American Economic Review*, Vol. 37, No. 1.

Donges, J. (1976), 'A Comparative Study of Industrialisation Policies in Fifteen Semi Industrial Countries', *Weltwirtschafliches Archiv*, Vol. 12, No. 4, pp. 626–59.

Dornbusch, R. and A. Reynoso (1989), 'Financial Factors in Economic Development', *American Economic Review: Papers and Proceedings*, Vol. 79, No. 2, pp. 204–9.

Duesenberry, J. S. (1962), *Income, Saving and the Theory of Consumer Behaviour*, Harvard University Press, Cambridge, Mass.

Dutt, A. K. (1991), 'Interest Rate Policy in LDCs: A Post Keynesian View', *Journal of Post Keynesian Economics*, Vol. 13, No. 2, pp. 210–32.

Easterly, W. and S. Rebelo (1993), 'Fiscal Policy and Economic Growth: An Empirical Investigation', *Journal of Monetary Economics*, Vol. 32, No. 3, pp. 417–58.

Eastwood, R. and R. Kohli (1999), 'Directed Credit and Investment in Small-Scale Industry in India: Evidence from Firm-level Data 1965–78', *Journal of Development Studies*, Vol. 35, No. 4, pp. 42–63.

Edwards, S. (1996), 'Why are Latin America's Saving Rates so Low? An International Comparison', *Journal of Development Economics*, Vol. 51, No. 1, pp. 5–44.

—— (1998), 'Openness, Productivity and Growth: What Do We Really Know?', *The Economic Journal*, Vol. 108, No. 447, pp. 383–98.

Enders, W. (1995), *Applied Econometric Time Series*, Wiley, New York.

Engle, R. and C. W. J. Granger (1987), Cointegration and Error-Correction Modeling: Representation, Estimation and Testing', *Econometrica*, Vol. 48, No. 2, pp. 283–307.

EPWRF (Economic and Political Weekly Research Foundation) (1995), 'Economic Reforms and Rate of Saving', *Economic and Political Weekly*, Vol. 30, Nos 18 and 19, pp. 1021–41.

—— (1996), *National Accounts Statistics of India, 1950–51 to 1994–95*, Sameeksha Trust, Bombay.

Ettori, F. (1990), *The Pervasive Effects of High Taxation of Capital Goods in India*, WPS 433, The World Bank, Washington, D.C.

Fazzari, S. M, R. G. Hubbard and B. C. Petersen (1988), 'Financing Constraints and Corporate Investment', *Brooking Papers on Economic Activity*, Vol. 1, pp. 141–95.

Feldstein, M. (1974), 'Social Security, Induced Retirement, and Aggregate Capital Accumulation', *Journal of Political Economy*, Vol. 82, No. 5, pp. 905–26.

—— (1995), 'Global Capital Flows: Too Little, Not Too Much', *The Economist*, 24 June, pp. 76–7.

Feldstein, M. and C. Horioka (1980), 'Domestic saving and International Capital Flows', *Economic Journal*, Vol. 90, pp. 314–29.

Ferderer, J. P. (1993), 'The Impact of Uncertainty on Aggregate Investment: An Empirical Analysis', *Journal of Money, Credit and Banking*, Vol. 25, No. 1, pp. 30–48.

Fielding, D. (1997), 'Aggregate Investment in South Africa: A Model with Implications for Political Reform', *Oxford Bulletin of Economics and Statistics*, Vol. 59, No. 3, pp. 349–69.

Fischer, S. (1993), 'The Role of Macroeconomic Factors in Growth', *Journal of Monetary Economics*, Vol. 32, No. 3, pp. 485–512.

Frankel, J. A. and Razin A. (1992), *Fiscal Policies and the World Economy* (2nd edn), The MIT Press, Cambridge.

Fry, Maxwell (1995), 'Financial development in Asia: some analytical issues', *Asian–Pacific Economic Literature*, Vol. 9, No. 1, pp. 40–57.

Gersovitz, M. (1988), 'Saving and Development', in H. Chenery and T. N. Srinivasan (eds), *Handbook of Development Economics*, Vol. 1, North Holland, Amsterdam, pp. 381–424.

Gertler, M. (1988), 'Financial Structure and Aggregate Economic Activity: An Overview', *Journal of Money, Credit and Banking*, Vol. 20, pp. 559–88.

Gertler, M. and S. Gilchrist (1994), 'Monetary Policy, Business Cycles and the Behaviour of Small Manufacturing Firms', *Quarterly Journal of Economics*, Vol. 109, No. 2, pp. 309–40.

Gibson, H. D. and E. Tsakalotos (1994), 'The Scope and Limits of Financial Liberalisation in Developing Countries: A Critical Survey', *Journal of Development Studies*, Vol. 30, No. 3, pp. 578–628.

Gilbert, C. (1989), 'LSE and the British Approach to Time Series Econometrics', *Oxford Economic Papers*, Vol. 41, No. 1, pp. 108–28.

—— (1990), 'Professor Hendry's Econometric Methodology', in C. W. J. Granger (ed.), *Modelling Economic Series: Readings in Econometric Methodology*, Clarendon Press, Oxford, pp. 279–303.

Goldar, B. (1997), 'Econometrics of Indian Industry', in K.L. Krishna (ed.), *Econometric Applications in India*, Oxford University Press, Delhi, pp. 53–107.

Goldar, B. and V. S. Renganathan (1990), *Liberalisation of Capital Goods Imports in India*, Working Paper No. 8, National Institute of Public Finance and Policy, New Delhi.

Gothoskar, S. P. (1988), 'New Approach in National Accounts', *Economic and Political Weekly*, September 24, Vol. 23, No. 39, pp. 2003–16.

Gramlich, E. M. (1994), 'Infrastructure Investment: A Review Essay', *Journal of Economic Literature*, Vol. 32, pp. 1176–96.

Granger, C. W. J. (1981), 'Some Properties of Time-series Data and their Use in Econometric Model Specification', *Journal of Econometrics*, Vol. 16, pp. 121–30.

—— (1987), 'Spurious Regression', *New Palgrave: A Dictionary of Economics*, Macmillan, London, pp. 444–5.

—— (ed.) (1990), *Modelling Economic Series: Readings in Econometric Methodology*, Clarendon Press, Oxford.

—— (1997), 'On Modelling the Long Run in Applied Economics', *Economic Journal*, Vol. 107, No. 440, pp. 169–77.

Granger, C. W. J. and P. Newbold (1974), 'Spurious Regressions in Econometrics', *Journal of Econometrics*, Vol. 2, No. 2, pp. 111–20.

Greenaway, D. and O. Morrissey (1992), 'Structural Adjustment and Liberalisation in Developing Countries: What Lessons have We Learned?', *Kyklos*, Vol. 46, No. 2, pp. 241–61.

Greene, J. and D. Villanueva (1991), 'Private Investment in Developing Countries', *IMF Staff Papers*, Vol. 38, No. 1, pp. 33–58.

Greene, W. (1999), *Econometrics*, Prentice-Hall, New York.

Grossman, G. and E. Helpman (1991), *Innovation and Growth in the Global Economy*, The MIT Press, Cambridge.

Gurley, J. G. and E. S. Shaw (1955), 'Financial Aspects of Economic Development', *American Economic Review*, September, Vol. 45, No. 4, pp. 515–38.

Hadjimetheou, G. (1987), *Consumer Economics after Keynes: Theory and Evidence of the Consumption Function*, Wheatsheaf Books, Brighton, U.K.

Hall, S. G. (1991), 'The Effect of Varying Length VAR Models on the Maximum Likelihood Estimates of Cointegrating Vectors', *Scottish Journal of Political Economy*, Vol. 38, No. 4, pp. 317–23.

Hanson, J. and S. Kathuria (eds) (1999), *India: A Financial Sector for the Twenty-first Century*, Oxford University Press, Delhi.

Haque, N., M. H. Pesaran and S. Sharma (1999), 'Neglected Heterogeneity and Dynamics in Cross-country Saving Regressions', *IMF Working Paper*.

Harrigan, J. and P. Mosley (1988), 'Evaluating the Impact of World Bank Structural Adjustment Lending', *Journal of Development Studies*, Vol. 27, No. 1, pp. 95–134.

Harrod, R. (1948), *Towards a Dynamic Economics*, Macmillan, London.

Helleiner, G. K. (1994), 'Introduction', in Gerald K. Helleiner (ed.), *Trade Policy and Industrialisation in Turbulent Times*, Routledge, London.

Hendry, D. F. (1996), *Dynamic Econometrics*, Oxford University Press, Oxford.

Hendry, D. F., A. Pagan and J. D. Sargan (1985), 'Dynamic Specification', in Z. Griliches and M. D. Intriligator (eds), *Handbook of Econometrics*, Vol. 2, North-Holland, Amsterdam.

Hoshi, T., A. Kashyap and D. Scharfstein (1991), 'Corporate Structure, Liquidity and Investment: Evidence from Japanese Industrial Groups', *Quarterly Journal of Economics*, Vol. 106, No. 1, pp. 33–60.

Hubbard, R. G. (1998), 'Capital-market Imperfections and Investment', *Journal of Economic Literature*, Vol. 36, No. 1, pp. 193–225.

Hubbard, R. G., J. Skinner and S. Zeldes (1994), 'The Importance of Precautionary Motives in Explaining Individual and Aggregate Saving', *Carnegie-Rochester Conference Series on Public Policy*, Vol. 40, pp. 59–125.

Hussein, K. A. and A. P. Thirlwall (1999), 'Explaining Differences in the Domestic Savings Ratio Across Countries: A Panel Data Study', *Journal of Development Studies*, Vol. 36, No. 1, pp. 31–52.

Ibarra, L. A. (1995), 'Credibility of Trade Policy Reform and Investment: The Mexican Experience', *Journal of Development* Economics, Vol. 47, No. 1, pp. 39–60.

Inder, B. (1993), 'Estimating Long-run Relationships in Economics: A Comparison of Different Approaches', *Journal of Econometrics*, Vol. 57, No. 1, pp. 53–68.

Jappelli, T. and M. Pagano (1989), 'Consumption and Capital Market Imperfections: An International Comparison', *American Economic Review*, Vol. 79, No. 3, pp. 1088–105.

Johansen, S. (1988), 'Statistical Analysis of Cointegration Vectors', *Journal of Economic Dynamics and Control*, Vol. 12, pp. 231–54.

Johansen, S. and K. Juselius (1990), 'Maximum Likelihood Estimation with Inference on Cointegration — With Application to the Demand for Money', *Oxford Bulletin of Economics and Statistics*, Vol. 52, No. 2, pp. 169–210.

Johnston, J. (1991), *Econometric Methods*, McGraw-Hill, New York.

Jones, C. I. (1994), 'Economic growth and the relative price of capital', *Journal of Monetary Economics*, Vol. 34, No. 3, pp. 359–82.

—— (1995), 'Time Series Tests of Endogenous Growth Models', *Quarterly Journal of Economics*, Vol. 110, No. 2, pp. 495–525.

—— (1998), *Introduction of Economic Growth*, W. W. Norton, New York.

Jorgenson, D. W. (1967), 'The Theory of Investment Behaviour', in Robert Ferber (ed.), *Determinants of Investment Behavior*, Columbia University Press, New York, pp. 129–55.

—— (1971), 'Econometric Studies of Investment Behaviour: A Survey', *Journal of Economic Literature*, Vol. 11, pp. 1111–47.

Joshi, V. (1998), 'Fiscal Stabilisation and Economic Reforms in India', in I. J. Ahluwalia and I. M. D. Little (eds), *India's Economic Reforms and Development: Essays for Manmohan Singh*, Oxford University Press, Delhi, pp. 147–68.

Joshi, V and I. M. D. Little (1994), *India: Macroeconomics and Political Economy, 1964–1991*, Oxford University Press, Delhi.

Joshi, V. and I. M. D. Little (1996), *India's Economic Reforms 1991–2001*, Clarendon Press, Oxford.

Joshi, V. and I. M. D. Little (1997), 'India: Reform on Hold', *Asian Development Review*, Vol. 15, No. 2, pp. 1–42.

Kaldor, N. (1957), 'A Model of Economic Growth', *Economic Journal*, Vol. 67, No. 268.

Ketkar, K. W. and S. L. Ketkar (1992), 'Banking Nationalisation, Financial Savings, and Economic Development: A Case Study of India', *Journal of Developing Areas*, Vol. 27, No. 1, pp. 69–84.

Keynes, J. M. (1936), *The General Theory of Employment, Interest and Money*, Macmillan, London.

—— (1937), 'The Ex-Ante Theory', *Economic Journal*, Vol. 47, No. 188, pp. 663–9.

Kimball, M. (1990), 'Precautionary Saving in the Small and the Large', *Econometrica*, Vol. 58, No. 1, pp. 53–73.

King, R. and R. Levine (1993), 'Finance and Growth: Schumpeter May be Right', *Quarterly Journal of Economics*, Vol. 108, No. 3, pp. 717–37.

Kohli, A. (1991), *Democracy and Discontent: India's Growing Crisis of Governability*, Cambridge University Press, Cambridge.

Krishnamurty, K., K. S. Krishnaswamy, and P. D. Sharma (1987), Determinants of Saving Rates in India', *Journal of Quantitative Economics*, Vol. 3, pp. 335–57.

Krishnamurty, K. and D. U. Sastry (1975), *Investment and Financing in the Corporate Sector in India*, Tata McGraw-Hill, Delhi.

Krueger, A. O. (1978), *Foreign Trade Regimes and Economic Development: Liberalisation Attempts and Consequences*, Ballinger, Cambridge, Mass.

—— (1982), *Trade and Employment in Developing Countries: Synthesis and Conclusion*, University of Chicago Press, Chicago.

—— (1980), 'Trade Policy as an Input to Development', *American Economic Review: Papers and Proceedings*, Vol. 70, No. 2, pp. 288–92.

—— (1992), *Economic Policy Reforms in Developing Countries*, Basil Blackwell, Oxford.

—— (1997), 'Trade Policy and Economic Development: How We Learn', *American Economic Review*, Vol. 87, No. 1, pp. 1–22.

Kumar, A. G., K. Sen and R. R. Vaidya (2001), 'Outward Orientation, Investment and Finance Constraints: A Study of Indian Firms', *Journal of Development Studies*, Vol. 37, No. 4, pp. 133–49.

Lal, D. and H. Myint (1996), *The Political Economy of Poverty, Equity and Growth*, Clarendon Press, Oxford.

Laumas, P.S. (1990), 'Monetization, Financial Liberalization, and Economic Development', *Economic Development and Cultural Change*, Vol. 38, pp. 377–90.

Lee, J-W. (1995), 'Capital Goods Imports and Long-run Growth', *Journal of Development Economics*, Vol. 48, No. 1, pp. 91–110.

Levine, R. (1997), 'Financial Development and Economic Growth: Views and Agenda', *Journal of Economic Literature*, Vol. 35, No. 2, pp. 688–726.

Levine, R. and D. Renelt (1992), 'A Sensitivity Analysis of Cross-country Growth Regressions', *American Economic Review*, Vol. 82, No. 4, pp. 942–63.

Lewis, W. A. (1954), 'Economic Development with Unlimited Supplies of Labour', *Manchester School*, Vol. 22, No. 2, pp. 139–91.

—— (1955), *Theory of Economic Growth*, Allen and Unwin, London.

—— (1984), 'Development Economics in the 1950s', in G. M. Meier and D. Seers (eds), *Pioneers in Development*, Oxford University Press, New York, pp. 121–37.

Lin, L-Y and W. T. Woo (1994), 'Saving Behaviour under Imperfect Capital Markets and the Current Account Consequences', *Economic Journal*, Vol. 104, No. 428, pp. 512–27.

Little, I. M. D. (1962), 'A Critical Examination of India's Third Five Year Plan', *Oxford Economic Papers*, Vol. 14, No. 1, pp. 1–24.

—— (1982), *Economic Development: Theory, Policy and International Relations*, Basic Books, New York.

—— (1999), *Collection and Recollections: Economic Papers and Their Provenance*, Clarendon Press, Oxford.

Little, I. M. D, D. Mazumdar and J. Page (1987), *Small Manufacturing Enterprises: A Comparative Analysis of India and Other Economies*, Oxford University Press, Oxford.

Little, I. M. D, T. Scitovsky, and M. F. G Scott (1970), *Industry and Trade in Some Developing Countries: A Comparative Study*, Oxford University Press, Oxford.

Loayza, N., H. Lopez, K. Schmidt–Hebbel, and L. Serven (1998), *Saving in the World: Stylized Facts*, The World Bank, mimeo.

Loayza, N., K. Schmidt–Hebbel and L. Serven (2000), 'What Drives Private Saving around the World?', *The Review of Economics and Statistics*, Vol. 82, No. 2, pp. 165–81.

Lopez, J. H., K. Schmidt–Hebbel and L. Serven (2000), 'How Effective is Fiscal Policy in Raising National Saving?', *The Review of Economics and Statistics*, Vol. 82, No. 2, pp. 226–38.

Lucas, R. E., Jr. (1976), 'Econometric Policy Evaluation: A Critique', *Carnegie–Rochester Conference Series on Public Policy*, Vol. 1, No. 1, pp. 19–46.

—— (1988), 'On the Mechanics of Economic Development', *Journal of Monetary Economics*, Vol. 22, No. 1, pp. 3–42.

Maddison, A. (1994), 'Explaining the Economic Performance of Nations, 1820–1989', in William J. Baumol, Richard R. Nelson and Edward N. Wolff (eds), *Convergence of Productivity: Cross-National Studies and Historical Evidence*, Oxford University Press, New York, pp. 20–61.

Mahmood, S. and G. Ranis (1992), *The Political Economy of Development Policy Change*, Blackwell, Oxford.

Mankiw, N. G. (1995), 'The Growth of Nations', *Brookings Papers on Economic Activity*, No. 2, pp. 275–326.

Mankiw, N. G., D. Romer, and D. Weil (1992), 'A Contribution to the Empirics of Economic Growth', *Quarterly Journal of Economics*, Vol. 107, pp. 407–38.

Marathe, S. S. (1989), *Regulation and Development: India's Policy Experience of Controls over Industry*, Sage Publications, Delhi.

Masson, P., T. Bayoumi, and H. Samiei (1995), 'Saving Behaviour in Industrial and Developing Countries', *IMF manuscript*.

McCombie, J. S. L and A. P. Thirlwall (1994), *Economic Growths and the Balance-of-Payments Constraint*, Macmillan, London.

McKinnon, R. I. (1973), *Money and Capital in Economic Development*, Brookings Institute, Washington, D.C.

McKinnon, Ronald I. (1979), 'Foreign Trade Regimes and Economic Development: A Review Article', *Journal of International Economics*, Vol. 9, No. 3, pp. 429–52.

Meier, G. M. (1984), 'The Formation Period', in M. M. Meier and Dudley Seers (eds), *Pioneers in Development*, Oxford University Press, New York, pp. 3–22.

Meier, G. M. and R. Baldwin (1957), *Economic Development*, John Wiley and Sons, New York.

Mills, T. C. (1990), *Time Series Techniques for Economists*, Cambridge University Press, Cambridge.

Ministry of Finance (1991), *Report of the Committee on the Financial System* (Narsimhan Committee Report), Government of India, Delhi.

Modigliani, F. (1970), 'The Life Cycle Hypothesis of Saving and Intercountry Differences in the Saving Ratio', in W. A. Eltis, M. F. Scott and J. N. Wolfe (eds), *Induction, Growth and Trade*, Clarendon Press, Oxford, pp. 197–225.

—— (1986), 'Life Cycle, Individual Thrift, and the Wealth of Nations', *American Economic Review*, Vol. 76, No. 2, pp. 297–313.

—— (1993), 'Recent Declines in the Savings Rate: A Life Cycle Perspective', in M. Baldassarri, L. Paganetto and E. S. Phelps (eds), *World Saving, Prosperity and Growth*, Macmillan, London, pp. 249–86.

Modigliani, F. and A. Sterling (1983), 'Determinants of Private Saving with Special Reference to the Role of Social Security: Cross Country Tests', in F. Modigliani and R. Hemming (eds), *The Determinants of National Saving and Wealth*, St. Martin's Press, New York, pp. 224–55.

Mohan, R. and V. Aggarwal (1990), 'Commands and Controls: Planning for Indian Industrialization, 1951–1990', *Journal of Comparative Economics*, Vol. 14, No. 4, pp. 681–712.

Mookherjee, D. (1995), 'Introduction', in D. Mookherjee (ed.), *Indian Industry: Policies and Performance*, Oxford University Press, Delhi, pp. 1–43.

Mundle, S. and M. G. Rao (1997), 'Public Expenditure in India: Trends and Issues', in S. Mundle (ed.), *Public Finance: Policy Issues for India*, Oxford University Press, Delhi.

Murphy, K., A. Shleifer, and R. W. Vishny (1989), 'Industrialisation and the Big Push', *Quarterly Journal of Economics*, Vol. 97, No. 4, pp. 1003–26.

Muscatelli, V. and S. Hurns (1995), 'Econometric Modelling Using Cointegrated Time Series', in L. Oxley, D. A. R. George, C. J. Roberts and S. Sayer (eds), *Surveys in Econometrics*, Basil Blackwell, Oxford, pp. 171–214.

Nagaraj, R. (1991), 'Public Sector Performance in the Eighties', *Economic and Political Weekly*, Vol. 26, No. 50, pp. 2877–83.

—— (1993), 'Macroeconomic Impact of Public Sector Enterprises: Some Further Evidence', *Economic and Political Weekly*, 16–23 January, Vol. 28, No. 304, pp. 105–9.

Nelson, C. R. and C. I. Plosser (1982), 'Trends and Random Walks in Macroeconomic Time Series: Some Evidence and Implications', *Journal of Monetary Economics*, Vol. 10, No. 1, pp. 139–62.

Oliner, S., G. Rudebusch, and D. Sichel (1995), 'New and Old Models of Business Investment: A Comparison of Forecasting Performance', *Journal of Money, Credit and Banking*, Vol. 27, No. 4, pp. 809–26.

—— (1996), 'The Lucas Critique Revisited: Assessing the Stability of Empirical

Euler Equations for Investment', *Journal of Econometrics*, Vol. 70, No. 3, pp. 291–316.

Owen, P. D. and O. Solis–Fallas (1989), 'Unorganized Money Market and Unproductive Assets in the New Structuralist Critique of Financial Liberalization', *Journal of Development Economics*, Vol. 22, No. 3, pp. 341–55.

Pagan, A. (1987), 'Three Methodologies: A Critical Appraisal', *Journal of Economic Surveys*, Vol. 1, No. 1, pp. 3–24.

—— (1995), 'The Three Econometric Methodologies: An Update', in L. Oxley, D. A. R. George, C. J. Roberts, and S. Sayer (eds), *Surveys in Econometrics*, Basil Blackwell, Oxford, pp. 30–41.

Pandit, B. L. (1991), *The Growth and Structure of Savings in India*, Oxford University Press, Delhi.

Patnaik, P. and S. K. Rao (1977), 'Towards an Explanation of a Crisis in a Mixed Underdeveloped Economy', *Economic and Political Weekly*, Vol. 12, No. 6, 7, and 8, pp. 205–18.

Patnaik, P. and C. P. Chandrasekhar (1996), 'Investment, Export and Growth: A cross Country Analaysis', *Economic and Political Weekly*, Vol. 31, No. 1, pp. 31–6.

Prabhat Patnaik and C. P. Chandrasekhar (1998), 'India: Dirigisme, Structural Adjustment, and the Radical Alternative', in D. Baker, G. Epstein and R. Pollin (eds), *Globalization and Progressive Economic Policy*, Cambridge University Press, Cambridge, pp. 67–91.

Perron, P. (1989), 'The Great Crash, the Oil Price Shock and the Unit Root Hypothesis', *Econometrica*, Vol. 57, pp. 1361–401.

Phillips, P. C. B. and B. E. Hansen (1990), 'Statistical Inference in Instrumental Variables Regression with $I(1)$ Processes', *Review of Economic Studies*, Vol. 57, No. 1, pp. 99–125.

Phillips, P. C. B. and M. Loretan (1991), 'Estimating Long-Run Economic Equilibria', *Review of Economic Studies*, Vol. 58, No. 2, pp. 407–36.

Pindyck, R. S. (1991), 'Irreversibility, Uncertainty and Investment', *Journal of Economic Literature*, Vol. 29, No. 3, pp. 1110–48.

Pindyck, R. S. and A. Solimano (1993), 'Economic Instability and Aggregate Investment', *NBER Macroeconomics Annual 1993*, The MIT Press, Cambridge, pp. 259–303.

Price, S. (1995), 'Aggregate Uncertainty, Capacity Utilization and Manufacturing Investment', *Applied Economics*, Vol. 57, No. 2, pp. 147–54.

Pritchett, L. (1996), 'Measuring Outward orientation in LDCs: Can it be Done?', *Journal of Development Economics*, Vol. 49, No. 2, pp. 307–35.

Pursell, G. (1992), 'Trade Policies in India', in D. Salvatore (ed.), *National Trade Policies*, Greenwood Press, New York.

Rakshit, M. (1983), 'On Assessment and Interpretation of Saving-investment Estimates in India', *Economic and Political Weekly*, Annual Number, Vol. 18, No. 19–2, pp. 753–76.

Rama, M. (1993), 'Empirical Investment Equations in Developing Countries', in Luis Serven and Andres Solimano (eds), *Striving for Growth after Adjustment*, The World Bank, Washington, D. C.

Rangarajan, C. (1994), 'Industrial Growth: Another Look', in D. Nayyar (ed.), *Industrial Growth and Stagnation: The Debate in India*, Oxford University Press, Delhi, pp. 289–317.

—— (1998), *Indian Economy: Essays on Money and Finance*, UBS Publishers, Delhi.

Ranis, G. and S. Mahmood (1992), *The Political Economy of Development Policy Change*, Basil Blackwell, Oxford.

Reserve Bank of India (RBI) (1982), *Capital Formation and Saving in India, 1950–51 to 1979–80*, (Report of the Working Group on Saving: Raj Committee Report).

—— (1985), *Report of the Committee on the Working of the Monetary System*, (Chakravarty Committee Report).

Riedel, J. (1988), 'Economic Development in East Asia: Doing What Comes Naturally?', in H. Hughes (ed.), *Achieving Industrialisation in East Asia*, Cambridge University Press, Cambridge, pp. 1–38.

Riedel, J. (1996), 'Explaining Economic Growth: The 'New View', in Theory and Practice', Unpublished paper, Paul H. Nitze School of Advanced International Studies, The Johns Hopkins University, Washington, D.C.

Rivera–Batiz, F. and P. M. Romer (1991), 'Economic Integration and Endogenous Growth', *Quarterly Journal of Economics*, Vol. 106, No. 2, pp. 531–56.

Robinson, J. (1962), 'A Model of Accumulation', in J. Robinson (ed.), *Essays in the Theory of Economic Growth*, Macmillan, London.

Rodrik, D. (1991), 'Policy Uncertainty and Private Investment in Developing Countries', *Journal of Development Economics*, Vol. 36, No. 3, pp. 229–43.

—— (1995a), 'Trade and Industrial Policy Reform', in J. R. Behrman and T. N. Srinivasan (eds), *Handbook of Development Economics*, Volume III, North Holland, Amsterdam, pp. 2927–82.

—— (1995b), 'Getting Interventions Right: How Korea and Taiwan Grew Rich', *Economic Policy*, Vol. 20, No. 1, pp. 55–107.

—— (1997), 'Trade Strategies, Exports and Investment: Another Look at East Asia', *Pacific Economic Review*, Vol. 2, No. 1, pp. 1–24.

—— (1999), *The New Global Economy and Developing Countries: Making Openness Work*, Overseas Development Council (distributed by Johns Hopkins University Press), Washington, D.C.

Romer, P. M. (1986), 'Increasing Returns and Long-run Growth', *Journal of Political Economy*, Vol. 94, No. 5, pp. 1002–37.

—— (1987), 'Growth Based on Increasing Returns due to Specialisation', *American Economic Review*, Vol. 77, No. 2, pp. 56–62.

—— (1990), 'Endogenous Technical Change', *Journal of Political Economy*, Vol. 98, No. 1, pp. 71–102.

—— (1992), 'Two Strategies for Economic Development: Using and Producing

Ideas', *World Bank Annual Conference on Development Economics*, The World Bank.

Roy, T. and K. Sen (1991), 'Changes in Saving Rate and its Implications for Growth', *Economic and Political Weekly*, Vol. 20, No. 16, pp. 1055–8.

Sargan, J. D. (1964), 'Wages and Prices in the United Kingdom: A Study of Econometric Methodology', in P. E. Hart and J. K. Whittaker (eds), *Econometric Analysis for Natural Economic Planning*, Butterworth, London.

Sarma, A. (1995), 'Performance of Public Enterprises in India', in D. Mookherjee (ed.), *Indian Industry: Policies and Performance*, Oxford University Press, Delhi, pp. 289–321.

Sarma, J. V. M. (1988), 'Investment Allowance and Private Corporate Investment in India', *Economic and Political Weekly*, Vol. 23, No. 43, pp. 2235–8.

Schmookler, J. (1966), *Invention and Economic Growth*, Harvard University Press, Cambridge, Mass.

Scott, M. F. G. (1976), 'Investment and Growth', *Oxford Economic Papers*, Vol. 28, No. 3, pp. 317–63.

—— (1981), 'The Contribution of Investment to Economic Growth', *Scottish Journal of Political Economics*, Vol. 28, No. 1, pp. 211–26.

—— (1989), *A New View of Economic Growth*, Clarendon Press, Oxford.

—— (1991a), 'A Reply to Denison', *Oxford Economic Papers*, Vol. 43, No. 2, pp. 237–44.

—— (1991b), 'A New View of Economic Growth: Four Lectures', *Policy Research Working Paper*, No. 131, The World Bank, Washington, D. C.

—— (1992), 'Policy Implications of a New View of Economic Growth', *Economic Journal*, Vol. 102, No. 412, pp. 621–32.

Sen, K. and R. R. Vaidya (1997), *The Process of Financial Liberalization in India*, Oxford University Press, Delhi.

Serven, L. and A. Solimano (1993), 'Debt Crisis, Adjustment Policies and Capital Formation in Developing Countries: Where Do We Stand?', *World Development*, Vol. 21, No. 1, pp. 127–40.

Shaw, E. (1973), *Financial Deepening in Economic Development*, Oxford University Press, New York.

Shetty, S. L. (1990), 'Saving Behaviour in the 1980s: Some Lessons', *Economic and Political Weekly*, Vol. 25, No. 11, pp. 555–60.

Solimano, A. (1992), 'How Private Investment Reacts to Changing Macroeconomic Conditions', in A. Chibber, M. Dailami, and N. Shafik, *Reviving Private Investment in Developing Countries: Empirical Studies and Policy Lessons*, North-Holland, Amsterdam.

Solow, R. M. (1956), 'A Contribution to the Theory of Economic Growth', *Quarterly Journal of Economics*, Vol. 70, No. 1, pp. 65–94.

—— (1957), 'Technical Change and the Aggregate Production Function', *The Review of Economics and Statistics*, Vol. 39, No. 3, pp. 312–20.

Solow, R. M. (1970), *Growth Theory*, Oxford University Press, Oxford.

—— (1994), 'Perspectives on Growth Theory', *Journal of Economic Perspectives*, Vol. 8, No. 1, pp. 45–54.

—— (2000), *Growth Theory: An Exposition*, 2nd edition, Oxford University Press, New York.

Srinivasan, T. N. (1994), 'Data Base for development Analysis: An Overview', *Journal of Development Economics*, Vol. 44, No. 1, pp. 3–27.

—— (1999), 'Trade Orientation Trade Liberalisation and Economic Growth', in Garry Saxonhouse and T. N. Srinivasan (eds), *Development, Duality and the International Economic Regime: Essays in Honor of Gustav Ranis*, University of Michigan Press, Ann Arbor.

—— (2000), *Eight Lectures on India's Economic Reforms*, Oxford University Press, Delhi.

Srinivasan, T. N. and J. Bhagwati (1999), 'Outward-orientation and Development: Are Revisionists Right?', Yale Growth Centre, Yale University (mimeo).

Srinivasan, T. N. and N. S. S. Narayana (1994), 'Economic Performance since the Third Plan and Its Implications for Policy', in D. Nayyar (ed.), *Industrial Growth and Stagnation: The Debate in India*, Oxford University Press, Delhi, pp. 89–110.

Srivastava, V. (1996), *Liberalization, Productivity and Competition: A Panel Study of Indian Manufacturing*, Oxford University Press, Delhi.

Stiglitz, J. and M. Uy (1996), 'Financial Markets, Public Policy, and the East Asian Miracle', *World Bank Research Observer*, Vol. 11, No. 2, pp. 249–76.

Swan, T. W. (1956), 'Economic Growth and Capital Accumulation', *Economic Record*, Vol. 32, No. 3, pp. 334–61.

Taylor, L. (1983), *Structuralist Macroeconomics: Applicable Models for the Third World*, Basic Books, New York.

—— (1988), *Varieties of Stabilization Experience: Towards Sensible Macroeconomics in the Third World*, Clarendon Press, Oxford.

Temple, J. (1998), 'Equipment investment and the Solow Model', *Oxford Economic Papers*, Vol. 50, No. 1, pp. 39–62.

—— (1999), 'The New Growth Evidence', *Journal of Economic Literature*, Vol. 37, No. 1, pp. 112–56.

Thirlwall, A. P. (1974), *Inflation, Saving and Growth in Developing Economies*, Macmillan, London.

—— (1976), *Financing Economic Development*, Macmillan, London.

Van de Stadt, H., A. Kapteyn and S. Van de Geer (1985), 'The Relativity of Utility: Evidence from Panel Data', *The Review of Economics and Statistics*, Vol. 67, No. 2, pp. 179–87.

Van Wijnbergen, S. (1982), 'Stagflationary Effect of Monetary Stabilization Policies: A Quantitative Analysis of South Korea', *Journal of Development Studies*, Vol. 19, No. 2, pp. 133–69.

Warman, F. and A. P. Thirlwall (1994), 'Interest Rates, Saving, Investment and Growth in Mexico 1960–90: Tests of the Financial Liberalisation Hypothesis', *Journal of Development Studies*, Vol. 30, No. 3, pp. 629–49.

Wickens, M. R. (1996), 'Interpreting Cointegrating vectors and Common Stochastic Trends', *Journal of Econometrics*, Vol. 74, No. 2, pp. 255–71.

Wickens, M. R. and T. S. Breusch (1988), 'Dynamic Specification, The Long Run and the Estimation of Transformed Regression Models', *Economic Journal*, Vol. 98, No. 390, pp. 189–205.

World Bank (1988), *Adjustment Lending*, PPR Policy and Research Papers No. 1, The World Bank, Washington, D. C.

—— (1989), *India: An Industrializing Economy in Transition*, The World Bank, Washington, D. C.

—— (1993), *The East Asian Miracle*, The World Bank, Washington, D. C.

Young, A. (1995), 'The Tyranny of Numbers: Confronting the Statistical Realities of the East Asian Growth Experience', *Quarterly Journal of Economics*, Vol. 120, No. 3, pp. 641–80.

Yule, G. U. (1926), 'Why do we Sometimes get Nonsense Correlations between Time-series?', *Journal of the Royal Econometric Society*, Vol. 89, No. 1, pp. 1–64.

Zeldes, S. (1989), 'Consumption and Liquidity Constraints: An Empirical Investigation', *Journal of Political Economy*, Vol. 97, No. 2, pp. 305–46.

Index